AMERICA PERCEIVED

AMERICA PERCEIVED

THE MAKING OF CHINESE IMAGES
OF THE UNITED STATES, 1945–1953

HONG ZHANG

Contributions to the Study of World History, Number 94

GREENWOOD PRESS
Westport, Connecticut • London

Library of Congress Cataloging-in-Publication Data

Zhang, Hong, 1962–
    America perceived : the making of Chinese images of the United States,
    1945–1953 / Hong Zhang.
        p.   cm—(Contributions to the study of world history, ISSN 0885–9159 ; no. 94)
        Includes bibliographical references (p.   ) and index.
        ISBN 0–313–31001–7 (alk. paper)
        1. United States—Relations—China.   2. China—Relations—United States.   3. United
    States—Foreign relations—1945–1953.   4. United States—Foreign public opinion, Chinese.
    5. Public opinion—China—History—20th century.   6. Urban youth—China—Political
    activity—History—20th century.   7. Anti-Americanism—China—History—20th century.   8.
    China—Politics and government—1945–1949.   I. Title.   II. Series.
    E183.8.C5Z423   2002
    327.73051′09′045—dc21   2001040591

British Library Cataloguing in Publication Data is available.

Library of Congress Catalog Card Number: 2001040591
ISBN: 0–313–31001–7
ISSN: 0885–9159

First published in 2002

Greenwood Press, 88 Post Road West, Westport, CT 06881
An imprint of Greenwood Publishing Group, Inc.
www.greenwood.com

Printed in the United States of America

The paper used in this book complies with the
Permanent Paper Standard issued by the National
Information Standards Organization (Z39.48–1984).

10 9 8 7 6 5 4 3 2 1

Copyright Acknowledgments

The author and publisher gratefully acknowledge permission for use of the following material:

Extracts from Hong Zhang. "*Fan Meifuri*: The Chinese Student Movement Opposing the U.S.
Rehabilitation of Japan, 1948." *The Journal of American-East Asian Relations* 5 (summer 1996):
183–208.

Extracts from Hong Zhang. "Chinese Intellectuals and the 'Resist America, Aid Korea' Political
Campaign." *Chinese Historians* 9 (1996): 38–74.

To my parents, Zhang Peiduo and Cheng Xiaoqin

CONTENTS

Photo essay follows page 118

ACKNOWLEDGMENTS

In the course of completing this project, I have benefited enormously from the assistance of many people and institutions. The research for this book was facilitated by the professional help of archivists and librarians in both the United States and China. I am especially thankful to those at the Hoover Institution, the U.S. National Archives, the Library of Congress, the Beijing Archives, and Nankai University in Tianjin.

My teachers, colleagues, and friends have been very supportive of me throughout the research, writing, and revising of this book. I am most indebted to my adviser, Michael Schaller, for his scholarly guidance and insightful suggestions. Special thanks also go to Gail Bernstein and James Millward for their intellectual and moral support during my years at the University of Arizona. I have received much encouragement and help from my colleagues, who have greatly enriched my academic life at the University of Central Florida.

Constructive suggestions from a number of scholars, including Rose Beiler, Bruce Pauley, Jeffrey Wasserstrom, and Joseph Yick, helped me prepare the manuscript for the final stage of publication. I especially wish to express my deep gratitude to Dr. Yick for his professional support and his critical and incisive comments on various parts of the project.

I would like to thank *The Journal of American-East Asian Relations* for permission to reuse in chapter 5 material that was published in its summer 1996 issue, and *Chinese Historians* for allowing me to quote from my "Chinese Intellectuals and the 'Resist America, Aid Korea' Political Campaign" (vol. 9, 1996).

I am also very grateful to the small number of retired college professors in China, who talked with me freely in the summers of 1997 and 1998 about their life as students in the late 1940s and offered me special insight into the Shen Chong Incident of 1946.

I wish to extend my gratitude to Heather Staines and Lori Ewen of Greenwood Publishing Group and to all those who have helped and supported me in this project.

Despite my great scholarly indebtedness to many people, I alone am responsible for any mistakes that may remain in this book.

Finally, I want to thank my family for their encouragement and support. I owe a deep debt to my parents, who taught me the importance of education and who have provided me with love and help at every stage of my life. I am most grateful to my husband, Dan, for his patience, understanding, and good humor.

ABBREVIATIONS AND ACRONYMS

Beida	Beijing University
CCP	Chinese Communist Party
CPV	Chinese People's Volunteers
GMD	Guomindang
FRUS	Foreign Relations of the United States
Jiaoda	Jiaotong University
Lianda	National Southwest Associated University or *Guoli Xinan Lianhe Daxue*
Meidi	American Imperialism
MFN	Most Favored Nation
NA	National Archives
SCAP	Supreme Commander for Allied Powers
UNIS	United States Information Service
Yanda	Yanjing University

INTRODUCTION

The years between the end of World War II and the outbreak of the Korean War witnessed the peak, decline, and end of American involvement and influence in China. These crucial "years of uncertainty" represented a significant turning point in the history of Sino-American relations.[1] While recent scholarly attention to this period has led to a more profound understanding of a turbulent and intricate phase in Chinese-American relations, most of the interpretations deal with the formal triangular relationship between the United States, the Chinese Nationalist Party (Guomindang, or GMD), and the Chinese Communist Party (CCP), often in the larger context of global politics.[2] This study moves beyond the policy- and diplomacy-oriented approach. Instead of rehashing the diplomatic history of the late 1940s and early 1950s, it places the shifting perceptions of the United States among a significant political group—the young, volatile, and politically sensitive urban Chinese—into a historical perspective through examining especially the origin, development, and eruption of their anti-American sentiment (*fanMei qingxu*) in the post–World War II period.[3] The ups and downs in their views not only affected the political fortunes of the two rival parties in China, the GMD and the CCP, but also contributed to the drastic turn in U.S.-China relations. A closer examination of the changing attitudes among politically active, young, educated Chinese toward the unfolding American involvement in East Asia in the postwar period will further demystify the Communist takeover of China in 1949. It will also contribute to a better understanding of a volatile age in Sino-American relations.

Furthermore, a study of the anti-American sentiment during the period in question will shed new light on the mind-set of educated Chinese, as their political thinking was entwined with class, cultural, and moral concerns. For example, ostensibly, their vehement response to the alleged rape of a college student by a U.S. marine in late 1946 reflected their nationalistic outrage. At a deeper level, however, it disclosed a cultural and class bias inherent in their thinking. In this sense, the anti-American outbursts also revealed how urban educated youths viewed themselves.

Studies regarding American images of China have amply demonstrated that the only certainty that has characterized the American views of China is the uncertainty, punctuated by a fluctuating "love/hate" syndrome.[4] Meanwhile, many young Chinese intellectuals also found themselves entertaining ambivalent feelings toward the United States during the first few decades of the twentieth century.[5] America was often viewed as both a relevant model and a threat to China.[6] In his *Beautiful Imperialist: China Perceives America*, David Shambaugh studies the Chinese images of America during a later period and concludes that ambivalence as manifested in the dichotomy of admiration and denigration typifies the Chinese perceptions of the United States.[7]

The conflicting sentiments of admiration and resentment toward the United States often served as a prism that reflected the understanding and thinking of the educated Chinese about their own country. For the most part, the views of young Chinese intellectuals toward the United States in the first half of the twentieth century developed in the general framework of their quest for "national salvation," an issue that dominated their political thinking. Their images of America were closely related to their concerns about China's destiny and often oscillated depending upon whether they perceived American involvement as assisting or impeding the achievement of Chinese independence from foreign control. Consequently, the United States alternated, in the eyes of many, between providing guidance or inspiration on the one hand and being an obstacle or even threat on the other.

Not only students educated in China but also American-trained Chinese students contributed to the making of Chinese images of the United States. From the late nineteenth century on, an increasing number of Chinese students went to America to study. The U.S. government promoted the education of Chinese students at American institutions of higher education, for it expected American-educated students to be "saturated with American sentiment"[8] and to act as transmitters of American values upon their return to China. However, direct exposure to things American often resulted in mixed emotions among these students, which was manifested in admiration for American material wealth, political power, scientific and technological development, efficiency, exuberant energy, and optimistic outlook; fascination with America's political system, family system, and customs; and resentment of American discriminatory immigration policy and racial prejudice against the Chinese and the perceived gap between American rhetoric and practice. The returned students and scholars wrote extensively about their impressions of American society, and their writings helped to shape Chinese perceptions of the United States.[9] The 1905 Chinese boycott of American goods reflected the influence and power of such writings.

If ambivalence and mixed emotions characterized the attitudes of many young Chinese intellectuals toward the United States during the early decades of the twentieth century, political militancy among radical students in Chinese colleges and to some extent high schools set the tone for the turn from the sentiment of "love" during World War II to that of "hate" in the postwar period and for the shaping of the larger public images of the United States. The fluctuations in the perceptions, therefore, testify to "the malleability of political language and imagery in general."[10]

The American public was largely oblivious to the growth of strong anti-American sentiment in China. In 1948, to correct the general American misperception that the United States enjoyed a high prestige in postwar China, the American Foundation of Foreign Affairs published a rare study of Chinese opinion on U.S. activities in the country. In the preface, William Neumann, research director for the project, cautioned against American "apathy or blindness to criticism from abroad." He maintained that, since the American government had provided considerable aid to the Chinese Nationalist government, the uninformed American "is likely to believe that American prestige is therefore high, and that his country has contributed to the welfare of China," when in fact "the contrary is closer to the truth."[11]

Hoping to see a strong, pro-American Chinese government, Washington had long urged the Nationalist government led by Chiang Kai-shek (Jiang Jie-shi) to implement reforms and broaden its base to attract Chinese intellectuals, whose support was solicited by the U.S. government itself.[12] Nevertheless, American policy toward East Asia in the postwar period served to alienate this numerically small yet politically articulate group of Chinese.[13] Even before the Communist takeover, the U.S. government had lost the battle for the hearts and minds of many young educated Chinese, and had, in a sense, "lost China." In an article titled "America Loses Chinese Good Will" published in early 1949, the historian Dorothy Borg asserted that "in terms of securing Chinese good will American policy has been a conspicuous failure."[14]

Intellectual activism has played a significant role in shaping the course of modern Chinese history. Historically, educated Chinese, or Confucian literati, saw themselves as the cream of the state, obligated to criticize openly any deviations from Confucian moral principles. Following historical precedents and inspired by a strong sense of patriotic duty, many modern Chinese intellectuals believed keenly that they were responsible for the fate of the nation and should speak out on behalf of the Chinese people. Despairing over a weak and unstable China that had lost its old luster, Chinese college students carried with them a sense of mission and played their part in fomenting change.[15] Student protesters of the first half of the twentieth century, however, moved sharply away from the traditional mode of literati remonstrations. Instead, they turned the streets into political stages to publicize their opinions dramatically and to elicit wider support for their views.[16]

The special position that educated youths occupied in their society made it imperative for any ruling party or aspiring political organization to take their views or outcries seriously. Historians have highlighted the prominent roles of college students in a country undergoing revolutionary change. In his influential book, *Student Nationalism in China*, John Israel establishes the importance of student nationalist outbursts in Chinese politics during the Nanjing decade (1927–37). He claims that the record of the student movement demonstrates that it "exerted a disproportionately strong influence on the course of China's history."[17] Jeffrey Wasserstrom's *Student Protests in Twentieth-Century China* focuses especially on the role and techniques of student protests in the Republican era (1912–49), during which educated youths continually articulated their challenge to the political authorities. Wasserstrom argues that student protests in Republican China were often subversive in nature and that even though they "did not constitute *physical* threats to the status quo, student protesters posed very real *symbolic* threats." Their words and deeds "raised doubts in the mind of the audience about the right of those in power to rule."[18] Student political activism in urban China played an important role in the ultimate Communist victory. In *Making Urban Revolution in China*, Joseph Yick establishes the salience of nonmilitary factors, such as the failure of the GMD to secure its urban bases and the allegiance of the urban populace, especially the educated youths, for the Nationalist government's collapse in 1949, in contrast to the CCP's successful mobilization of students in its political confrontation with the GMD.[19]

However, even though college students featured prominently in the political and cultural movements of Republican China, they were not a singular entity and one can hardly encompass them under one blanket term of "national student culture." Not only did students themselves come from diverse social and cultural backgrounds, but also the various institutions of higher education during the Republican period emerged from distinct social and cultural backgrounds and developed their own individual values, styles, and political leanings.[20] Against the backdrop of cultural and social diversities, college campuses nevertheless proved to be highly politically charged centers and witnessed intense polarization in the late 1940s.

Driven largely by a sense of national dignity and pride, by a fervent desire for full equality in foreign relations, by frustration with the devastating Civil War, and by an ingrained sense of their special social role, many politically committed young Chinese, who were among the most ardent of Chinese nationalists, became highly critical of postwar U.S. policy toward China and Japan. The vigorously expressed anti-American sentiment in GMD-controlled urban China is a subject largely overlooked in the standard historical treatment of Sino-American relations.[21] The issue, however, had significant implications for the outcome of the CCP-GMD power struggle and for the subsequent collision and estrangement between Communist China and the United States. In the short run, the American assistance gave the GMD an upper hand in its competition with the CCP for territorial control in the wake of the Japanese surrender. In the long run, however, American aid and presence were not significant enough to turn the war tide in the favor of the GMD. Nevertheless, they were visible and disconcerting enough to place the U.S. government as the primary target of Chinese nationalism. Furthermore, the surging anti-American sentiment among radical youths placed the Nationalist government in an untenable position, for it fell under heavy attack from young nationalists for having failed to bolster the prestige and dignity of China. Politically active young Chinese were especially critical of what they saw as the GMD's supine policy toward the United States.

While the student anti-American outbursts were detrimental to the cause of the GMD, whose leaders appeared incapable of gratifying the nationalist demand, the CCP not only stimulated and capitalized upon them, but also greatly benefited from them. By claiming to stand at the forefront of the "student patriotic movement," the Communists made effective propaganda and allied themselves with politically influential members of Chinese society. In this sense, the movement figured significantly in easing the way of the Communists into urban China in 1949 despite their power concentration in the rural areas during and immediately after World War II. Ironically, the American endeavors to establish a pro-U.S. "democratic" China inadvertently undermined the cause of the GMD and contributed to the Communist urban victory. Furthermore, the CCP's successful alliance with politically active students during the late 1940s helped set the stage for the making of Chinese images of America during the Korean War.

In brief, during the late 1940s, Chinese youths launched a mounting wave of protest demonstrations and rallies against the U.S. government. Amid the surging anti-American sentiment, antipathy largely replaced admiration and the view of America as an obstacle to the achievement of China's political aspirations prevailed. In no other period in modern Chinese history did nonofficially sponsored anti-American sentiment manifest itself in such a virulent form. It revealed a most tangible strain in Chinese-American relations at the popular level. The negative sentiment was shaped by a combination of real and imagined insults and by the larger political, economic, and cultural contexts. The growing anti-American sentiment in the post–World War II period would be pushed to the forefront by the newly established Communist government and the image of an imperialistic United States working tenaciously against the interest of Chinese people persisted beyond the Civil War years.

NOTES

1. Dorothy Borg and Waldo Heinrichs, eds., *Uncertain Years: Chinese-American Relations, 1947–1950* (New York: Columbia University Press, 1980), vii.

2. Outstanding among the recent works include Dorothy Borg and Waldo Heinrichs, *Uncertain Years*; Harry Harding and Yuan Ming, eds., *Sino-American Relations, 1945–1955: A Joint Reassessment of a Critical Decade* (Wilmington, Del.: A Scholarly Resources Imprint, 1989); William Whitney Stueck, Jr., *The Road to Confrontation: American Policy toward China and Korea, 1947–1950* (Chapel Hill: University of North Carolina Press, 1981); Nancy B. Tucker, *Patterns in the Dust: Chinese-American Relations and the Recognition Controversy, 1949–1950* (New York: Columbia University Press, 1983); Steven I. Levine, *Anvil of Victory: The Communist Revolution in Manchuria, 1945–1948* (New York: Columbia University Press, 1987); Zi Zhongyun, *Meiguo duiHua zhengce de yuanqi he fazhan, 1945–1950* (The origins and development of U.S. policy toward China, 1945–1950) (Chongqing: Chongqing Chubanshe, 1987); Michael Schaller, *The U.S. Crusade in China, 1938–1945* (New York: Columbia University Press, 1979); Odd Arne Westad, *Cold War and Revolution: Soviet-American Rivalry and the Origins of the Chinese Civil War* (New York: Columbia University Press, 1993); Chen Jian, *China's Road to the Korean War: The Making of the Sino-American Confrontation* (New York: Columbia Uni-

versity Press, 1994); and Shu Guang Zhang, *Mao's Military Romanticism: China and the Korean War, 1950–1953* (Lawrence: University Press of Kansas, 1995).

3. Jon W. Huebner's concise article "Chinese Anti-Americanism, 1946–1948" was among the first works to deal exclusively with the subject of the anti-American phenomenon among Chinese intellectuals in the late 1940s. Based essentially on *Chinese Press Review* and secondary sources, Huebner's brief discussion of the non-Communist anti-American sentiment in the city of Shanghai offers a preliminary study of this important aspect of Sino-American relations. See Huebner, "Chinese Anti-Americanism, 1946–1948," *The Australian Journal of Chinese Affairs* 17 (January 1987): 115–25.

4. Noteworthy among works of this nature include Harold R. Isaacs's classic *Scratches on Our Minds: American Images of China and India* (New York: John Day Company, 1958); T. Christopher Jespersen, *American Images of China, 1931–1949* (Stanford: Stanford University Press, 1996); Warren I. Cohen, "American Perceptions of China," in *Dragon and Eagle: United States-China Relations, Past and Future*, ed. Michel Oksenberg and Robert B. Oxnam (New York: Basic Books, 1973), 54–86; Richard Madsen, *China and the American Dream: A Moral Inquiry* (Berkeley and Los Angeles: University of California Press, 1995); and Jeffrey N. Wasserstrom, "Big Bad China and the Good Chinese: An American Fairy Tale," in *China Beyond the Headlines*, ed. Timothy B. Weston and Lionel M. Jensen (Lanham, Md.: Rowman & Littlefield Publishers, 2000), 13–35.

5. In the context of modern China, the term "intellectual," or *zhishi fenzi*, literally translated as "elements with knowledge," in its broadest meaning refers to anyone who was educated. The historian Y.C. Wang defines twentieth-century Chinese intellectuals as "'educated men' in distinction to the masses who are uneducated." See Y.C. Wang, *Chinese Intellectuals and the West, 1872–1949* (Chapel Hill: University of North Carolina Press, 1966), vii. According to the 1979 edition of the Chinese encyclopedia, *ci hai*, an "intellectual" means "anyone who labors with his brain and is in possession of certain cultural or scientific knowledge, workers in literature and arts, teachers, physicians, etc." See Yueh Tai-yun, *Intellectuals in Chinese Fiction* (Berkeley: Institute of East Asian Studies, 1988), 5. Since Chinese students formed a crucial part of the intellectual community or the intelligentsia, in this book the term "intellectuals" refers not only to teachers, professors, journalists, scholars, and other professional people, but especially to college and in some cases high school students.

6. For arguments on this thesis, see also David Shambaugh's article "Anti-Americanism in China," in *Anti-Americanism: Origins and Context*, ed. Thomas P. Thornton, special issue of *The Annals of the American Academy of Political and Social Science* 497 (May 1988): 142–56; Michael Hunt's "Themes in Traditional and Modern Chinese Images of America," in *Mutual Images in U.S.-China Relations*, ed. David Shambaugh, Occasional Paper, no. 32, Wilson Center, 1988, 1–17. Two notable studies that offer especially early Chinese images of America are Michael H. Hunt's *The Making of a Special Relationship: The United States and China to 1914* (New York: Columbia University Press, 1983) and R. David Arkush and Leo O. Lee, trans. and eds., *Land without Ghosts: Chinese Impressions of America from the Mid-Nineteenth Century to the Present* (Berkeley: University of California Press, 1989).

7. David Shambaugh, *Beautiful Imperialist: China Perceives America, 1972–1990* (Princeton: Princeton University Press, 1991), 3.

8. Jerome B. Grieder, *Intellectuals and the State in Modern China: A Narrative History* (New York: The Free Press, 1981), 215.

9. For an excellent collection of Chinese writings about American society and people, see Arkush and Lee, *Land without Ghosts*. In his article "The Unofficial Envoys:

Chinese Students in the United States, 1906–1938," Hongshan Li argues that years of education in this country usually failed to inculcate favorable images in Chinese students. Rather, the students became resentful of America's China policy. See Hongshan Li and Zhaohui Hong, eds., *Image, Perception, and the Making of U.S.-China Relations* (Lanham, Md.: University Press of America, 1998), 145–67.

10. John W. Dower, *War without Mercy: Race and Power in the Pacific War* (New York: Pantheon Books, 1986), xi.

11. Thurston Griggs, *Americans in China: Some Chinese Views* (Washington, D.C.: Foundation for Foreign Affairs, 1948), preface.

12. For a brief discussion of the futile American effort to "build up the Chinese liberals," see Thomas D. Lutze, "America's Japan Policy and the Defection of Chinese Liberals, 1947–1948," in *George C. Marshall's Mediation Mission to China, December 1945–January 1947*, ed. Larry I. Bland (Lexington, Va.: George C. Marshall Foundation, 1998), 461–97.

13. During the Republican period of 1912 to 1949, the Chinese student population in higher education constituted less than 0.01% of the whole population. In other words, only about 40,000 out of a population of 400,000,000 were able to receive a college education. See Philip West, *Yenching University and the Sino-American Relations, 1916-1952* (Cambridge: Harvard University Press, 1976), 90.

14. Dorothy Borg, "America Loses Chinese Good Will," *Far Eastern Survey* 18 (February 23, 1949), 45.

15. For discussions on this issue, see Merle Goldman, *China's Intellectuals: Advice and Dissent* (Cambridge: Harvard University Press, 1981), 3–10; and Merle Goldman, Timothy Cheek, and Carol Lee Hamrin, eds., *China's Intellectuals and the State: In Search of a New Relationship* (Cambridge: The Council on East Asian Studies, Harvard University, 1987), 1–3. For a good general examination of the relationship between Chinese intellectuals and modern Chinese politics, see Grieder, *Intellectuals and the State in Modern China*.

16. See Jeffrey N. Wasserstrom, *Student Protests in Twentieth-Century China: The View from Shanghai* (Stanford: Stanford University Press, 1989), for an excellent discussion of students' dramatic and effective utilization of streets as political stages.

17. John Israel, *Student Nationalism in China, 1927–1937* (Stanford: Stanford University Press, 1966), 9. In *Rebels and Bureaucrats: China's December 9ers* (Berkeley: University of California Press, 1976), Israel and Donald Klein establish the connection between emotional patriotism just prior to the Sino-Japanese War (1937–1945) and the conversion of urban Chinese intellectuals to the rural-based Communist movement in Yan'an. In *The Politics of Depoliticization in Republican China: Guomindang Policy towards Student Political Activism, 1927–1949* (Berne, Germany: Peter Lang, 1996), pp. 23–31, Jianli Huang provides a brief discussion of student activism in twentieth-century China.

18. Wasserstrom, *Student Protests in Twentieth-Century China*, 18.

19. Joseph K.S. Yick, *Making Urban Revolution in China: The CCP-GMD Struggle for Beiping-Tianjin, 1945–1949* (Armonk, N.Y.: M.E. Sharpe, 1995).

20. Wen-Hsin Yeh's book, *The Alienated Academy,* presents an interesting study of campus culture in individual Republican institutions and of the relationship between the social, political, and cultural orientation of an individual college and the student response to the larger national events during Republican China. The author identifies four major types of higher educational institutions in Republican China: state-sponsored universities, western missionary colleges, private Chinese colleges, and government-sponsored institutions; see *The Alienated Academy: Culture and Politics in Republican*

China, 1919–1937 (Cambridge: Harvard University Press, 1990), 3.

21. Some studies of the student movement during the Chinese Civil War period have, however, discussed the issue to some extent. See, for example, Suzanne Pepper, *Civil War in China: The Political Struggle, 1945–1949* (Berkeley: University of California Press, 1978), 52–58, 72–78; Jessie G. Lutz, "The Chinese Student Movement of 1945–1949," *Journal of Asian Studies* 31 (November 1971): 89–110; Yick, *Making Urban Revolution in China*, 94–103, 116–18; and Wasserstrom, *Student Protests in Twentieth-Century China*, 139–42, 261–63. While these works provide insight into the shifting Chinese intellectuals' views of and attitudes toward the U.S. government's involvement in China in the postwar period, the foci of these studies dictate that the authors can give the subject only preliminary treatment.

1

AMERICA AS BOTH INSPIRATION AND OBSTACLE

The young United States rose to prominence when the old "Middle Kingdom" experienced drastic decline. In the midst of China's economic, political, military, and international weaknesses, the wealthy and strong "flowery flag country" (*huaqi guo*, the term used by early Chinese to refer to the United States, after the "flowery-looking" American national flag) appealed to different groups of Chinese for different reasons. For example, in the mid-nineteenth century, immigrant workers referred to this faraway land as the "mountain of gold" (*jinshan*) full of economic opportunities, while reform-minded officials saw it as a possible model for China's own technological development. Around the turn of the twentieth century, the United States became a popular destination for Chinese students, who went there to acquire necessary skills to help strengthen their own country. Many of them were destined to play an important part in China's development.[1] While their direct exposure to things American shaped their own views of the United States, their ambivalence toward a country both alluring and disappointing also helped mold as well as reflected the general Chinese intellectual opinion. Meanwhile, many politically minded young intellectuals in China found the history of American independence an inspiring example for China's own political aspirations and American president Woodrow Wilson's call for world justice directly relevant to their own yearning for political independence. However, the juxtaposition of expectations with realities often induced in young educated Chinese a paradoxical combination of admiration, fascination, disillusionment, and even resentment. Consequently, in their search for national unity and strength, they oscillated between perceiving the United States as an inspiration and as an obstacle.

EDUCATIONAL MISSIONS TO AMERICA

The Opium War of 1839–42, initiated by Britain over the opening of China's door for trade in general and over China's anti-opium campaign in particular, ended in China's defeat and its entrance into a century of "unequal treaties" and concessions. The war and China's subsequent defeat at the hands of Western powers disclosed a militarily discredited and internationally humiliated China, shaken in its illusion of supreme status. Convinced of the superiority of Western weapons, some high-ranking scholar-officials in China began to push for programs of learning Western military technology so that China could better deter further Western aggression.[2] Reform-minded Chinese officials were impressed by the achievements of the United States, which rose to power, wealth, and great prominence within only one hundred years.[3] Moreover, in 1868 the United States concluded the Burlingame Treaty with China, which specified among other issues mutual rights of residence and attendance at public schools by citizens of both countries. The reciprocal nature of the treaty terms pleased the Chinese officials.[4]

Urged by Viceroys Zeng Guofan and Li Hongzhang, the Qing court set up an educational program in 1872 to send 30 Chinese boys between the ages of 12 and 16 each year to study defense- and technology-related subjects in the United States. Therefore, *Meiguo*, the Beautiful Country, which is the Chinese name for the United States, became the first country to which China sent students abroad. The boys were to stay in this country for 15 years. Upon completing their studies, they would return to China and be at the service of the Qing government. Supporters of this program hoped that it would allow the government to have an ever-increasing body of skilled engineers who would help build railroads, set up telegraph lines, construct warships, and manufacture guns and ammunitions.[5] The group of 30 Chinese boys became the first Chinese students to study in the United States.

Li Hongzhang, the prominent Qing statesman, believed that it was of great significance and urgency for China to build the basis of self-strengthening by sending young students to the United States to learn specific Western skills. Li lamented that "it is a matter of not only distress but also shame for a big country like China to lack independence and power."[6] The boys were there to acquire "military science, ship-building techniques, mathematics, and engineering, and so on, so that China can be familiar with all the technical specialties of the West and have its own experts."[7] Between 1872 and 1874, 120 Chinese boys were sent to the Untied States to study. However, the mission did not turn out to be as fruitful as Li had hoped. The U.S. government refused to allow the select group of boys to move on to the military academies at Annapolis and West Point upon the completion of their high school education. On the other hand, the Qing court also received disturbing reports concerning the young students' "undesirable" behavior, including incompetence in classical Chinese learning, conversion to Christianity, and even marriage to American women. This educational mission, which began in 1872 and allowed over 100 Chinese boys to study in the United States, was abruptly ended in 1881. Li subsequently sent promising students to countries such as

Germany, France, and Britain, where the governments did not object to training Chinese students in military and naval affairs.[8]

About two decades later, in 1894, the first Sino-Japanese War broke out; this also ended in China's crushing defeat, and produced a far greater shock in China than the previous defeats by the Western powers, generating profound repercussions. The defeat not only demonstrated China's weakness, but also shattered its traditional self-image as the center of civilization and morality. It had been humiliating enough for the Chinese to be beaten by the Western powers. But now worst of all they had been humbled by a previously scorned Asian neighbor, which China had long regarded as its cultural protégé. This served as a powerful awakening and some of the literati began to vigorously demand political and social reforms. There arose calls for educational reforms from people who deemed the existing examination system, with its emphasis on Confucian teachings, to be outmoded.

In 1905, the Qing court abolished the traditional civil service examination based on classical education, a move that paved the way not only for the establishment of more higher educational institutions, but also for the introduction of new curricula and teaching methods. The American curriculum, together with those of other Western nations, then became a point of reference. Along with the introduction of new courses, including natural and social sciences, mathematics, and English, such Western ideas as democracy, social Darwinism, and socialism exposed Chinese youths to new modes of thinking.

Around the turn of the century, more Chinese started to go to the West and to Japan to study. The number of Chinese students in the United States had remained small until 1908, when the U.S. government turned its share of the Boxer Indemnity, which it had attained in the settlement following the antiforeign, anti-Christian Boxer Uprising (1898–1901), into a scholarship program.[9] It allowed 100 Chinese students to go to the United States each year to pursue higher education.[10] Part of the fund was allocated to build a preparatory school, known as Qinghua College, in Beijing in 1909 to facilitate the study abroad program. Selected high school graduates would first go through a short, American-run preparatory program at Qinghua before being sent to the United States.[11]

Through the Boxer Indemnity fund and other official and private avenues, more Chinese students had the opportunity to study in the United States. By 1910, the United States had acquired the reputation for being "the Chinese Mecca of Education."[12] By 1915, there were more than 1,200 Chinese students in American schools and colleges, of whom about 800 were in colleges and universities.[13] The number of Chinese students in the United States grew steadily until by 1949 around 36,000 had been to schools there.[14]

Most of the Chinese students studying abroad during this period cherished a strong sense of mission and were pushed by an urge to acquire necessary skills to help strengthen their country.[15] A large number of returned students found employment in college teaching and government service,[16] and some became prominent leaders in industry and finance.[17] In his memoirs, K.S. Hao, an American-educated Chinese, maintains that "almost all the overseas Chinese students at that time thought of nothing but learning knowledge that would be useful and beneficial to their country, that could be effectively and quickly learned, and that could offer immediate and fundamental solutions to the problems of their country." They would then return to China "to contribute what they [had] learned upon the completion of their studies." Dr. Wellington Koo, an American-trained jurist who later became a well-known diplomat for the Nationalist government, likewise asserted in a 1912 speech that Chinese students in America selected courses and majors with serving, or rather, saving their country, as their primary goal.[18]

Chinese students and visitors who went to America were intrigued by what they saw and found much to praise. They envied its material wealth, marveled at its rapid technological development, and complimented its optimistic and forward-looking people. As No-yong Park, who went there in 1921, wrote, "The typical American is young and energetic, progressive and optimistic, and is a great 'booster,' a hard-working man, a good sport, and a genius as an organizer." The Americans "are the ones who live in the future tense."[19] The American accomplishments often so overwhelmed the Chinese visitors and students that some of them were turned into "Americophiles." A senior Chinese student, J.L. Huang, while studying at Vanderbilt University in Nashville, Tennessee, concluded a laudatory speech in an annual oratorical contest in 1924 by saying: "America! America! The time is come! The hour is struck! The destiny of the whole world is in your hands! Turn the key, and turn it right!"[20] He subsequently became a persistent promoter of the idea of a special American relationship with China. Some students, such as Huang, developed a lifelong sense of identity with American cultural ideas and values.

Direct as well as indirect Chinese exposure to things American, however, often resulted in mixed emotions. The growing prosperity and power of the United States contrasted sharply with an enfeebled and unstable China lacking in independence and lagging behind in modernization. China's weakness, its inferior position in the international realm, and the image of China as "the sick man of Asia" (*dongya bingfu*) all rendered Chinese students sensitive and bitter. Accordingly, they felt more keenly the urgent need for China to revitalize itself.

Those Chinese who had the opportunity for a short visit to the United States also often harbored ambivalent feelings about the country. Liang Qichao (1873–1929), a preeminent scholar and a famous reformer, after touring the United States in 1903 wrote his informative *Notes from a Journey to the New Continent* (*Xin dalu youji*), which influenced significantly the thinking of many early twentieth-century Chinese intellectuals. His work demonstrates a mixture of views toward the United States. He was both intrigued and troubled. While admiring American political and economic developments, he cautioned the Chinese to be alert to the signs of American jingoism, to American imperialistic designs, and to President Theodore Roosevelt's call for a more powerful American presence in the Pacific area. Liang also concluded that democracy and the American republican system, with its diffusion of power, did not apply to the Chinese political situation.[21]

The existence of racial prejudice in the United States often struck deep in the hearts of the Chinese. Western concepts of race reached China when its intellectuals were most concerned with the issue of national salvation. Among the various new ideas introduced to China from abroad, the philosophy of social Darwinism, with its emphasis on the "survival of the fittest" races among human societies, introduced and interpreted by the prominent British-educated scholar Yan Fu, gained prominence. The social Darwinian discourse on race significantly impacted the thinking of Chinese intellectuals. The issue assumed particular relevance to Chinese students who went to America where they encountered a society in which Chinese were openly discriminated against.[22] The Chinese writer Qi Youzi published a popular story in early 1905 titled "Bitter Student," which depicted the bias that Chinese students experienced in the United States.[23] Some arriving students and visitors suffered ill-treatment immediately upon their entry into the United States on Angel Island in the middle of San Francisco Bay. Chih Meng, having won a five-year scholarship to study in the United States in 1919, claimed, "In California we had our first experiences with racism. Three barbershops in the Bay Region refused to cut our hair because we were Asiatics. What hurt most was that the YMCA in Los Angeles declined to rent us transient rooms for the same reason."[24]

The writings of Wen Yiduo, who studied in the United States between 1922 and 1925, and who would later become a renowned scholar and turn into a radical intellectual in the 1940s, also revealed vividly a strong sense of racial consciousness.[25] He wrote home saying that "the US is not a place for me to stay in long." He continued with a bitter tone that "for a young Chinese of principle, the flavour of life here cannot be described. When I come home at the end of the year after next, I shall tell you all about it beside our fireside and I shall weep bitterly to get rid of the accumulated indignation and frustration in my heart."[26] Wen would hold a lifelong bitterness toward racial injustice in the United States.[27] In this sense, resentment constituted an element of many Chinese students' experiences in the United States even when the American government acted altruistically.

As sojourners in a distant land with different customs, Chinese students became keenly conscious of their own "Chineseness." Loneliness, homesickness, and feelings of alienation instilled in them a heightened sense of patriotic attachment to their own country.[28] Furthermore, for many, the discrimination against the Chinese in the United States was a direct reflection of China's own political and military weakness and national humiliations. Already imbued with a strong feeling of national consciousness, embittered now by the racial prejudice they had witnessed or experienced, and disillusioned by the perceived gap between American preaching and practice, some would return to China carrying with them not only feelings of admiration but also those of distrust or even animosity toward the United States.[29] Consequently, a few decades later, when the newly founded Communist government initiated a nationwide effort to eradicate Western-educated intellectuals' "worship America" mentality, it inflamed a smoldering bitterness that had been in existence in the minds of some for a long time.

MESSAGES CONVEYED BY *UNCLE TOM'S CABIN*

If an American education did not necessarily produce Chinese students "saturated with American sentiment," the passage in the United States Congress of a series of exclusion laws targeting especially Chinese laborers, along with the anti-Chinese riots, aroused deep resentment in China.[30] With the spread in coastal China of stories and the corpus of literature on the intensified hostility toward

Chinese labor in the United States in the late nineteenth and early twentieth centuries, some Chinese writers of that period uttered a cry of dismay and indignation, and even compared the harsh American treatment of Chinese labor with the previous enslavement of blacks in America. Lin Shu (1852–1924), the most famous translator of English and American novels during the first two decades of the twentieth century, rendered Harriet Beecher Stowe's *Uncle Tom's Cabin* into Chinese, under the title *A Black Slave's Cry to Heaven (Heinu yutianlu)*.[31] It became the first American novel ever translated into Chinese. Lin was most concerned at the time with the rapid deterioration of China's strength and the fate of China. The wretched experience of the black slaves in the United States seemed to be a dire sign of what might befall the Chinese in the future. In the afterword, Lin claimed that he had not translated this book to elicit tears from the reader, but rather to warn about the dark fate of the yellow race and "to cry out for the sake of our people because the prospect of enslavement is threatening our race."[32]

Being at the receiving end of American racial intolerance, very few Chinese visitors and students in the United States could ignore the issue. On the other hand, a feeling of superiority buttressed by China's past grandeur and by tradition, combined with a sense of shame over China's existing weakness, rendered many Chinese unwilling to relate the Chinese plight to the black minority. As one scholar argues, Chinese students' experiences in the United States heightened their racial consciousness, but few questioned the premises of racial hierarchy. While seeking to improve the Chinese position in the hierarchy, they often revealed prejudices against other races, especially American blacks.[33] For example, during his trip to the United States in 1903, the eloquent Liang Qichao was indignant that the Chinese laborers were being excluded from the United States, while the blacks were there to stay. He thus claimed, "true, the type of Chinese [excluded from America] are lowly and undisciplined. But are they not better than the blacks?" In an article introducing *Cry to Heaven*, another Chinese writer, Ling Shi, insisted that this book be read extensively in China in order to awaken the Chinese to the national crisis. He further claimed that "all the tears that I had shed for the blacks in reading *Cry to Heaven* were actually tears for our yellow race. While I was crying for the blacks' past plight, I was actually crying for the yellow people's present plight."[34] The book was finished in 1901, one year after the United States and seven other foreign powers put down the antiforeign Boxer Uprising in northern China. A popular book in China, it conveyed a gloomy image of the United States.[35]

Out of patriotic spirit and grave concern for China's future, Lin Shu and others hoped that the novel could inspire the Chinese to fight for freedom. Based on this book, the Spring Willow (*Chun Liu*) Society, organized by Chinese students in Japan, put on a five-act play in Tokyo for three days in 1907. The primary motivation for the play was to arouse the nationalistic fervor of the Chinese students in Japan.[36] Many intellectuals at the time sensed keenly the need for a unified and strong China in order for the Chinese to be treated with respect and dignity abroad. Meanwhile, in the eyes of many, the United States constituted a land not only of opportunity and great wealth, but also of violence and intense hatred.

THE 1905 BOYCOTT

The issue that cast the biggest shadow over Sino-American relations in the late nineteenth and early twentieth centuries was the American immigration policy toward China. In response to the increasingly strict Chinese exclusion laws and regulations enacted by the United States Congress, to the stories and literature of ill-treatment suffered by Chinese laborers, and also to the humiliation and hardship experienced by Chinese students and merchants at the port of entry, Chinese merchants and students joined together in launching a boycott of American goods and services in 1905, the first widespread and politically charged economic movement organized against a foreign country in Chinese history.

The 1905 boycott represented a fresh Chinese response to national humiliations through essentially concerted economic action. While the movement originated in Shanghai, it quickly spread to major coastal cities in the south, and to Beijing and Tianjin in the north. Those who provided momentum to the movement included students, merchants, cultural figures, labor leaders, educated women, and overseas Chinese. Out of this political agitation in the form of organized economic action emerged Chinese nationalist fervor. Propaganda poems, novels, essays, newspaper articles, and even some local operas (mostly in the southeastern coastal cities) deplored bitterly the plight of Chinese labor in the United States, attacked the American exclusion policy, and contended sensationally that cheap American goods reaching the China market had taken away the jobs of Chinese laborers who then had to migrate to the United States to make a miserable living.[37] One organizer of the movement, Feng Xiawei, even committed suicide in front of the American consulate in Shanghai in order to stimulate others to continue the boycott.[38] Feng's martyrdom fueled the movement. Thousands of people went to the memorial meetings held for Feng while patriotic articles were written in his memory.[39]

A number of educated women played an active role in the anti-American boycott. They wrote articles, made public speeches, and distributed pamphlets advising women not to buy such American products as perfume, face powder, and soap. In Shanghai, they organized mass meetings urging women to boycott American goods, and asking the American government to repeal discriminatory immigration policies.[40] A few political activists also saw the movement as a good opportunity to challenge traditional Chinese family patterns, to interest Chinese women in political issues, and to instill in them a sense of national crisis. Handbills with such titles as "For the Chinese Women" were distributed. Lin Guanhong, the writer of the essay "A Plea to the Two Hundred Million Fellow Sisters," called on Chinese women to unite and boycott American goods. Lin claimed that she was overwhelmed with great joy over the nationwide development of the movement to resist the U.S. exclusion immigration policy. She further argued that the success of the movement, which involved national dignity and honor, would greatly enhance China's international status.[41] In another article encouraging Chinese women to boycott American goods, the author, Zhi Qun, asserted that the boycott movement, a prelude to national unity, offered Chinese women an opportunity to gain their rights:

If women join the movement to resist American goods, they will establish the basis for their independence. Chinese women, with their bound feet, have been depending on their husbands for their livelihood, and have spared no time and energy to worry about the national issues. Now if they can join the movement to boycott American goods, they will then fulfill certain obligations as members of the nation. Isn't this the beginning of achieving women's independence?[42]

The movement had such a wide appeal in the coastal cities at the time that some rhymes were concocted for children to sing on the street. One of the popular children's songs goes as follows:

> Listen, listen, and listen to my song.
> Every day my dad said, let's boycott American goods.
> Every night my mom said, I hate American goods.
> I then also hated American goods, so I destroyed
> our American cigarettes and perfume.
> My mom became mad at me for doing so.
> But my dad praised me excessively.
> Everyone else looks at me with wonder.
> And says I did the right thing, because the
> American law barring the Chinese is too cruel.
> Sisters and brothers, please don't use American goods.
> If children all over the country learn from me,
> We shall have no more fear of American guns and cannons.
> We will make it impossible for American goods to be sold here.
> The American merchants will then have no business to do.
> And the Americans will have to make a compromise with us.
> Listen to me everyone, and don't laugh at me.
> Think carefully about what I have said, and you will have no regret.[43]

Involvement of different social classes made the 1905 boycott movement a popular one. Merchants in Shanghai, Guangdong, Tianjin, Xiamen, and other coastal cities organized the boycott, which enjoyed the enthusiastic support of patriotic students from China's modern schools. For example, students from Shanghai took to the streets giving public lectures and distributing handbills. Young people from two American-run missionary schools there quit to show their support of the boycott. One of the schools, the Qingxin Academy, had to be dissolved as a result.[44] Actors, singers, storytellers, and cartoonists also participated in the movement in ways that both educated and entertained the public.[45] Chinese newspapers, especially those in Shanghai, gave wide coverage to the boycott.[46]

The movement, which lasted for about six months in some cities, resulted in losses to American and Chinese merchants and posed a threat to American economic, cultural, religious, and political interests in China.[47] The boycott also alerted policymakers in Washington to the growing Chinese resentment of racial discrimination and violence in the United States. President Roosevelt issued orders to immigration officials demanding fair treatment and warm courtesy toward Chinese teachers, students, merchants, and travelers to the United States.[48]

Although largely symbolic and with little effect on American exclusion policy, the boycott against the sale and use of American products helped promote among the participating Chinese a sense of unity, heightened their national sentiment, and enhanced their awareness of the importance of organizing themselves to publicize their grievances. In a sense, the 1905 boycott, in focusing Chinese public attention on the issue of American discrimination against the Chinese, planted the seed of the American "loss of China." Viewing the anti-Chinese phenomenon in the United States as an obvious reflection of China's weakness, many educated Chinese began to search more vigorously for means to strengthen their motherland. The patriotic rhetoric and the participation of the broad spectrum of social groups in the movement therefore evinced a growing sense of Chinese nationalism.

An equally significant consequence of the movement was that active student involvement in the boycott led to a new awareness on the part of Washington of students' political, social, and cultural significance. The U.S. government thus displayed a special interest in promoting and sponsoring the education of Chinese students in America. It assumed that students educated in this country would better appreciate its culture and values, and would therefore serve as strong spokesmen of the American way of life upon returning to China and help cement ties between the two countries. Looking upon Chinese students as potential transmitters of American values in China and upholders of Sino-American friendship, the U.S. government took the concrete step of allocating the excessive part of the Boxer Indemnity to the education of Chinese students in the United States. Beginning in 1908, a record number of students began to arrive in the country to be enrolled in colleges and universities. "The underlying assumption," as the historian Michael Schaller argues, "was to make Chinese accept American values, to become more like Americans." Good Chinese meant those who were converted to Christianity and devoted themselves to making over their own culture in the American image.[49] However, as discussed previously, the American-educated students largely failed to meet these expectations and held ambivalent feelings toward *Meiguo*, the Beautiful Country.

INSPIRATION OR OBSTACLE

During the early twentieth century, the issue of national revitalization assumed a new urgency among urban Chinese intellectuals and students. The end of the Qing imperial rule and the founding of the republic failed to usher in a representative government capable of leading China to a new era, but saw further political disintegration as evinced by President Yuan Shikai's frustrated monarchical ambitions and the ensuing turbulent era of warlord rule. Meanwhile, the penetration of foreign powers into China continued unabated. On the other hand, all manner of foreign ideologies continued to flow into China and were avidly scanned and absorbed by the Chinese eager to find a way to inject energy and vibrancy into their country. Many politically conscious Chinese were convinced that if China did not strengthen itself, it would be subdued by stronger nations and would experience the extinction of the nation (*wangguo*). Propelled by a long-held sense of their special social responsibility, domestic political instability, and foreign encroachments, they became highly conscious of the compelling need to save China. They believed that "bringing an end to the crisis of the state was the precondition for lifting China out of danger and building a modern China."[50] The iconoclastic New Cultural Movement of the early twentieth century was the outcome of such a search.

Frustrated with China's continued weakness, and in their eager pursuit of national autonomy and political renewal, many young intellectuals seriously questioned and challenged the validity of traditional Chinese values and institutions, and urged a wholesale introduction of Western science and ideologies. Many believed that an intellectual revolution to reconstruct China through the adoption of Western science and democracy would be a panacea to save China. In May 1919, the intellectual movement was translated into the first nationwide student protests. Bitter disillusionment with the decision made by the peacemakers at the post–World War I Versailles Conference to transfer the former German concessions in Shandong to Japan triggered a mass student demonstration in Beijing on May 4, 1919, an epoch-making date in modern Chinese history. Protest demonstrations, strikes, and boycotts against Japanese goods then spread all over China. The decision at Versailles not only dashed the Chinese expectations for an improved international position, but also led to a new intellectual and political awakening, which manifested itself especially in skepticism and uncertainties about Western democracy and even about the Western civilization that had embroiled itself in a disastrous world war, and in intellectuals' further and deeper political involvement.[51]

The May Fourth Movement ushered in a decade of rising nationalist fervor. Chinese students stood at the forefront of the political trend for change. Although coming from diverse social and economic backgrounds, they experienced a new sense of freedom away from the confines of their homes. Congregated in a new campus environment in large cities, they gradually developed their own distinct social identity through forming discussion groups and societies, in which they exchanged new ideas concerning pressing social and political issues. T.C. Wang refers to the growth of a sense of social solidarity among the students and their constant intellectual probing during the early decades of the twentieth century as the unfolding of a "youth movement" in China.[52] Chinese nationalism, broadly defined as a strong desire to see a unified, independent, and rejuvenated China and as a distinct identification with the Chinese nation, served as "the force that created the paradoxical unity of all participants."[53] While sharing the common goal of saving China, young intellectuals, however, differed in their projected solutions.[54] For example, while many after 1919 began to adopt a critical reappraisal of Western democracy, some continued to view it as being directly relevant to China. The most famous upholder of Western values and attitudes was probably Hu Shi, an eminent American-returned scholar.[55] In 1919, Hu Shi's former mentor at Columbia University, John Dewey, a philosopher and educator, and a proponent of pragmatism, was invited to visit China, a trip made possible by

Hu Shi and some of Dewey's other Chinese followers. Dewey went on a lecture tour of 11 provinces in China in 1919–20. He promulgated the virtues of education and the idea that individual development formed the basis of a democratic society. He found in China eager listeners. A major newspaper in Beijing published Dewey's lectures under the name "Five Major Lectures by Dewey" (*Duwei wuda yanjiang*). They proved to be so popular that they were reprinted 10 times within two years.[56] However, in the course of the 1920s, even though Dewey's message of gradual reform remained influential among some westernized individuals, its popularity quickly waned.[57] As one historian argues, Dewey's method "struck some listeners as irrelevant to a China sunk in poverty, fragmented by cynical warlords, and struggling to achieve control of its own affairs."[58] The American model thus seemed far from being a cure-all for the Chinese situation.

In their desperate search for answers to unify and liberate a China beset by imperialism and internal strife, the generation of young intellectuals, who had tasted political power during the dynamic May Fourth demonstrations, began to respond to the foreign stimuli. Experiencing a profound sense of national disgrace from China's helplessness in the face of imperialistic incursions, many however lost confidence in Western liberal reforms and scientific progress as the applicable methods to save China. For example, the unequal treaty system that emerged from the cultural and power confrontations between China and the West shielded the Western community of merchants and missionaries and fostered the growth of Western influence and privileges in China.[59] Among other things, China had to grant Westerners "extraterritoriality," which meant that they were exempt from Chinese laws and were subject only to the jurisdiction of their own countries. The students denounced especially the abuses of extraterritoriality in the anti-imperialist movement in the 1920s.[60]

The introduction of Western notions of national independence, sovereignty, and equality to China, together with the humiliating imposition of unequal treaties and the demonstration of foreign military might, nurtured Chinese nationalism and heightened intellectuals' opposition to foreign incursions and privileges in China.[61] While endeavoring to resolve their inner tensions over the necessity to adopt Western ideas, many Chinese intellectuals revealed a patriotic ardor. In time their nationalistic fervor led them to grapple with cultural influences from the West as they became more conscious of China's need to recapture national dignity and identity. Western presence and contact, accompanied by frustrations with domestic political uncertainties and impatience with the faltering pace of China's movement to gain freedom of action in the international realm, served as a strong catalyst for the Chinese patriotic movement during the early decades of the twentieth century. Many intellectuals believed that the recovery of lost territories, the abolition of the unequal treaties, and an end to foreign interference were the prerequisites for China's survival in the modern world. In this context, antiforeignness grew into a distinct patriotic sentiment among urban and educated groups in the 1920s. For example, a cartoon in a 1925 issue of *Dongfang zazhi* (Journal of the East) depicted a "civilized" West wearing a mask of friendship to hide its menacing true self.[62]

For the most part, young intellectuals in the 1920s shared a fervent enthusiasm for national salvation and experienced a common patriotic concern for China's fate. Fired by a strong desire to save China, many looked to the radical solutions promoted by the Chinese Nationalist Party and the Chinese Communist Party, and constituted an important part of tangible political forces of the two political parties. As the decade went on, large-scale protests broke out against what the students perceived to be the political, economic, and cultural encroachments upon China on the part of the imperialist powers. "Down with the imperialists and their running dogs [lackeys]" became the students' credo for a long time to come.

With regard to their views toward the United States during the early decades of the twentieth century, many young intellectuals found themselves in a conflicting position and entertained ambivalent feelings. The asymmetrical relationship between the two nations often induced in them a paradoxical combination of admiration and suspicion, which manifested itself as admiring Western scientific progress and those foreign social and political ideas relevant to a struggling nation (*chongyang*), while repudiating the West (*paiwai*) for its encroachment upon China. The juxtaposition of the "love and hate" perceptions of the United States among politically conscious Chinese can be understood in terms of this general framework.

America was viewed as both a relevant model and a threat to China.[63] On the one hand, the United States stood out as a nation of science and freedom. At the beginning of the twentieth century, many Chinese intellectuals, who believed that the Chinese would learn to stand up for themselves through learning from the American experience, found particularly inspiring the history of American independence in light of China's national crisis. Zhang Zongyuan, a Chinese student studying in the United States, rendered the first few volumes of Edward Channing's *A History of the United States* into Chinese. He renamed his translation *A History of American Independence*, as he translated only the part related to the American independence movement. When the book was published in 1902, it became so popular that it had to be reprinted within three months.[64]

The first half of the twentieth century also witnessed a great influx of Western, especially American, missionary activities in China. Social services, including hospitals and schools established by missionary boards, flourished. American-sponsored Christian schools and colleges took in thousands of students each year, introducing to them American ways of life. In their efforts to educate and "uplift" China, Americans were motivated essentially by the desire to export their benevolence, to bring light to the benighted Chinese, and to remake China in the American mode, while often failing to understand Chinese nationalistic aspirations.[65] In time, many Americans became strong believers in the special American role in China. According to a pamphlet produced by the American Information Committee in 1939, "American institutions and ideals fired the minds of countless Chinese youths who sought to reconstruct their country along similar lines." It further asserted that the "returned students have absorbed much of American ideals, methods, and ideas of government and industry, and they have a warm place in their hearts for America. They have put their stamp in molding the China of tomorrow."[66] Convinced that the Chinese cherished special fondness for things American, most Americans in China found disturbing the rise of the student anti-foreign movement in the 1920s. Meanwhile, American diplomats in China often denied the legitimacy and authenticity of Chinese nationalism and attributed it to Communist agitators, who "exploited the ignorance and passivity of less developed peoples."[67]

The American notion of a special relationship with China, promulgated especially by American missionaries, businessmen, and diplomats in China, raised expectations among some Chinese, who seemed to reciprocate the American feeling and cherished an affinity with the United States.[68] For example, in a meeting organized by the Chinese Student Activities Council of Greater New York in 1925, Hu Shi echoed the American line of thinking in terms of the relevance of an American model for China. He affirmed that the "thousands of Chinese students educated in American schools and trained in American industries constituted the best salesmen of American products, material, intellectual, and spiritual."[69] Jiang Menglin, who, together with Hu Shi, had studied under John Dewey at Columbia University, believed that the United States was distinctly different from other Western powers in its relations with China. In his autobiography, he asserts that "in days of old, when the West fought for colonial empire in the East, all the important Western Powers except America at various times wronged China." He continued: "The only thing Americans got from China was extraterritoriality, but what she had done for China is far more and will be remembered for generations to come."[70] As the historian Akira Iriye put it, many Chinese of this period looked upon the United States as "more than just one of the powers; America impressed them as a nation endowed with special resources that were relevant to the young republic."[71]

The American Open Door policy first promulgated at the turn of the twentieth century, though primarily concerned with keeping the "China Market" open for American trade and maintaining American political, religious, and cultural interests in China, was viewed by some Chinese as a demonstration of American goodwill toward China. For example, Wu Tingfang, the Chinese minister to the United States from 1897 to 1912, interpreted the Open Door and the Equal Economic Opportunity as almost altruistic.[72]

The American educational model remained consistently relevant during the first few decades of the twentieth century.[73] Even during the period of the 1920s when general hostility toward the foreign presence prevailed, American influence in the educational sphere was still extensive. When, in 1924, one student at Nankai University questioned the relevance of American-style Chinese educational methods to the issue of saving the country and criticized blind adoration of things American in Chinese education, he nevertheless revealed the prevalence of American influence in China:

We ask what a middle school teacher does and the answer is to teach students English, mathematics, and other knowledge to prepare them for university education. Why university education? The answer is to get a diploma. . . . The university teachers teach American politics, American economy, American commerce, American railway, American this, American that. . . . The student, when he graduates, also goes to the U.S. and somehow manages to secure a master's or doctoral degree. After he returns to China, he steps into the shoes of his teachers and perpetuates the revolving educational system. Only this revolving is one stage higher than the first kind. The difference between these two is that the middle school teacher plays a Chinese-American hoax, while the university teacher bluffs through his Americanism.[74]

A general review of the major Chinese intellectual journals of the 1920s proves that many Chinese still held "enthusiastically favorable" images of America, which impressed them as representing the future.[75]

The greatest contribution made by the American-returned students was probably in the field of education. By the thirties and forties, not only was an American curriculum the popular one in Chinese schools, but an American degree also became almost a stepping-stone to a position in the leading universities in China. Students returning from America dominated college faculty positions.[76] For example, out of the 83 full professors in Qinghua University in 1937, 74 had been to the United States to study. Only one received his education solely in China.[77] Meanwhile, information on various aspects of American life and culture as published through newspaper and journal articles was made increasingly available to literate, urban Chinese.

Nevertheless, the United States constituted one of the foreign powers that enjoyed special privileges in China and severely challenged its national integrity. In the specific American connection, Chinese intellectuals also experienced recurrent disappointments and disillusionment. For example, President Woodrow Wilson's Fourteen Points and New Diplomacy, with their emphasis on world justice and national self-determination, along with the convening of the Versailles Peace Conference, had afforded Chinese intellectuals high expectations of a new age of equality among nations and that China would finally gain a proper place in the international community. Accordingly, an image of America standing up for China surfaced. In December 1918, Chen Duxiu, the vanguard of the New Cultural Movement, stated that the various speeches made by Wilson were most "open-minded and righteous." Wilson, asserted Chen, was "the number-one good man on earth." Chen believed that Wilson's fundamental point was to prevent the powers from impinging upon the principles of equality and freedom.[78]

The dashing of the hopes, as manifested most painfully in the transfer of control over the former German concession in Shandong to Japan, created a gap between American rhetoric and reality. As a result, not only feelings of disappointment arose among Chinese intellectuals over the failure of Wilsonian idealism, but also misgivings regarding the sincerity of America's supposed concerns about China, and fear of the Western powers' continuing incursions on China. In an article titled "The Secret Diplomacy and the Robbers' World," Li Dazhao, another prominent figure of the May Fourth Movement, wrote angrily, "Wilson! Did you oppose the secret diplomacy? Now where are your points?! All have gone with the wind. I really feel sorry and ashamed of you."[79] Meanwhile, a disillusioned Chen Duxiu turned to communism as a solution to China's ills. Together, he and Li Dazhao became the cofounders of the Chinese Communist Party in 1921.

The American desire to "uplift" China clashed with the Chinese aspiration to seek an end to foreign interference and regain national independence.[80] Furthermore, the

American upholding of the unequal treaties, the Chinese exclusion policies in the United States, and American attitudes of racial superiority induced many Chinese to question the American rhetoric of benevolence and friendship. Favorable images of the United States, however, prevailed during World War II when a common enemy drew China and the United States closer together than before.

WARM FEELINGS DURING THE SINO-JAPANESE WAR

Japan became the principal target of Chinese national hostility in the 1930s, when it posed a severe threat to China's political independence and national security. Japanese aggression constituted a significant element in further stimulating Chinese nationalism. College and high school students, together with people from other walks of life, increasingly lodged protests against the advancing menace of Japan and participated in patriotic activities. Beginning in late 1931, large-scale student demonstrations against Japan repeatedly broke out. On December 9 and 16, 1935, the students in Beijing held the most significant nationalistic demonstrations since the May Fourth Movement, demanding that the Nationalist government take a strong stand against Japanese aggression. Students also formed patriotic associations of various kinds and were engaged in protests, public lectures, and anti-Japanese plays, which led to growing agitation.[81]

A full-scale war with Japan erupted in the summer of 1937. On July 17, Chiang Kai-shek declared to the nation that, despite China's ill preparation for fighting the Japanese, it had reached the "limit of endurance," and that the Chinese "must throw every ounce of energy into the struggle for national survival and independence."[82] In the immediate years that followed, the Chinese recognized American sympathy for China's war of resistance, but wished that American support would go beyond futile protests against Japanese aggression and would provide China with more concrete assistance.

The Japanese attack upon Pearl Harbor in December 1941 finally brought China powerful allies and in particular threw the United States and China together. For the majority of Chinese it instilled hope and confidence in a complete victory over Japan. Meanwhile, President Franklin D. Roosevelt visualized a future Asia where the United States and the Chinese Nationalist government would cooperate to construct a new order, thus enabling China to function as a major force in balancing power in postwar Asia.[83] Furthermore, the United States also made some political headway toward recognizing China as a major power. In January 1943, Chiang Kai-shek announced blissfully that the United States and Great Britain had abolished extraterritoriality and related unequal treaties with China. The treaties compromising Chinese sovereignty had been a constant reminder of Chinese weakness. Now, in the midst of the war, the unequal treaties became null and void.[84] Chiang could not but express his joy over the abrogation of the treaties and claimed that America and Britain had "lighted a new light to guide man's progress on the road to equality and freedom for all peoples."[85] The inspired Chinese viewed the abolition of the "unequal treaties" as a most significant step for China's entering the international community on an equal basis.

In 1943, the United States also revised its immigration policy, enabling a token number of Chinese to immigrate there. Later in the year, the Moscow Declaration acknowledged China as one of the "Big Four."[86] The Cairo Declaration that followed pledged the restoration of Manchuria, Taiwan, and the Pescadores to China. President Roosevelt was thus able to say, in his Christmas Eve message: "Today we and the Republic of China are closer together than ever before in deep friendship and in unity of purpose."[87] The political reality bolstered the expectation of many educated Chinese of an elevated position for their country in the postwar world. The earlier images of China as a weak country, suffering from imperialistic aggression, gave way to a more confident view of China's place in the postwar world as one of the leading powers. The American talk of China as one of the "Big Four" and of international justice corresponded with the Chinese thinking of their country's postwar status. Despite the existence of visible strains in official wartime Sino-American relations,[88] many Chinese thought warmly of the United States as a powerful ally of China. One Chinese reporter described people's feelings toward America in the Nationalist government's wartime seat, Chongqing, as follows:

I was in Chungking [Chongqing] throughout the eight war years, and every July 4th I could observe that many Chinese felt just as jubilant as the Americans. "Meikuojen" (The American people) were most popular even among the Chinese country folks on rural districts. Common talk among the Chinese on that day was of the gigantic American army and production and "America—indeed, a Land of Plenty."[89]

When news of President Roosevelt's death reached China, all major newspapers mourned for days, and paid high tributes to Roosevelt's character and achievements.[90]

With Japan's unconditional surrender in August 1945, China seemed to be emerging as an independent nation at long last. Foreign powers' unequal treaties with China had been relinquished, which erased the vestige of China's semicolonial status. The political reality in China in the wake of World War II, however, served as a blow to the high expectations cherished by the politically conscious Chinese. Far from fulfilling a vigorous function in the postwar world, and with civil war imminent, China seemed to be on the verge of political breakdown. Meanwhile, the prominent role the U.S. government played in Chinese politics incurred strong opposition among politically engaged educated youths as they began to criticize bitterly American "interference" in Chinese affairs. The late forties thus saw the disappearance of warm Chinese feelings toward America as demonstrated during World War II and the growth of visible intellectual hostility toward the U.S. government, which became the primary target of Chinese nationalism.

NOTES

1. Weili Ye's *Seeking Modernity in China's Name: Chinese Students in the United States, 1900–1927* (Stanford: Stanford University Press, 2001) is a recent study of Chinese students' encounter with the American society in the early twentieth century and the important role they played in China after returning to that country.

2. Frederick Wakeman, Jr., *The Fall of Imperial China* (New York: The Free Press, 1975), 163–98.

3. Zhongguo shixuehui, ed., *Yangwu yundong* (Self-strengthening movement) (Shanghai: Shanghai chubanshe, 1961), 565.

4. Thomas E. LaFargue, *China's First Hundred: Educational Mission Students in the United States, 1872–1881* (Pullman: Washington State University Press, 1987), 32–33.

5. Ibid., 13.

6. Yang Yusheng, "Cong yangwu re dao diyue chao" (From the self-strengthening craze to the 1905 boycott), *Meiguo yanjiu* (American studies), no. 3 (1991): 78–79.

7. Ibid., 79. For a more detailed discussion on this issue, see also Y.C. Wang, *Chinese Intellectuals and the West, 1872-1949* (Chapel Hill: University of North Carolina Press, 1966), 74–76.

8. Jonathan D. Spence, *The Search for Modern China*, 2d ed. (New York: W.W. Norton, 1999), 218–19; see also Luo Rongqu, "Meiguo yu xifang zichanjieji xinwenhua shuru Zhongguo" (The influx of American and Western bourgeois new cultures to China), in *Zhongwai wenhua jiaoliushi* (A history of cultural exchanges between China and foreign countries), ed. Zhou Yiliang (Henan: Henan renmin chubanshe, 1987), 656. For a study of the experiences of the 100 Chinese students during their stay in the United States and after their return to China, see LaFargue, *China's First Hundred*.

9. For discussions of the Boxer movement that broke out in 1898, see Chester C. Tan, *The Boxer Catastrophe* (New York: Octagon Books, 1967); Joseph W. Esherick, *The Origins of the Boxer Uprising* (Berkeley and Los Angeles: University of California Press, 1987).

10. U.S. altruism can be viewed from both sides. Colin MacKerras asserts that this educational plan actually meant that "under the guise of generosity, the Americans used money, paid to them to help invade China in 1900, for the purpose of imposing their own values on Chinese intellectuals." MacKerras, *Western Images of China* (Hong Kong: Oxford University Press, 1989), 76.

11. Yi-rong Young Liu, "Chinese Intellectuals' Sense of Mission and Their Attitude toward Foreign Study," (Ph.D. diss., University of California at Los Angeles, 1985), 52.

12. Jerome B. Grieder, Hu Shih and the Chinese Renaissance: Liberalism in the Chinese Revolution, 1917–1937 (Cambridge: Harvard University Press, 1970), 36; R. David Arkush and Leo O. Lee, trans. and eds., Land without Ghosts: Chinese Impressions of America from the Mid-Nineteenth Century to the Present (Berkeley and Los Angeles: University of California Press, 1989), 98.

13. Chow Tse-tsung, *The May Fourth Movement: Intellectual Revolution in Modern China* (Cambridge: Harvard University Press, 1960), 26.

14. Lyman P. Van Slyke, "Culture, Society, and Technology in Sino-American Relations," in *Dragon and Eagle: United States–China Relations: Past and Future*, ed. Michel Oksenberg and Robert B. Oxnam (New York: Basic Books, 1978), 140. Between the years of 1938 and 1945 when China was engaged in the war with Japan, the Chinese government drastically reduced the number of students going to study in the United States.

15. In *Chinese Intellectuals and the West*, Y.C. Wang argues that engineering was the most popular field among Chinese students between 1905 and 1952; see pp. 168–69 of his book. Interestingly, college students in China during this period concentrated mainly on the legal and liberal arts fields. See Suzanne Pepper, *Radicalism and Education Reform in 20th-Century China: The Search for an Ideal Development Model* (New York: Cambridge University Press, 1996), 81.

16. Pepper, *Radicalism and Education Reform in 20th-Century China*, 83.

17. Ye, *Seeking Modernity in China's Name*, 2.

18. See Liu, "Chinese Intellectuals' Sense of Mission," 79–80.

19. No-yong Park, "A Chinese View of the American Character," in *America in Perspective: The United States through Foreign Eyes*, ed. Henry Steele Commager (New York: Random House, 1947), 334–35.

20. J.L. Huang Collection, Box No. 1, Hoover Institution Archives Holdings on China. In *China and the West: Society and Culture 1815–1937* (Bloomington: Indiana University Press, 1979), 78–79, Jerome Chen provides more examples on this. For instance, Chang Po-ling (Zhang Boling), the famous early-twentieth-century Chinese educator, highly praised American material wealth and scientific progress, and ascribed them to American leaders' untiring public service, marvelous experiences, physical strength, capability, and work ethic, attributes that he believed were beyond the attainment of Chinese officials.

21. See Arkush and Lee, *Land without Ghosts*, 81–84, for more details on Liang's trip to the United States; Jerome B. Grieder also provides useful illustrations on Liang's 1903 tour of the United States in "Liang Ch'i-chao 1873–1929 and Hu Shih 1891–1962," in *Abroad in America: Visitors to the New Nation, 1776–1914*, ed. Marc Pachter and Frances Wein (Reading, Mass.: Addison-Wesley, 1976), 279–92. Kang Youwei (1858–1927), a key leader of the reform movement of 1898, a prominent figure in the intellectual movement of modern China, and mentor of Liang Qichao, also looked upon the progress that the United States had made in science and technology as spectacular, even though he did not think that the American republican system could apply to the Chinese autocratic situation. Kang commented in 1898 that "of all the countries on earth, none is as prosperous and contented as the United States of America, but her republican political system is different from China's [autocratic] system." (Kung-chuan Hsiao, *A Modern China and a New World: Kang Yu-wei, Reformer and Utopian, 1858–1927* [Seattle: University of Washington Press, 1975], 209.)

22. Ye, *Seeking Modernity in China's Name*, 85–86.

23. Qi Youzi, "Ku xuesheng" (Bitter student), in *FanMei Huagong jinyue wenxueji* (Collected literature on opposition to the American treaty excluding Chinese laborers), ed. A Ying (Beijing: Zhonghua shuju chuban, 1960), 273–309.

24. Chih Meng, *Chinese American Understanding: A Sixty-Year Search* (New York: China Institute in America, 1981), 102.

25. Personal hardship and political and social injustice politicized and radicalized Wen Yiduo, and turned him into a fierce opponent of the status quo. In July 1946, he was gunned down on the street by GMD secret agents for his outspoken views against the Nationalist government's move toward the Civil War and the GMD's suppression of political dissidents. See John Israel, *Lianda: A Chinese University in War and Revolution* (Stanford: Stanford University Press, 1998), 378–79.

26. Chen, *China and the West*, 160.

27. Ye, *Seeking Modernity in China's Name*, 105–7.

28. Frank Dikötter, *The Discourse of Race in Modern China* (Stanford: Stanford University Press, 1992), 157.

29. See Jerome B. Grieder, *Intellectuals and the State in Modern China: A Narrative History* (New York: The Free Press, 1981), 215. Tu Wei-ming argues that many American-trained students "experienced psychological tension between their romantic promulgation of the liberal-democratic ideal and their painful memories of discriminatory treatment during stays in America." (See Tu, "Chinese Perceptions of America," in *Dragon and Eagle*, 99.)

30. In 1882, the United States Congress passed the Chinese Restriction Act prohibiting the entry of Chinese laborers into the United States for a period of 10 years, which was the first time that America had restricted immigration. The Scott Act of 1888 limited the return

of those Chinese laborers who had temporarily visited China. The Geary Act of 1892 renewed the exclusion act for another 10 years. In 1902, Congress passed a bill permanently excluding Chinese laborers. Although Chinese students, along with teachers, merchants, officials, and travelers for pleasure or curiosity, belonged to the five special classes of Chinese exempt from the exclusion regulations, they often received ill-treatment at the point of entry, and some were refused entry and sent back.

31. Lin Shu could read only Chinese. Therefore, he collaborated with others versed in Western languages in translating Western works into Chinese. For the translation of *Uncle Tom's Cabin*, for example, he had to depend on Wei Yi's oral rendition.

32. See Lin Shu's afterword in *Land without Ghosts*, 79.

33. Ye, *Seeking Modernity in China's Name*, 108.

34. Quoted from Tao Jie, "Heinu yu tian lu—diyibu yicheng zhongwen de Meiguo xiaoshuo" (A black slave's cry to heaven—the first American novel translated into Chinese), *Meiguo yanjiu*, no. 3 (1991): 129.

35. See Arkush and Lee, *Land without Ghosts*, 77.

36. Tao Jie, "Heinu yu tian lu," 133.

37. See articles collected in A Ying's *FanMei Huagong*.

38. See Wang Yao, "FanMei yundong zai Zhongguo wenxue shang de fanying" (The anti-American movement as reflected in modern Chinese literature), *Guangming ribao*, December 16, 1950. For a study of the impact of Feng's martyrdom on the boycott, see Sin-kiong Wong's "Die for the Boycott and Nation: Martyrdom and the 1905 Anti-American Movement in China," *Modern Asian Studies* 35 (July 2001): 565–88.

39. A Ying, *FanMei Huagong*, 696–99.

40. For more details, see Liu Jucai, *Zhongguo jindai funu yundongshi* (A history of modern Chinese women's movement) (Beijing: Zhongguo funu chubanshe, 1989), 255–62.

41. Lin Guanhong, "Jinggao er wan wan tongbao jiemei" (A plea to the two hundred million fellow sisters), in *FanMei Huagong*, 648.

42. Zhi Qun, "Zhengyue zhi jinggao er" (Second warning on fighting the Chinese exclusion law), in *FanMei Huagong*, 650–51.

43. Chu E, "Zhengyue geyao" (A rhyme on fighting the exclusion law), in *FanMei Huagong*, 677.

44. See Chen Xulu et al., *Jindai Zhongguo bashinian* (The Chinese history of the last eighty years) (Shanghai: Shanghai renmin chubanshe, 1983), 433; Jeffrey N. Wasserstrom, *Student Protests in Twentieth-Century China: The View from Shanghai* (Stanford: Stanford University Press, 1991), 41.

45. Wong, "Die for the Boycott and Nation," 587.

46. Zhang Chunwu, *Guangxu 31 ZhongMei gongyue fengchao* (The 1905 agitation against the Sino-American labor treaty) (Taibei: Taiwan shangwu yinshuguan, 1965), 53.

47. For two careful studies of the American exclusion policy at home versus the Open Door policy in China, see Delber L. McKee, *Chinese Exclusion versus the Open Door Policy, 1900–1906: Clashes over China Policy in the Roosevelt Era* (Detroit: Wayne State University Press, 1977) and Michael H. Hunt, *The Making of a Special Relationship: The United States and China to 1914* (New York: Columbia University Press, 1983), especially chapters 3, 7, and 8.

48. See Hongshan Li, "The Unofficial Envoys: Chinese Students in the United States, 1906–1938," in *Image, Perception, and the Making of U.S.-China Relations*, ed. Hongshan Li and Zhaohui Hong (Lanham, Md.: University Press of America, 1998), 145–46.

49. Michael Schaller, *The United States and China in the Twentieth Century* (New York: Oxford University Press, 1979), 22. For arguments along this line, see Hongshan Li, "The Unofficial Envoys," 145–63.

50. Michael H. Hunt, "Chinese National Identity and the Strong State: The Late Qing–Republican Crisis," in *China's Quest for National Identity*, ed. Lowell Dittmer and Samuel S. Kim (Ithaca: Cornell University Press, 1993), 62.

51. For detailed treatments of the May Fourth Movement, see Chow, *The May Fourth Movement*; Joseph T. Chen, *The May Fourth Movement in Shanghai* (Leiden: E.J. Brill, 1971); and Lin Yu-sheng, *The Crisis of Chinese Consciousness: Radical Anti-Traditionalism in the May Fourth Era* (Madison: University of Wisconsin Press, 1979).

52. Tsi C. Wang, *The Youth Movement in China* (New York: New Republic, 1927).

53. Lucien Bianco, *Origins of the Chinese Revolution, 1915–1949* (Stanford: Stanford University Press, 1967), 19.

54. Modern Chinese nationalism consisted of multilayered connotations, which cannot be easily defined. For a study about the complexity of Chinese nationalism, see articles in *Chinese Nationalism,* ed. Jonathan Unger (Armonk, N.Y.: M.E. Sharpe, 1996).

55. Having graduated from the Qinghua preparatory school, Hu Shi was sent to America on the Boxer Indemnity fund in 1910, and received a Ph.D. in philosophy from Columbia University in 1917. A student of John Dewey and perhaps the most famous Chinese intellectual educated in the United States, Hu Shi remained one of the firmest defenders of Wilsonian idealism and argued against charges of Western "materialism and spiritual impoverishment." See Chen, "Liang Ch'i-chao and Hu Shih," 279–93. For a study on Hu Shi's role in the New Cultural Movement, see Grieder, *Hu Shih and the Chinese Renaissance*, 75–169.

56. See Luo, "Meiguo yu xifang zichanjieji xinwenhua shuru Zhongguo," 663.

57. Dewey's other well-known Chinese disciples included Jiang Menglin, Tao Xingzhi, and Chen Heqin.

58. Van Slyke, "Culture, Society, and Technology in Sino-American Relations," 142–43.

59. For a careful study of the foreign settlements in Shanghai and the desire of Westerners to continue their privileged and "spoilt" life in a rapidly changing China, see Nicholas R. Clifford, *Spoilt Children of Empire: Westerners in Shanghai and the Chinese Revolution of the 1920s* (Hanover, N.H.: Middlebury College Press, 1991). In *China Perceived: Images and Policies in Chinese-American Relations* (New York: Alfred A. Knopf, 1974), John K. Fairbank examines the anti-American nature of the Chinese revolution of the twentieth century in the context of the identification of the Westerners with the old ruling class in China. Having acquired an upper-class status, the foreigners in China joined the traditional Chinese rulers. The inculcating of Western values then turned the modern Chinese revolutionaries against the old order. Since the foreigners in China were part of the old order, the attack on the latter would inevitably involve the former. See pp. 61–84 of the book.

60. The following comments by an American working as a bank teller in a Chinese port city suggested the bitter sentiment toward extraterritoriality: "If a Chinaman does not at once make room for me in the street I would strike him forcibly with my cane in the face. . . . Should I break his nose or kill him, the worst that could happen would be that he or his people would make complaints to the consul, who might impose the fine of a dollar for the misdemeanor, but I could always prove that I had just cause to beat him." (See Hugh Deane, *Good Deeds and Gunboats: Two Centuries of American-Chinese Encounters* [San Francisco: China Books & Periodicals, 1990], 2.) Sun Yat-sen later lamented that foreign powers had subjected China to the status of a "hypocolony," a situation worse than a colony because it had become "not the slaves of one country, but of all." (Sun Yat-sen, *San-min Chu-i: The Three Principles of the People*, trans. Frank W. Prince [Shanghai: Institute of Pacific Relations, 1927], 38, 123.)

61. John F. Cleverley, *The Schooling of China: Tradition and Modernity in Chinese Education* (Boston: George Allen and Unwin, 1985), 49.

62. See Ka-che Yip, *Religion, Nationalism, and Chinese Students: The Anti-Christian Movement of 1922–1927* (Bellingham: Western Washington University, 1980), 43.

63. In her article "Chinese Intellectuals and the United States: The Dilemma of Individualism vs. Patriotism," *Asian Survey* 29 (July 1989): 645–54, Chinese historian Yuan Ming briefly discusses the complex images of Chinese intellectuals toward the United States as a consequence of their pursuit of individual enlightenment and national salvation.

64. See Yu Danchu, "Meiguo dulishi zai jindai Zhongguo de jieshao he yingxiang" (The introduction and impact of the history of American independence on modern China), *Shijie lishi* (World history), no. 2 (1987): 60–81.

65. James C. Thomson Jr., *While China Faced West: American Reformers in Nationalist China, 1928-1937* (Cambridge: Harvard University Press, 1969), 5.

66. The American Information Committee, *Japan over China–America's Gain or Loss?* (Shanghai, 1939), 6.

67. Quoted from David Wilson, "The United States and Chinese Nationalism during the 1920s," *Chinese Historians* 5 (fall 1992): 39.

68. Michael Hunt's *The Making of a Special Relationship* remains the most outstanding study on this subject. In his book, he defines the American "open door constituency" as those businessmen, missionaries, and diplomats "with a common commitment to penetrating China and propagating at home a paternalistic vision (conventionally associated with the open door) of defending and reforming China," xi.

69. See Meng, *Chinese American Understanding*, 215. For a discussion of the firm belief in the relevance of the American model for the enlightenment of China held by Hu Shi and some other Chinese with a similar educational background, see Q. Edward Wang, *Inventing China Through History: The May Fourth Approach to Historiography* (Albany: State University of New York Press, 2001), 67–73.

70. See Chiang Monlin (Jiang Menglin), *Tides from the West: A Chinese Autobiography* (New Haven: Yale University Press, 1947), 269.

71. Akira Iriye, *Across the Pacific: An Inner History of American-East Asian Relations* (New York: Harcourt, Brace & World, 1967), 129.

72. Chen, *China and the West*, 82.

73. In the early thirties, the League of Nations sent an educational mission to China to conduct a general survey of public education in China. The mission reported on the pervasive influence of the American model in the field of Chinese education: "A notable characteristic of contemporary China is the cultivation by a group of the specific tendencies of some foreign culture, whether it come from America, Germany, France or some other nation. . . . The officials responsible for public education in China simply identified American education and modern educational system. The old Chinese system of education seemed to them not only obsolete and in great need of reform, but also of a nature to be condemned. Without any transition, therefore, the teaching programmes and methods of the United States were made to supersede the centuries-old wisdom and learning of China. There are extremists who would like to see China Americanised." See The League of Nation's Mission of Educational Experts, *The Reorganisation of Education in China* (Paris: League of Nations' Institute of Intellectual Co-operation, 1932), 25.

74. Quoted from Yip, *Religion, Nationalism, and Chinese Students*, 10.

75. Tu, "Chinese Perceptions of America," 94.

76. Kwang-ching Liu, *Americans and Chinese: A Historical Essay and a Bibliography* (Cambridge: Harvard University Press, 1963), 35. In *Radicalism and Education*

Reform in 20th-Century China, pp. 59–64, Pepper also discusses the influence of American-returned students on the Chinese educational system.

77. Arkush and Lee, *Land without Ghosts*, 143.

78. Li Zhancai, "Shi xi Wusi shiqi Meiguo duihua yingxiang" (An analysis of American influence on China during the May Fourth era), *Zhongguo xiandaishi* (History of modern China), no. 1 (1994): 68.

79. Quoted from Yuan Ming, "Chinese Intellectuals and the United States," 651.

80. Chiang Kai-shek provided a revealing view of what he perceived to be the discrepancy between American profession of high ideals and American practice in an interview with an American reporter, Lewis Garnett, in 1926: "Thinking men in China hate America more than they hate Japan. Japan talks to us in ultimatums; she says frankly that she wants special privileges. . . . We understand that and know how to meet it. The Americans come to us with smiling faces and friendly talk, but in the end your government acts just like the Japanese. And we, disarmed by your fair words, do not know how to meet such insincerity." Quoted in Harold R. Isaacs, *Scratches on Our Minds: American Images of China and India* (New York: The John Day Company, 1958), 202. At around the same time, Mao Zedong, influenced by the student national movement in the 1920s and disenchanted with U.S. foreign policy, also began to look upon the Americans as one of the "foreign powers" who employed "a pretense of 'amity' in order that they may squeeze out more of the fat and blood of the Chinese people." Cited in Hunt, *The Making of a Special Relationship*, 304.

81. For a thorough discussion of patriotic student movements during this period, see John Israel, *Student Nationalism in China, 1927–1937* (Stanford: Stanford University Press, 1966).

82. Chiang Kai-shek, *The Collected Wartime Messages of Generalissimo Chiang Kai-shek, 1937–1945*, ed. and trans. George Kao (New York: The John Day Company, 1946), 22.

83. Tang Tsou, *America's Failure in China, 1941–50* (Chicago: University of Chicago Press, 1963), 41–43.

84. The Allies abolished the treaties also for the purpose of keeping China in the war against Japan. Also, Westerners could not enjoy special rights in coastal areas controlled by the Japanese anyway. For a study of the beginning, development, and abolition of extraterritoriality in China, see Wesley R. Fishel, *The End of Extraterritoriality in China* (Berkeley and Los Angeles: University of California Press, 1952).

85. Chiang, *The Collected Wartime Messages of Generalissimo Chiang Kai-shek*, 734.

86. U.S. Department of State, *The China White Paper: August 1949* (1949; reprint, Stanford: Stanford University Press, 1967), 37.

87. Ibid.

88. For example, the United States' "Europe First" strategy evoked disappointment on the part of the Nationalist government. China's low war priority and the difficulty in transporting supplies over the Hump after the fall of the Burma road made it impossible for the United States to provide the substantial aid desired by the Nationalist government, which then felt ignored and discriminated against. Meanwhile, given its "Europe First" strategy, the United States counted on China to engage a large number of Japanese troops, but the Nationalists considered that it had done its share of fighting and that it was now time for others to bear the main burden. Therefore, neither side gave priority to the war they shared and both attempted to use each other to occupy the Japanese while they focused on more important concerns. The difference in military strategic considerations constituted one of the discrepancies in the wartime policies between the two nations.

89. C.Y.W. Meng, "An Interpretation of Student Anti-US Demonstrations," *The China Weekly Review* (3 August 1946): 79.

90. See Yang Yusheng, "Dayang bian gaigechao de dongfang xiaoying" (The effect of the reform movement at the other side of the Pacific on the East), *Meiguo yanjiu*, no. 2 (1991): 105–8.

2

URBAN CHINESE RESPONSE TO THE AMERICAN MILITARY PRESENCE, 1945–1946

When the Sino-Japanese War ended in August 1945, the Chinese people hoped that domestic peace and national unity might at long last be within sight. But this desire soon proved to be illusory, as China found itself at the crossroads of war and peace again. Japan's defeat prompted a race between Nationalists and Communists for control of Japanese-occupied territories, enemy weapons, and military supplies. The Nationalist forces, confined largely to the southwest when the war ended abruptly, were less favorably posited in the scramble. The American government immediately assumed the responsibility for arranging for the surrender and repatriation of the Japanese troops in China, and came to the aid of the Nationalists in their reoccupation effort.

The subsequent presence of American troops in China, especially the occupation of north China by U.S. marines, compounded an already volatile political situation, became the target of inflaming Chinese nationalistic, anti-American sentiment, and constituted an important chapter in Sino-American relations. Upon the departure of the Soviet occupation forces from Manchuria in April 1946, the American troops became the most conspicuous foreign presence in China.[1] The direct contact between them and Chinese civilians resulted in significance far greater than the limited American military involvement in China entailed. It acted as a prism through which the politically sensitive Chinese perceived the postwar Sino-American relationship. The political magnification of the issues related to the prolonged stay of American servicemen in China served as a turning point in the unfolding urban Chinese perception of the United States in particular and Sino-American relations at large.

FROM TERRANOVA TO LARRINAGA

Two homicides, 125 years apart, illustrate the shift in the power balance that occurred in Sino-American relations. In the first case, on September 23, 1821, a six-pound pottery jar fell off the deck of the American ship *Emily*, anchored off Whampoa, Guangdong, and killed a boatwoman selling fruit in a small dinghy alongside the ship. Upon discovery and examination of the body, the Chinese authorities charged that the owner of the jar, Francisco Terranova, a seaman on board *Emily*, had intentionally thrown the jar at the woman after being shortchanged. They claimed that the jar hit the woman in the head, causing her to fall off the boat and drown. Terranova denied the charge, and his shipmates testified that he had nothing to do with the woman's death.

The Chinese provincial governor general and the district magistrate were determined to exercise justice by making the foreigners observe Chinese laws. Meanwhile, major American merchants and captains in the port city of Canton organized an emergency committee, which agreed to submit the case to Chinese jurisdiction and requested a fair trial in return. The Chinese authorities then consented to leave Terranova in American custody and to hold the trial on board *Emily*. During the trial, however, the Chinese magistrate grew impatient over the American insistence on cross-examining the Chinese witnesses and on listening to testimony for the accused, and he ended the trial abruptly. The magistrate left with the demand that Terranova be surrendered to him. The governor general subsequently issued an embargo on trade with the Americans until Terranova was handed over to the Chinese authorities for a retrial in the city.

The dire consequences of halting trade forced the emergency committee to allow the Chinese officials to take away Terranova on October 24. Terranova was tried by the magistrate with no Americans present. He confessed to hurling the jar overboard with no intention of doing any harm, and was found guilty of murder. At dawn on the fourth day after his delivery to the Chinese, he was taken to the execution ground and strangled. Trade then resumed.

The Terranova incident was the first conflict involving extraterritoriality between China and the United States. By threatening to terminate trade between the two countries, the Chinese authorities were able to settle the case their way. The event suggests that in these early days of contact between the two countries, American political influence in China was negligible.[2]

In the second case, over one hundred years later, on September 22, 1946, on a Shanghai city street, Julian Larrinaga, a civilian working as a seaman in the U.S. Navy, quarreled with a Chinese rickshaw puller, Zang Dayaozi, after refusing to pay Zang the fare. Immediately confronted by a group of angry-looking rickshaw pullers, Larrinaga called upon Edward Roderick, a coxswain in the U.S. Navy, to come to his aid. After Roderick struck Zang with his fist, Zang fell to the pavement and sustained a concussion. He died early next morning from the injury. Roderick was charged with having struck and caused the death of Zang.[3]

This time, the Chinese authorities held little sway over the trial and sentencing of the American sailor, because Roderick, a member of the U.S. military force, was not subject to the Chinese law. Although China and the United States signed a treaty on January 11, 1943, which relinquished American extraterritorial rights as well as related special privileges in China,[4] a few months later, on May 21, 1943, the Chinese and American authorities exchanged notes concerning criminal jurisdiction over American armed forces stationed temporarily in China. The Sino-American Military Service Agreement provided that the service courts and the military and naval authorities of the United States held exclusive jurisdiction over criminal offenses committed by members of the American armed forces in China, and thus exempted the American troops in China from the Chinese Criminal Code.[5] Consequently, only the U.S. Navy held jurisdiction over Roderick. On November 12, 1946, a general U.S. Navy Court Martial tried him in Shanghai, while Larrinaga, a civilian, was subject to the Chinese Criminal Code and was tried in the Shanghai District Court for having instigated the assault leading to Zang's death. He was sentenced to one year and nine months' imprisonment.[6] Roderick pleaded not guilty to the charge of manslaughter. After several days of trial the naval court acquitted him, on the ground, as explained by Rear Admiral W.A. Kitts, that the Chinese witnesses had difficulty identifying Roderick. During the subsequent trial for Larrinaga, however, Roderick appeared before the Shanghai District Court as a witness and admitted that he had struck Zang in order to aid Larrinaga who was surrounded by a group of angry rickshaw pullers, and that Zang fell immediately to the ground.[7]

The Chinese Ministry of Foreign Affairs then lodged a formal complaint to the U.S. embassy about the way in which the American naval authorities in China handled the case and demanded a retrial of Roderick's case, as Roderick had in the subsequent Chinese court confessed complicity in the death of Zang. The letter of complaint asserted that the procedures for the trial of Roderick had violated the provisions of the Sino-American Military Service Agreement because the naval court had failed to cooperate with the Chinese authorities in obtaining testimony from the Chinese witnesses and it did not invite Chinese representatives to witness Roderick's trial. Also, the letter argued that the naval authorities neglected to ask the Shanghai District Court to furnish information relevant to the case.[8] The U.S. Navy Headquarters in Shanghai refuted the official Chinese protest, and concluded that since Roderick, a member of the U.S. military forces, was subject exclusively to U.S. laws, to put him in "double jeopardy" on the same charge would be a breach of U.S. laws. The case thus came to an end, but conflicts between American servicemen and Chinese civilians continued.

The difference in the handling of the two homicide cases highlights a change in the locus of power between China and the United States. While the Terranova case demonstrates a degree of presumptuousness on the part of Chinese officials, the case of Roderick reflects American assertiveness, and in the eyes of politically sensitive Chinese, American disregard of justice for the Chinese and indifference to China's newly gained sovereignty. The death of Zang Dayaozi and the acquittal of Edward Roderick were widely and critically reported and commented upon in local newspapers. The Zang Dayaozi incident and other conflicts involving American troops and local Chinese in the immediate postwar years provoked Chinese resentment of American military presence in China and gave rise to anti-Americanism among politically conscious urban Chinese.

MARINES IN NORTH CHINA

As the Third Marine Amphibious Corps of the U.S. Pacific Fleet was undergoing extensive training in Guam and Okinawa in preparation for an invasion of the Tokyo Plain, World War II came to an abrupt end. Immediately afterwards, all the units received orders to get ready for reassignment to north China. To the great relief of the marines, they met no resistance from the supposedly hostile Japanese forces when they landed in the key cities in north China in late September and October 1945. On the contrary, they received a warm welcome from the local Chinese. Upon the marines' arrival, flag-waving and cheering crowds greeted them for days.[9] Upon reaching the city of Tianjin, for example, the marines and their trucks had to force their way through streets packed with welcoming crowds to reach their billets.[10]

The U.S. marines were not new to north China. As part of the 1901 Boxer Protocol in the aftermath of the antiforeign, anti-Christian Boxer Movement, foreign powers, including the United States, secured the right to station their troops permanently in the Legation Quarter in Beijing to prevent future antiforeign movements from threatening the lives of foreigners in the diplomatic quarters. Soon afterwards, a contingent of U.S. marines assumed the duty of garrisoning the American Legation (elevated to the status of embassy in 1935) and guarding the railway line from Beijing to the sea so that more troops could be brought in for the protection of the Legation if needed.[11] Of the various foreign military contingents stationed in Beijing, the U.S. marine detachment, with over 500 men at its peak forming six companies, was the largest.[12]

China duty in those days entailed adventure, excitement, travel, pursuit of pleasure, an easy yet exotic life, and "high living," and was therefore a coveted one.[13] The low cost of living in China allowed almost all the marines to hire Chinese servants, often simply called "boys," to conduct daily chores for them, which included cooking, cleaning, making beds, running errands, and polishing their shoes. The relatively light guard duties left the marines, officers as well as enlisted men, much time for social, athletic, and cultural activities. On the other hand, "booze and women," easily available and quite affordable, appeared first on the list of "vices" marines engaged in. Consequently, venereal disease became a common curse for marines in China. In the end, the coveted China assignment with its idle garrison duty had a debilitating effect on the marines.[14]

Meanwhile, since 1912, units from the Fifteenth Regiment of the U.S. Army were stationed in Tianjin, a city about 60 miles southeast of Beijing and known as the gateway to Beijing. Troops of the Fifteenth Regiment guarded the railroad to Beijing until February 1938 when they were recalled to the United States due to the war situation in China.[15] More than 200 marines from the Beijing Embassy Guard were then dispatched to Tianjin to replace them. By November 1941, shortly before Japan bombed Pearl Harbor, most marines had withdrawn from China.

Immediately after Pearl Harbor, however, the remaining marines in north China were forced to surrender to the Japanese and were then thrown into prison camps.[16] Four years later, following the end of the war, marines returned triumphantly to China in much greater numbers, but on a different, and more murky and dangerous mission.

In the wake of World War II, American ground and naval forces in China reached about 113,000 at their peak, which included the landing in north China of some 53,000 marines fresh from the Pacific Theater.[17] The immediate tasks of the American forces in China were to occupy such key ports as Shanghai, Dagu, Canton, and Qingdao and to assist the Guomindang (GMD) government in accepting the surrender of the Japanese military forces and personnel and in disarming and repatriating them to Japan. More significantly, they were to aid the Chinese Nationalists in their competition with the Communists to take over cities and strategic areas formerly held by Japanese troops by air- and sea-lifting half a million Nationalist forces to the coastal cities, to central and north China, and to Manchuria.[18] Major naval leaders also hoped to use the marines as a counterforce to possible Soviet advance in north China.[19]

By assisting in the transport of Nationalist forces to reestablish sovereignty over occupied territories in north China, American troops helped neutralize the Chinese Communist forces operating in the region.[20] Meanwhile, before the Nationalists could consolidate their hold over north China, U.S. marines, functioning as an occupation force there, had occupied Tianjin, Beiping, Qingdao, and their environs, assumed garrison duties, secured the seaports and airfields, and guarded railroads, bridges, and coal mines in these areas.[21] Although the marines were supposed to remain neutral and to avoid direct military involvement, the fact that their presence strengthened the position of the GMD while significantly weakening that of the Chinese Communist Party (CCP) in northern China soon invited passive Communist resistance.[22]

MARINES ON THE OUTPOSTS

For the American servicemen stationed on the isolated outposts assuming responsibility for the Nationalists in guarding vital coal and supply trains, railroads, and bridges, life was lonely, boring, and potentially dangerous.[23] The marines' occupation of coastal north China prevented the Communist forces active in the region from assuming control of cities and vital supply and communication lines; it also forced them to retreat temporarily to the countryside, and thus proved to be a thorn in the side of the Communists. Consequently, the Communists viewed the marines' presence in north China with strong misgivings, even though initially they had expressed a willingness to cooperate with the American troops.[24]

Although avoiding open military engagement and overt hostilities, the CCP forces soon began a series of harassing attacks on the marines, destroying rail tracks and bridges, and firing on marine-guarded trains.[25] Consequently, marines had to remain on constant alert against raiding Communists and common village thieves who would steal such items as oil drums, vehicles, ammunition, and fuel for a good profit in the black market.[26] Communication with local villagers was almost nonexistent.[27] One marine officer later recalls that "lack of communication and an unclear situation resulted in numerous warning shots being fired, particularly at night, at dim figures who could have been innocent farmers or reconnoitering Communists."[28]

When the Nationalist troops reached north China in late 1945, they demonstrated no eagerness to relieve the marines of their guard duties. Instead, they were keen on reestablishing control in Manchuria where the Communists had already established a foothold. This necessitated a continuing deployment of marines to the exposed outposts.

The cease-fire agreement between the Communists and the Nationalists that went into effect in January 1946 eased the tension somewhat between the marines and the Communists. However, Communist raids and ambushes increased significantly in the middle of 1946 when the Civil War erupted in Manchuria upon the Soviet departure. By then, the CCP leaders had become disillusioned with the Marshall Mission.[29] As they were getting ready for a final military showdown with the Nationalists, the Communists believed that the marines in north China posed a real as well as a potential threat to their military confrontation with the GMD.

Against the backdrop of heightened CCP resentment of American military presence, the most serious armed clash took place on the highway at Anping, a small town between Beiping and Tianjin, on July 29, 1946. Communist soldiers ambushed a motor convoy of supplies escorted by the marines, killing three and wounding eleven.[30] The CCP leaders hoped that these attacks could slow down the redeployment process of the Nationalist troops assisted by the marines and hasten the withdrawal of American forces from China.

For marines on the outposts, the hazardous China duties were exasperating. While the real war was over, they were, however, placed in the tenuous position of refraining from direct military involvement in a Chinese civil war, and yet apparently taking the side of the GMD, thus serving as the target of Communist ambushes.[31] Whereas the nebulous nature of the China mission further aggravated the unpleasant guard duties, the American postwar demobilization also hit the marine detachments, as an increasing number of long-timers were qualified to return home. They were replaced either with regulars scraped together hastily or with new and inexperienced draftees or not replaced at all.[32] The trend of demobilization not only affected the morale of the remaining marines; the retrenchment also meant that their positions were even more vulnerable since they were spread thinner along miles of railroad.[33] Due to the grim facts associated with guard duties, a system was developed to rotate marines at the dreary yet dangerous outposts so that they could have some fun and rest in such cities as Beiping and Tianjin for a few days before they went back to the lonely rail lines.[34]

Real as well as potential armed clashes with Communist forces made marines' exposed positions untenable. In the wake of the Anping Incident, the U.S. Navy decided to turn over bridge, coal mine, and train guard duties to the Nationalist troops, and to concentrate marines in urban centers, including Beiping, Tianjin, Dagu, Qinhuangdao, and Qingdao.[35] By the time the Chinese Civil War flared up in late 1946, marines had largely withdrawn from their exposed outposts and into cities.[36] The relatively large congregations of marines in the cities, however, significantly increased the number of conflicts between them and urban Chinese, and thus affected the Chinese perception of the Americans.

U.S. MILITARY PRESENCE IN URBAN CHINA: DEVELOPMENT OF FRICTION

Upon arriving in urban China, American sailors, soldiers, and marines displayed some degree of curiosity about their exotic surroundings and things Chinese. For example, fascinated with the two-wheeled, man-powered rickshaws that were used widely in Chinese cities, many were eager to go for rides in them, and sometimes they would pull Chinese rickshaw pullers for fun.[37] Just out of combat and with money to burn, they celebrated wholeheartily. On the other hand, American servicemen also meant good business for many Chinese shopowners since the former "invaded these shops, paid excessive prices, but all came out with large parcels and seemed happy and contented."[38]

City life appeared not too bad for officers as well as enlisted men. As Colonel Henry Aplington recalled: "There were twice-weekly dinner dances and Sunday afternoon tea dances at the officers' club. Service clubs were opened for the men, and there were nightclubs and bars to suit every taste."[39] Meanwhile, American servicemen toured famous historic sites, visited Chinese theaters, sampled Chinese cuisine, patronized stores for items such as silk, brocades, artifacts, and various other kinds of souvenirs to send home, and frequented nightclubs, dancing halls, bars, and brothels.[40]

The aura of mutual appreciation that accompanied the initial arrival of American troops was short lived, however, and was soon replaced by a mutual dislike developed between many American servicemen and urban Chinese. If the potentially dangerous and ambiguously defined duty at the exposed, overextended outposts deepened the marines' desire to get out of China, their exhilaration over the urban surroundings also faded away after they encountered the bleak reality. To their dismay, they found old women hobbling around on small, pointed bound feet, shabby-looking men or women selling their starved children at ridiculously low prices on the streets, and hungry-looking children as well as adults searching their garbage cans for leftover food. For marines, a war-ravaged China in the midst of political and military crises and beleaguered by a dysfunctional economy, abject poverty, and squalor soon lost its exotic luster. Disbelief and shock over the wretched existence of countless Chinese around them replaced their sense of novelty.

In the prewar years, the China mission had attracted mainly marines who were seeking adventure and excitement in a land shrouded in mystery and exoticism in the American imagination. The great majority of the marines in postwar China, however, were not careerists. Recruited to the Marine Corps by the call of war, many on the China mission had already fought long and hard in the Pacific War. Echoing the domestic call to "bring the boys home," they longed to return to the United States as soon as possible to resume the normal life of peacetime.[41]

The plunge into such teeming Chinese cities as Beiping, Tianjin, Nanjing, Shanghai, and Wuhan of an unprecedented large number of American soldiers, sailors, and marines in the immediate post–World War II period brought American servicemen into direct daily contact with local Chinese. Different languages, cultural backgrounds, customs, economic statuses, and races highlighted the conspicuous presence of American servicemen in the midst of the urban Chinese population, and promised friction between the two groups.

Well aware of the potential trouble, the marine authorities encouraged and promoted athletic and cultural activities among their servicemen. They hoped that the recreational pursuits would help maintain the marines' morale, keep them physically fit, and provide an outlet for their pent-up energies, which could otherwise be directed to urban brothels, and thus expose them to undesirable elements of Chinese society as well as to venereal disease, and tarnish their reputation among local Chinese. The marine authorities also designated certain entertainment and service quarters as "out of bounds" areas due to sanitary and safety reasons.[42] *Marine's Guide to North China* warned the servicemen about security breaches, asked them not to wander about alone, and encouraged them to check out local culture and cuisine.[43] Despite the marine authorities' efforts to steer their young men to "healthy" pursuits, many soon made frequent trips to the "red-light district."

American servicemen on leave dealt frequently with lower-class urban Chinese whose services they needed. They came into regular contact with two groups especially: pullers for rickshaws and pedicabs, and prostitutes. GIs found rickshaws and pedicabs a cheap and convenient way to take them to various places. Pullers for rickshaws and pedicabs also found GIs a good source of income and eagerly sought them out. Frequent dealings, however, often led to arguments over payment, and sometimes even tragic deaths as in the case of rickshaw puller Zang Dayaozi. While GIs sometimes suspected rickshaw pullers of overcharging, local Chinese newspapers often reported cases of GIs refusing to pay the fare or beating up pullers. In an attempt to ease the tensions between the two groups, and perhaps embarrassed by the unseemly sight of a large number of man-pulled vehicles rushing on the crammed streets of Shanghai, the GMD officials even issued a ruling to reduce and eventually eliminate rickshaws in the city.[44] The ruling also reflected a typical GMD indifference to the livelihood of the urban poor.

A major GI hangout that often involved the service of rickshaw and pedicab pullers was urban brothels. While GIs' frequent trips to "pleasure houses" caused concern among their superiors, their visits to prostitutes also did not endear them to the moralistic Chinese, who viewed them as lascivious men lacking in moral qualities. The newly developed Chinese image of American servicemen as debased womanizers also reflected negatively on the young Chinese women whom they patronized. As the latter were often seen riding with the Americans in their jeeps, the Chinese even coined a term "jeep girls" (*jipu nulang*), which carried a derogatory tone. In fact, any Chinese girl "careening through the streets in open-topped jeeps" with drunken Americans was often "automatically regarded as little better than a prostitute."[45] The commonly held Chinese view was that no well-brought-up girls of decent families would willingly mingle with drunken, ill-mannered, and lustful American soldiers (*Meiguo dabing*).

In cartoons and picture books, "jeep girls" often appeared as immodest-looking young women with long wavy hair, tight-fitting dresses, and high heels.

Drunken GIs waving beer bottles and shouting, "Yield!" when their jeeps drove through busy streets became a familiar scene in major cities. In her memoirs *To the Storm*, Yue Daiyuan recalls that even though she was only a teenager at the time, she found the behavior of GIs "unbearably offensive" and often wondered how they could act this way in her country.[46] Accidents caused by GI-driven jeeps and trucks as well as bickering between American servicemen and Chinese rickshaw pullers contributed to a large number of conflicts between American military personnel and local Chinese. An official Chinese report claimed 1,500 cases of Chinese injuries and deaths involving the Americans stationed in China during the 11-month period between September 1945 and July 1946. Between September 12 of 1945 and January 10 of 1946, 495 jeep incidents accounted for 226 Chinese injured by the American servicemen, an average of 4 incidents and 2 casualties per day.[47]

The U.S. diplomatic and military services in major Chinese cities frequently received reports of incidents and disorderly behavior on the part of American servicemen. Most of the incidents were either settled locally by the concerned American and Chinese authorities or ignored. For example, a jeep driven by a marine killed Xu Zhendong, a high school teacher in Beiping, in October 1946. Fearful that this incident might incite public outcry, Hu Shi, president of National Beijing University (commonly known as Beida) and Chinese ambassador to the United States during World War II, wrote a personal letter to J. Leighton Stuart, who became American ambassador to China in June 1946, informing him that Xu was survived by his old parents, his wife, and seven children.[48] A good teacher, Xu was popular with his students. Hu Shi suggested that some embassy official or marine officer pay a visit to the principal of the late Xu's high school and offer money to aid the victim's family. These gestures, Hu believed, would "do much toward easing the anti-American feeling, which, artificially fanned up, is affecting the middle school youths, especially after the death and funeral of Mr. Hsu Chentung [Xu Zhendong]."[49] This incident constituted one of an extended chain of events involving American servicemen and Chinese civilians.[50]

In the immediate postwar China, the presence of American bases, military services, and army post offices in China, the numerous incidents related to American servicemen and jeeps, and the fact that the American military and naval personnel were exempt from the Chinese Criminal Code served to remind the Chinese of the days of extraterritoriality, seemed to overshadow China's new status as one of the "powers," and hurt Chinese national pride. The conduct of some American servicemen further aggravated the situation, and constituted a source of friction.[51] Stories of American jeeps and trucks injuring and killing Chinese pedestrians and rickshaw pullers and of rowdy drunken GIs brawling in cafes and assaulting Chinese women received considerable critical coverage in the Chinese newspapers of almost every political color.

Although the incidents triggered no widespread public demonstrations at first, they aroused resentment and fostered Chinese anti-American sentiment at the popular level. In the eyes of the Chinese, the incidents did not stem simply from reckless behavior on the part of American troops, but also reflected American insensitivity and arrogance. They became issues of national pride, thus provoking particular exasperation from the Chinese who were keenly conscious of the lowly position China had occupied in the past hundred years. When Wang Changhua, a lawyer, was killed by a jeep, the Bar Association of Beiping and Tianjin started a movement urging the American military authorities to punish the marine driver and to evacuate American forces from China. After Wang's family rejected an American offer of money, a local newspaper published an article titled "Good as the U.S. Dollar Is, It Cannot Buy People's Lives."[52]

One newspaper article even hinted that Americans were more contemptuous of Chinese than other foreigners were. It maintained that "motor vehicles running in the streets of Beiping and Tianjin are plenty. Why is it that all those that have killed and injured people have been U.S. vehicles? There were formerly also many foreign-owned motor vehicles in Beiping and Tianjin. Why did they not kill so many people? This is a matter that calls for our most careful consideration."[53]

In denouncing the American sense of racial superiority as manifested in the arrogant ways GIs behaved in China, the Chinese nevertheless revealed their own racism. The liberal *Lianhe wanbao* (United evening news), while suggesting mistakenly that American blacks always meekly accepted white exploitation, indicated that it was an outrage for the Americans to treat the Chinese on the same level as the American blacks. While sensationally comparing each new incident to a dagger driving deeper into the hearts of Chinese people, it argued that unlike American blacks, the Chinese could not stand the endless wrongs inflicted on them by the American soldiers, and that they had the right to demand nationals of other countries to treat them as equal human beings.[54]

Possibly because of the numerous incidents caused by American jeeps and trucks, the city of Beiping launched a "Traffic Safety Week" starting October 27, 1946.[55] The inadequacy of traffic rules and lights in the Chinese cities and the nonchalant way many Chinese pedestrians walked on the streets had also contributed to the large number of traffic incidents. Most Chinese believed that motor vehicles should yield the right of way to pedestrians and bicycle riders. Should an accident occur, the driver ought to be held responsible. One editorial in an official newspaper even urged the Chinese to learn to walk in a "modern" way.[56]

The descent upon urban China of a large number of American troops corresponded with the inception of a new era in China's relationship with the foreign powers. The abolition of the unequal treaties in 1943 signaled the end of the unequal relationship between China and foreign powers, which had, among other things, denied the Chinese the right to try foreigners for crimes that were against the Chinese laws. Postwar American marines, soldiers, and sailors therefore encountered an urban China highly sensitive to its newly gained international status and to any sign or indication of unequal treatment in the immediate post-extraterritorial period.

ADVENTURES OF SANMAO

In *Adventures of Sanmao, the Orphan*, comic strips created by the famous cartoonist Zhang Leping in 1947, American GIs also figured significantly. The depictions typified the negative Chinese images of American military personnel developed in post–World War II urban China: reckless, drunken, lascivious, and haughty, American GIs held little regard for Chinese lives and property and posed a serious threat to Chinese women, who were in danger of either being raped or led astray as in the case of "jeep girls." Powerless Chinese, such as the little orphan boy Sanmao, albeit indignant toward the ill-behaved American GIs and sailors, could do nothing to stop their offenses, while the rich and powerful Chinese would do nothing but bow to them obsequiously.[57]

The cartoon "Chaos" illustrates, among other things, students protesting against hunger and persecution, policemen beating, killing, and arresting people on the street, rich people fleeing the city, hungry people rioting for rice, and a desperate Chinese grocery store owner hanging himself. In their midst, American servicemen also appear prominently on the scene and contribute significantly to the general chaos: an American jeep with a "jeep girl" and a GI holding a huge liquor bottle is running into a Chinese girl; one GI is knocking down a Chinese man and his son, while another is grabbing his wife; a GI is holding a gun against a Chinese in a bank, while another is dancing with a Chinese girl in a dance hall (see Figure 1).

"Clobbered" shows that drunken American soldiers hold little regard for the Chinese: a hungry and miserable Sanmao stands outside a bar when an evil-looking American sailor holding a whiskey bottle comes out of the bar and hits Sanmao on the head with the bottle. After knocking down a bleeding Sanmao on the ground, the sailor continues threatening Sanmao by waving the bottle at him (see Figure 2).

In the cartoon "There Is Always a Bigger Bully," a well-dressed Chinese beats Sanmao with his cane for standing in his way. His cane, however, accidentally hits a government official walking behind him. When the angry official beats the now apologetic-looking man, his cane accidentally hits the American GI walking behind. The angry-looking GI kicks the official so hard that the falling official knocks over the rich Chinese. However, instead of protesting against the rude behavior of the American bully, they obsequiously bow to him with solicitous smiles on their faces (see Figure 3). When falling asleep on the sidewalk in the middle of rain, Sanmao dreams of pushing all three of the bullies into the river with a big splash. Awakened suddenly, Sanmao realizes to his chagrin that the splash in his dream is actually made by an American jeep rushing by (see Figure 4).

Immediately after the publication of *Adventures of Sanmao*, the homeless, parentless boy, Sanmao, became an immensely popular figure, and was a household name in China for decades afterwards. Apart from Sanmao being a loveable, warmhearted little boy who fought courageously against extremely adverse circumstances, the cartoon book, with its implicit yet powerful denunciation of the GMD rule and the ill behavior of American servicemen, also received official endorsement after the Communist takeover. This approval partially contributed to the sale of millions of copies of *Adventures of Sanmao* over the years.

THE RESPONSE FROM *STARS AND STRIPES*

In response to cases of misconduct involving American troops, the editorials of the Shanghai branch of the American military newspaper, *Stars and Stripes*, also made harsh comments on the unsavory behavior of certain GIs and sailors, criticized them for acting "like bums on the main street of Shanghai," and concluded that their performances had brought "a considerable measure of discredit on the Army, the Navy, and the United States."[58]

Another editorial article, "Losing Face," again deplored the unbecoming conduct of certain servicemen, and claimed that their unseemly behavior had tarnished the reputation of the U.S. military forces in China. The writer of the article stated:

To correct an American disgrace on the streets of Shanghai, the Navy has taken the drastic step of barring shore leave to crews of several ships in the Wangpoo [Huangpu River]. There can be nothing but sympathy for the many sailors who have behaved themselves and have been a credit to the uniform they wear. . . . Many of us have been ashamed of sailor behavior like hitting ricksha men, and throwing torpedoes at coolies' feet. Acting quite different from the way they would be at home. Somehow they have forgotten that (whether they like it or not) they are Uncle Sam's best ambassadors. The U.S. is judged all over the world by the manner in which its men in uniform conduct themselves. All of us have been blackened whenever a single GI in Navy blue or Army khaki, has acted out of line. Our enemies and even our friends think we are bums and bullies and ruffians. All because a few Americans think that they are the super-race, the owners of the world who can do as they please wherever they are—especially when they are away from home.[59]

In the midst of constant grievances against Americans stationed in China, the editor of the newspaper was only too happy to cite an anonymous letter written by a Chinese. The author expressed thanks to an American officer who came to his rescue when he was attacked by a dozen street urchins armed with bamboo sticks.[60]

GMD'S DILEMMA VERSUS CCP'S POLITICAL WEAPON

The increasing number of conflicts between American military personnel and Chinese civilians put the Nationalist government in a quandary. Since the GMD leaders needed to cultivate American goodwill and perceived advantages in the continued stay of U.S. troops in China, they attempted to mitigate the disputes that arose between American servicemen and local Chinese. However, when the incidents eventually assumed nationwide and nationalistic magnitude, the official attempts to calm the heated Chinese reaction not only failed to placate the aroused emotions but also incurred contempt for and resentment of the GMD among politically active young Chinese in particular and urban Chinese at large for its inability to uphold Chinese national interests. The reliance upon American military assistance, therefore, found the Nationalist government in the untenable position of being incapable of gratifying the nationalist demand.

Abhorring the presence of American military forces in China, the Communist leaders also realized the political sensitivity and expediency precipitated by the issue and used it to their advantage. Although the CCP leaders initially welcomed General George Marshall's mediating efforts, their disenchantment with Marshall's mission and the continuing American support of the GMD rendered them more critical of the U.S. government than ever before. When fighting erupted in Manchuria in mid-1946, Communist newspapers and broadcasts no longer held any restraint in attacking the GIs as well as the U.S. government for disregarding Chinese dignity, and the GMD government and its leader Chiang Kai-shek for inviting the "wolf" to China (*yinlang rushi*). Projecting itself as the upholder of Chinese national interest, the CCP also launched an anti-American propaganda campaign in the Communist-controlled territory in which it demonstrated American "atrocities" in posters. In October 1946, a representative from the Hoover War Library reported that a nine-year-old boy in Yan'an attempted to explain to him the differences between American progressives and reactionaries. The representative noted that wherever he went he saw walls plastered with large atrocity posters, showing numerous different versions of murders, rapes, and arson committed by GIs. The toddlers were taught to chant "*Meijun tuichu Zhongguo*" (American troops get out of China).

One day, the American saw in a shop a pile of 1937–39 newspapers that he wanted to purchase. But the shopowner refused to sell them to him. When he offered to pay more, the shopowner turned angry and proceeded to give the onlookers a tirade on "foreign oppression, forced buying, and despoiling of the country" and asked the American to leave the shop.[61]

On the other hand, even though the Communist propaganda contributed to the anti-American climate, it appears evident that many urban Chinese harbored some real grievances against the American military presence in China at the time. For their own political interests, the Communists managed to inflame the sore points, magnify the issues, whip up anti-American sentiment, and endeavor to transform local complaints into national protests. By doing so, the CCP hoped to further alienate the GMD politically, reduce the American involvement, and gain public support for its own anti-imperialist stand.

The U.S. troops, especially the marines, constituted a conspicuous foreign presence in China, and represented an integral part of the American China policy in the immediate postwar period. Fresh from the Pacific War, the marines were abruptly thrust into an environment politically perplexing and unstable and culturally alien and alienating. Enmeshed in political and military mires, China was full of pitfalls. The American servicemen were ill prepared for the drastic transition and for the challenges posed by their new roles as partial peacekeepers in a country on the threshold of another war. Serving only limited military functions in China, they became the target of Communist verbal blasts as well as sabotage.

Harassed and censured by the Communists, the American troops' presence soon incurred disapproval and even outrage from the Chinese who had initially warmly welcomed them. Suffering from cultural as well as political alienation, the demoralized American soldiers and sailors were caught in an increasingly hostile environment, which they were anxious to escape. Exposed to a highly volatile environment, their experience in China was often punctuated with homesickness, bewilderment, irritation, disdain, and resentment.

Since GIs were the ones who came into direct contact with local Chinese, they often inadvertently served as cultural and political representatives of the United States. The development of ill feelings between the two groups tarnished the image of the United States in the eyes of a large number of urban Chinese. The latter then translated their discontent with the American military presence not only to the U.S. government, but also to the Nationalist government for soliciting the American assistance and for its inability to uphold Chinese interests.

As an instrument of the U.S. government, the GIs' China mission politically impacted the unfolding Chinese Civil War and further destabilized an already chaotic society. In the end, the prolonged American military presence turned out to be a political liability to the GMD, while the CCP capitalized on the issue and transformed it into a significant weapon against the GMD and the U.S. government.

When the flames of civil war began to engulf China, American troops had little reason to remain in China since the U.S. government had no intention of making China a major battlefield for American soldiers. By June 1947, except for a contingent of marines who stayed on in the port city of Qingdao, all had withdrawn from China.

NOTES

1. Soviet troops invaded Manchuria following the Soviet Union's declaration of war on Japan on August 8, 1945. Within weeks they occupied the entire northeast. Keenly aware of the strategic significance of the region, both the CCP and the GMD were determined to fill the power vacuum upon the evacuation of the Soviet army from Manchuria. When the Soviets postponed their scheduled departure and denied the entry of the Nationalist troops into Manchuria under all kinds of pretexts, the U.S. and Nationalist governments, however, grew nervous over the Soviet intentions. Meanwhile, the Communist forces poured into Manchuria, and received from the Soviets large quantities of captured Japanese arms. It was not until late November 1945 that the Soviets and the GMD reached an agreement, allowing American forces to transport the Nationalist forces into Manchuria to reestablish the GMD authority there. By this time, however, the Communist forces had already penetrated the vast Manchurian countryside. Although the Nationalists regained control of cities as well as the major communications lines, these were often compared to urban islands surrounded by the sea of Communist countryside. Immediately upon the complete Soviet evacuation in May 1946, civil war erupted in Manchuria. For more details, see Steven I. Levine, *Anvil of Victory: The Communist Revolution in Manchuria, 1945–1948* (New York: Columbia University Press, 1987).

2. For a more detailed account of the Terranova incident, see William J. Donahue, "The Francis Terranova Case," *The Historian* 43 (February 1981), 211–24; see also Michael H. Hunt, *The Making of a Special Relationship: The United States and China to*

1914 (New York: Columbia University Press, 1983), 1–2; Jonathan D. Spence, *The Search for Modern China*, 2d ed. (New York: W.W. Norton, 1999), 126–29.

3. From Rear Admiral W.A. Kitts of United States Pacific Fleet to Shanghai District Attorney, Cao Liang Kan, July 2, 1947, RG59, 893.00/7-247, National Archives (hereafter, NA).

4. See Wesley R. Fishel, *The End of Extraterritoriality in China* (Berkeley and Los Angeles: University of California Press, 1952).

5. U.S. Department of State, *Foreign Relations of the United States [FRUS], 1943, China* (Washington, D.C.: Government Printing Office, 1972), 699.

6. *Xin wan bao*, March 26, 1947.

7. From Ministry of Foreign Affairs at Shanghai Office to U.S. Consulate General in Shanghai, March 28, 1947, RG59, 893.00/3-2847, NA.

8. From Ministry of Foreign Affairs at Shanghai Office to U.S. Consulate General in Shanghai, March 28, 1947, RG59, 893.00/3-2847, NA; from Chinese Ministry of Foreign Affairs to American Embassy, June 26, 1947, RG59, 893.00/6-2647, NA.

9. A.A. Vandegrift, *Once a Marine: The Memoirs of General A A. Vandegrift* (New York: W.W. Norton, 1964), 301.

10. Henry I. Shaw, *United States Marines in North China, 1945–1949* (Washington, D.C.: U.S. Marine Corps, 1968), 2.

11. U.S. marines had also established a presence in the city of Shanghai since early 1927 in the name of protecting American lives and property in response to the impending arrival of Nationalist soldiers in the midst of China's Northern Expedition. See Nicholas R. Clifford, *Spoilt Children of Empire: Westerners in Shanghai and the Chinese Revolution of the 1920s* (Hanover, N.H.: Middlebury University Press, 1991), 204–5, 229–30.

12. The six companies included three rifle companies, a headquarters, a service company, and a mounted detachment. See Roger B. Jeans and Katie Letcher Lyte, eds., *Good-Bye to Old Peking: The Wartime Letters of U.S. Marine Captain John Seymour Letcher* (Athens: Ohio University Press, 1998), 3–4.

13. John A. White, *The United States Marines in North China* (Millbrae, Calif: John A. White, 1974), 10. For a firsthand description of the "good life" marines in Beijing had lived prior to World War II, see Jeans, *Good-Bye to Old Peking*.

14. George B. Clark, *Treading Softly: The U.S. Marines in China from the 1840s to the 1940s* (Pike, N.H.: The Brass Hat, 1996), 59.

15. Jeans, *Good-Bye to Old Peking*, 2.

16. Clark, *Treading Softly*, 82.

17. U.S. Department of State, *The China White Paper: August 1949* (1949; reprint, Stanford: Stanford University Press, 1967), 694.

18. General Albert Wedemeyer, in charge of the U.S. military operations in China during and immediately after the war, described vividly the magnitude of the American operations in a letter to General Dwight Eisenhower: "Whole armies, spearheading the reoccupation, were airlifted in American planes to Shanghai, Nanking and Peiping. From the Pacific came part of the U.S. 7th Fleet, which later assisted in carrying Chinese troops into northern China, and 53,000 marines who occupied the Peiping-Tiantsin area. The air redeployment of the Chinese occupational forces, which was undertaken by the 10th and 14th Air Forces, was unquestionably the largest troop movement by air in the world's history. Thousands of Chinese soldiers were carried to key cities to accept local surrenders and disarm the enemy." Quoted from Michael Schaller, *The U.S. Crusade in China, 1938–1945* (New York: Columbia University Press, 1979), 265.

19. Edward J. Marolda, "The U.S. Navy and the 'Loss of China,' 1945–1950," in *George C. Marshall's Mediation Mission to China, December 1945–January 1947*, ed. Larry I. Bland (Lexington, Va.: George C. Washington Foundation, 1998), 410.

20. China's war with Japan witnessed the accumulation of strength of the Chinese Communists in north China. The retreat of Chiang's government to the remote southwest left a vast vacuum for Communist organizers, who employed the opportunity by working behind the Japanese lines. The Communist area included portions of Shenxi, Gansu, and Ningxia provinces. By 1944, although the Japanese occupied the main cities and lines of communications in north China, the Communists controlled much of the countryside. They utilized the nationalist sentiment and mobilized the rural masses into fighting a guerrilla war against Japan. Meanwhile, the campaigns of land and social reform carried out during the Sino-Japanese War established support for the Communists in the rural areas. During the course of the war, Communist numbers and territory expanded rapidly. Membership in the CCP increased from about 40,000 to about 1.2 million by the end of the war in 1945. In 1937, the manpower of the Communist army ranged from estimates of 45,000 to 90,000. By 1945, the number was between 500,000 and 900,000. Even taking the lower figures as valid, they indicate a large increase. (See Chalmers A. Johnson, *Peasant Nationalism and Communist Power: The Emergence of Revolutionary China, 1937–1945* [Stanford: Stanford University Press, 1962], 73–74.)

21. Beijing or Peking, the "northern capital," was the capital of the last imperial dynasty, the Qing dynasty. It continued to serve as the seat of the various republican governments until 1927 when Chiang Kai-shek made Nanjing, the "southern capital," the seat of the Nationalist government. Between 1928 and 1949 when the national capital was elsewhere, Beijing was called Beiping or "northern peace."

22. For further discussions of the postwar marine presence in north China from the political and military viewpoints, see Schaller, *The U.S. Crusade in China*, 262–88; James Readon-Anderson, *Yenan and the Great Powers: The Origins of Chinese Communist Foreign Policy, 1944–1946* (New York: Columbia University Press, 1980), 102–19; Shu Guang Zhang, *Deterrence and Strategic Culture: Chinese-American Confrontation, 1949–1959* (Ithaca: Cornell University Press, 1992), 20–21, 38–39; and Shaw, *United States Marines in North China*. For a study of the marines' sojourn in Qingdao, see Zhiguo Yang, "U.S. Marines in Qingdao: Society, Culture, and China's Civil War, 1945–1949," in *China and the United States: A New Cold War History*, ed. Xiaobing Li and Hongshan Li (Lanham, Md.: University Press of America, 1998), 181–206.

23. Henry Aplington II, "China Revisited," *Marine Corps Gazette* 57 (July 1973): 30.

24. In an internally circulated report issued on October 29, 1945, and titled "Guideline on the Treatment of American Troops in China and Instructions on Related Issues," the CCP Central Committee emphasized that the Communists should welcome and cooperate with the American troops as long as the latter respected the Communist interests. However, if the American troops acted in ways that were detrimental to the Communist interests, the Communists should then reject the American actions by claiming that the Americans were interfering with China's internal affairs. But on normal diplomatic occasions, the Communists should let the Americans know that the CCP had always insisted on friendly cooperation with the United States. See Tao Wenzhao, *Zhong-Mei guanxishi, 1911–1950* (The history of Chinese-American relations, 1911–1950) (Chongqing: Chongqing chubanshe, 1993), 390–91.

25. Shaw, *United States Marines in North China*, 2–3.

26. Michael Peterson and David Perlmutt, *Charlie Two Shoes and the Marines of Love Company* (Annapolis, Md.: Naval Institute Press, 1998), 33–34.

27. An exception was the development of friendship between a company of U.S. marines stationed in Qingdao and the village boy Tsui Chi Hsii (Cui Zhixi), whom the marines fondly called "Charlie" or "Charlie Two Shoes." Alone, alienated, and fearful in a strange land, the marines befriended Charlie, who charmed them with his friendliness and his bright and infectious smile. For the lonely marines, Charlie provided a human link they desperately needed. Charlie lived with the marines in their compound until 1949 when the last marines left Qingdao. See Peterson, *Charlie Two Shoes.*

28. Aplington, "China Revisited," 30.

29. For discussion on the Marshall Mission, see chapter 3.

30. U.S. Department of State, *Foreign Relations of the United States [FRUS], 1946, The Far East: China* (Washington, D.C.: Government Printing Office, 1972), 9:1418.

31. Policymakers in Washington deliberated among themselves about the level of the marine involvement in Chinese affairs, and most of them found the idea of a large-scale military engagement in China undesirable. As Schaller argues, "emotionally, they believed that a pro-American China was vital to the security of the United States. But they intellectually recoiled at the idea of involvement in a major Asian land war," having just ended a major war. See Schaller, *U.S. Crusade in China*, 285.

32. Vandegrift, *Once a Marine*, 307; Aplington, "China Revisited," 29.

33. Craig M. Cameron, *American Samurai: Myth, Imagination, and the Conduct of Battle in the First Marine Division, 1941–1951* (New York: Cambridge University Press, 1994), 217.

34. Shaw, *United States Marines in North China*, 11.

35. James Forrestal, *The Forrestal Diaries* (New York: Viking Press, 1951), 175–76.

36. U.S. Department of State, *China White Paper*, 694.

37. David Strand's book, *Rickshaw Beijing: City People and Politics in the 1920s* (Berkeley: University of California Press, 1989) provides an excellent study of urban life, politics, and social stratification as symbolized by rickshaw pullers, who formed a large part of the urban laboring poor of Republican China.

38. Arch Carey, "British Businessmen in China, 1903–1948," unpublished manuscript, Box 2, Part III: 11–12, Hoover Institution Archives Holdings on China.

39. Aplington, "China Revisited," 27.

40. Carey, "British Businessmen in China," 12.

41. Vandegrift, *Once a Marine*, 295.

42. Zhiguo Yang, "U.S. Marines in Qingdao: Military-Civilian Interaction, Nationalism, and China's Civil War, 1945–1949" (Ph.D. diss., University of Maryland, 1998), 128.

43. Cameron, *American Samurai*, 211.

44. Xixiao Guo, "The Climax of Sino-American Relations, 1944–1947" (Ph.D. diss., University of Georgia, 1997), 279–80.

45. John Israel, *Lianda: A Chinese University in War and Revolution* (Stanford: Stanford University Press, 1998), 367–68. See also Yue Daiyun and Caroline Wakeman, *To the Storm: The Odyssey of a Revolutionary Chinese Woman* (Berkeley and Los Angeles: University of California Press, 1985), 17.

46. Yue, *To the Storm*, 17.

47. See *Wen hui bao*, October 24, 1946.

48. Stuart (1876–1962) was born into a missionary family already two generations in China. Through arduous personal efforts, he founded Yanjing University, an elite Christian college in China, and served as its president for many years. In 1946, Stuart, the missionary and educator, became a politician and a diplomat when he assumed the position of U.S. ambassadorship to China. He left China in August 1949 shortly before the founding of the People's Republic of China. For further discussions on Stuart, especially his relationship with Yanjing University, see Philip West, *Yenching University and Sino-Western Relations, 1916-1952* (Cambridge, Mass.: Harvard University Press, 1976); for more on Stuart's life and work in China, see John Leighton Stuart, *Fifty Years in China: The Memoirs of John Leighton Stuart, Missionary and Ambassador* (New York: Random House, 1954).

49. See Memorandum for the Naval Attaché, December 11, 1946, Marshall Mission File, RG59, NA.

50. Ill feelings of this sort were not confined to the Chinese alone. Complaints of discipline problems on the part of American servicemen and even outbursts of anti-American riots or demonstrations also took place in Germany, Japan, Taiwan, and France in the late 1940s and 1950s. In the aftermath of an anti-American incident in Taiwan in 1957, both the American secretary of state and secretary of defense noted that difficult relations between American servicemen stationed overseas and the local population constituted a serious international problem. For more details on this issue, see Buel W. Patch, *Anti-Americanism and Soldiers Overseas* (Washington, D.C.: Editorial Research Reports, 1957).

51. As historian Lyman P. Van Slyke puts it, "All too frequently, the conduct of American GI's in China—among whom 'slopehead' or 'slopey' became a common epithet for the Chinese—was such as to inspire ill-feeling." (Van Slyke, "Culture, Society, and Technology in Sino-American Relations," in *Dragon and Eagle, United States-China Relations: Past and Future* [New York: Basic Books, 1973], 147.)

52. The article published in a Beiping newspaper was quoted by *Wen huibao*, October 19, 1946.

53. *Wen hui bao*, October 19, 1946.

54. *Lianhe wanbao*, October 2, 1946.

55. *Wen hui bao*, October 28, 1946.

56. Quoted from *Wen hui bao*, October 22, 1946.

57. See Zhang Leping, *Adventures of Sanmao, the Orphan* (Hong Kong: Joint Publishing Co., 1981), 136.

58. *Stars and Stripes*, Shanghai, January 11, 1946.

59. Ibid., February 23, 1946.

60. Ibid., February 16, 1946.

61. See the section "Chinese Communist Party—Poster Campaigns" in *Press Publications of Records of the Office of Chinese Affairs, 1945-1955*, reel 3.

3

INTELLECTUAL OPINION ON AMERICAN POLITICAL AND ECONOMIC INVOLVEMENT

The bitter and at times bloody conflicts between the Chinese Communist Party (CCP) and the Guomindang (GMD) reached back to the 1920s. The outbreak of the Sino-Japanese War in China in 1937 brought about cooperation between the Chinese Communists and the Nationalists. However, even though they formed a united front against Japanese aggression, the GMD and the CCP maintained their basic distrust of each other. In this sense, collaboration signified nothing more than a *modus vivendi* and came into existence only under the extreme pressure from a formidable foe. After the "New Fourth Army Incident" in 1941, in which the Nationalists wiped out thousands of Communist soldiers, the wartime collaboration progressively worsened.[1] When Japan surrendered in August 1945, the GMD and the CCP began a fierce race to seize Japanese-occupied territories and enemy weapons and supplies, which resulted in numerous clashes between the Nationalist and Communist troops. A civil war appeared imminent.

The Chinese domestic crisis, however, invited American political involvement. Because the American military presence in the immediate post–World War II period had failed to subdue the Communists, Washington sought a political solution to the China dilemma with the Marshall Mission (December 1945–January 1947). Coinciding with the prevailing Chinese mood for peace, the American endeavor initially received warm responses from educated Chinese. However, the continuing U.S. support of the ruling party in various forms compromised the supposedly impartial mediation effort by General George Marshall and soon turned Chinese public opinion against American involvement. In the end, the famous

Marshall Mission represented the culmination of the ill-fated American attempts at mediating between the two contending Chinese parties for a political settlement of their profound discord. Despite General Marshall's arduous efforts, the American mission failed to avert the outbreak of the Chinese Civil War, and afforded the Chinese Communists and politically conscious students and intellectuals with one more reason to denounce the American interference in Chinese affairs.

Toward the end of 1946, the signing of the Sino-American Commercial Treaty reinforced the suspicion and distrust of many Chinese intellectuals and businessmen about American involvement in China, since they perceived the treaty as detrimental to Chinese economic and political interests. Their outcries against the treaty not only mortified the Nationalist government, but also added another element of discord in the unfolding unofficial Chinese-American relations.

In brief, American political, military, and economic activities in the immediate postwar China, albeit on a limited scale, largely failed to generate Chinese goodwill, proved to be a liability to the GMD cause, and reinforced the CCP propaganda line of the evil alliance between an imperialistic America and a reactionary, warmongering GMD. Furthermore, American activities in China heightened educated youths' frustration with the U.S. China policy, and paved the way for the eruption of nationwide anti-American student demonstrations in the coming years. While the American involvement was not significant enough to turn the political and military tide in favor of the GMD, it was tangible enough to turn intellectual opinion in urban China against the U.S. government.

AMERICAN MEDIATION EFFORTS

During World War II, the U.S. government had anticipated that a unified and pro-American China would be a stabilizing force in postwar East Asia. By the fall of 1945, however, Washington was more concerned about the spread of Soviet influence in East Asia and was apprehensive about the imminent prospect of renewed upheaval in China.[2] Fearful that a chaotic and divided China would allow for the Soviet expansion into Manchuria, President Harry Truman sent highly respected U.S. Army Chief of Staff General Marshall as his special representative to China in late 1945. Marshall's task was to mediate a settlement between the GMD and the CCP and to bring about a coalition government.

Marshall's mission, however, was not the first attempt on the part of the American government to mediate between the two rival Chinese parties. During the war years, the Roosevelt administration was concerned with the adverse effect of the internal Chinese rivalry on the Allied war effort and on the American blueprint in postwar Asia where the United States and a pro-American China would cooperate to construct a new order. Vice President Henry Wallace's trip to China in June 1944 was the first official American effort to urge conciliation between the Chinese Nationalists and the Communists. Later in the year, Patrick Hurley, serving first as the personal envoy of President Roosevelt and then as the U.S. ambassador to China, undertook a mission to mediate between the two political rivals, which drew the United States directly into the whirlpool of the murky Chinese politics. However, the virulent nature of the CCP-GMD rivalry and Hurley's misconception, naiveté, and ignorance of China's political realities doomed the American efforts.[3]

After the Japanese surrender in August 1945, more seemingly promising negotiations resumed with the Communist leader Mao Zedong's trip to Chongqing, the wartime capital of the Nationalist government. But the talks were empty of content and did not lead anywhere. Each side then prepared for the final engagement. In November 1945, a frustrated Hurley abruptly resigned, and his mission ended in complete failure. With the aim of achieving domestic dominance, both the CCP and the GMD would only agree to a political settlement that could work to their own interests. Meanwhile, Hurley's principle of promoting unity through sustaining the GMD government and his support of the GMD's point of view over the differences between the two contenders assured the GMD leader, Chiang Kai-shek, of continued American support and made him recalcitrant in his demands and the CCP resentful. In the end, Hurley abandoned any efforts as a mediator and pushed for a policy of full American support for the GMD.[4]

Like its predecessor, the Truman administration also underestimated the deep antipathy between the two political rivals and overestimated the role the U.S. government could play in Chinese politics. General Marshall aimed to prevent a civil war in China by urging the CCP and the GMD to agree to a cease-fire and to form a coalition government to resolve their differences. His efforts immediately confronted long-standing and deep-rooted CCP-GMD disputes. The Communists would only agree to a coalition in which they could share real power and which would recognize the independence of their army, while the Nationalist Party insisted that the CCP subject itself to the GMD rule. The profound enmity and political differences between the two sides eventually prevented them from reaching any kind of political accommodation.

Furthermore, Marshall's mission, supposedly impartial, was compromised from the very beginning. The United States recognized the Nationalist government as the only legitimate government in China, and strove to integrate the Communist armed forces into the Nationalist army, while continuing programs of aid and support to the GMD exclusively. These included an extension of the Lend-Lease agreement and the sale of surplus war materials to the GMD. In the end, continued American support of the GMD forces bolstered Chiang Kai-shek's confidence that he could crush his longtime rival through military means, and further deepened the Communists' suspicion of American intentions.

Despite the inconsistency inherent in Marshall's mission and the extremely volatile political situation he was caught in, Marshall endeavored to act as evenhandedly as possible. His mission did achieve some initial success, as the CCP and the GMD came to a tenuous cease-fire agreement on January 10, 1946. Meanwhile, the Executive Headquarters was set up in Beiping to direct truce teams for field investigations and help supervise the agreement between the Chinese Nationalists and Communists. It consisted of three commissioners, one

American as chairman, one representative from the Chinese Nationalist government, and one representative from the Chinese Communist Party.[5]

With the onset of Marshall's mission, a large number of U.S. marines assisted in Marshall's political efforts to bring about a coalition government in China. When Marshall succeeded in securing a temporary cease-fire agreement between the two contending Chinese parties, many marines helped enforce the truce agreement by providing personnel for the Executive Headquarters and for its truce teams, which conducted field investigations. To facilitate the mediation, Marshall also placed an embargo on arms shipments to the Nationalist government that lasted from August 1946 to May 1947 and pushed to reduce the level of American forces in China. However, since Chiang had received enough American military support before the cutoff, these measures did not have any real effect.[6]

The truce turned out to be a short-lived one. Very soon the GMD and the CCP started accusing each other of violating the cease-fire order. After June 1946, the situation in north China, and especially in Manchuria, progressively worsened as the Communists and the Nationalists intensified their fighting. Nationalist forces appeared to gain the upper hand in north China and Manchuria over the course of the year. Having failed to avert the Chinese Civil War, a disappointed Marshall ended his yearlong effort and returned to the United States in January 1947.[7] Discouraged with the ongoing political upheaval in China, the Truman administration no longer wished to get too heavily enmeshed in the China quagmire. The wartime American image of a postwar Asia, where the United States and a pro-American China would cooperate to construct a new order, vanished before a weak and war-wrecked China. Caught in a bloody civil war, China no longer appeared capable of serving as a stronghold against communism in Asia. Thereafter, Washington shifted its policy in East Asia and looked upon a politically and economically stabilized Japan as a potential buffer against Soviet expansion. On the other hand, Washington could not simply dismiss the GMD. Political and ideological considerations sustained the link between the two. In the end, American political involvement simply added one more element of bitterness in Sino-American relations. While the failure in forestalling the outbreak of the Chinese Civil War frustrated and disillusioned the United States, Chiang Kai-shek abhorred the mediation because it departed from unconditional American support and deterred him from launching an immediate military offensive against the Communists.[8] On the other hand, American concern about the CCP-GMD rivalry initially raised hopes on the part of the Communist leader Mao Zedong; the shattering of these expectations only rendered him more resentful of the United States.[9]

MIXED EMOTIONS: INTELLECTUALS' RESPONSE

The bleak political reality in China disenchanted politically conscious educated Chinese who had yearned to see a powerful and united postwar China and hoped that the CCP and the GMD could resolve their differences through peaceful means. Many, however, had once placed hopes in the American government to help bring about "a strong, united and democratic China," as asserted in President Truman's statement on American policy toward China on

December 15, 1945.[10] They welcomed Marshall's arrival on the China scene to settle the GMD-CCP differences and looked upon Marshall as the "messiah for peace."[11]

In the remote southwest city of Kunming where congregated the brightest of China's intellectual elite, who had reached there shortly after the outbreak of the Sino-Japanese War, and where was located the National Southwest Associated University (*Guoli xinan Lianhe daxue*, commonly known as *xinan Lianda* or simply *Lianda*), the most famous of the wartime universities in China,[12] Truman's statement was published in almost every major newspaper. Immediately, it became the central topic among the intellectuals. They found especially appealing Truman's call for the convocation of "a national conference of representatives of major political elements" to seek an early settlement of China's internal strife and to effect the unification of China. Even though Truman made it clear that the United States would continue recognizing the Nationalist government as the sole legal government in China, he did suggest that the GMD government as a "one-party government" should broaden its base to "include other political elements in the country."[13] This especially excited many intellectuals who were conscious of the fact that the Chiang regime needed American support. They hoped that pressure from the United States might lead to a united China through means of peaceful unification.[14] Professor Fei Xiaotong, a distinguished sociologist at Lianda, wrote an open letter, signed by him and several other professors there, welcoming Marshall's arrival. In the letter, the words "democracy," "peace," and "freedom" appeared repeatedly.[15]

On the other hand, Truman's statement and the announcement of Marshall's mission shook Chinese self-esteem and evoked in Chinese editorials expressions of national shame. In the wake of Truman's statement and the appointment of General Marshall as Truman's special envoy to China, many nonofficial editorials in big cities such as Shanghai, Chongqing, and Wuhan reiterated the theme of China's "loss of face" when it was the American government that expressed the need for democracy and peace in China. The influential *Dagong bao* (L'impartiale), for example, asserted that Truman's statement shamed the Chinese, who should try to solve their own problems. It continued, "Do not let our friends give us more advice or interfere with our affairs."[16]

Many of China's intellectuals were at the moment articulate middle-of-the-roaders. Although small in number, they figured significantly in the political arena. Regarding peace and democracy as prerequisites for unity and national reconstruction, they were against any political party appearing to call for war, and their shift of political loyalty could be of crucial importance in the unfolding confrontation between the CCP and the GMD. In the immediate aftermath of the end of the Sino-Japanese War, liberal intellectuals saw a great opportunity to exert political influence.[17] Some also joined the Democratic League, which was composed of a number of groups of different political leanings. The League opposed civil war and one-party dictatorship, and supported some form of coalition government. With no military forces or territory of its own, it nevertheless hoped to work as a third force and to serve as a mediator between the two major political parties.[18]

While the slogan "peace, democracy, unification, and reconstruction" reflected the mood of the intellectual community in the wake of the Japanese surrender, the Nationalist government saw national unification, that is, the end of the Communist armed opposition, as its top priority.[19] To facilitate its takeover of north China and to preempt Communist advance into the region, the GMD turned to defeated Japanese and puppet troops to maintain order before the arrival of the American troops as well as its own. The use of Japanese and puppet troops, the occupation of key Chinese cities and strategic areas by American troops, and the American assistance in transporting Nationalist soldiers to southeast and north China allowed the GMD to regain control of urban China and to keep the Communists out of the cities and communications lines. With larger and better-equipped armies, Chiang Kai-shek appeared to enjoy the upper hand in the power struggle and seemed eager to settle the political differences through military means.

In the immediate postwar period, confronting the militarily superior GMD forces, the CCP catered to, and worked hard to influence, political opinion in minor political parties and among intellectuals by advocating a coalition government, since by doing so it would have little to lose. If the GMD spurned the Communist call for reorganizing the Nationalist government into a coalition in which the Communists could share real power, it would strengthen the CCP claim that the GMD desired nothing less than a total war. If the GMD accepted the Communist proposal, the CCP would gain much-needed time from such a coalition in which it could mobilize and expand its military forces. Either way, the Communists stood to gain.[20] As one historian points out: "Peaceful negotiation and armed struggle were simply two complementary methods [for the CCP] to deal with the GMD."[21]

Meanwhile, even though many intellectuals still harbored doubts about communism, their longing for peace seemed to push them more to the side of the Communists because of the latter's call for a coalition government, while the GMD appeared to prefer a military settlement of the CCP-GMD rivalry, and was thus seen as an obstacle to peace. Being on the sidelines, the CCP could attack at will the GMD's weak points. Although the CCP was also actively preparing for a final military confrontation with the GMD for national power, it drew considerably less fire from cultural and academic circles.

Furthermore, the Nationalist government's poor performance upon taking over urban China also disenchanted many of its supporters among the intellectuals. The ruling party's somewhat popular war image waned immediately with the end of the war. Criticism of governmental practices, somewhat suppressed under the threat of Japanese invasion, all surfaced after Japan's surrender.[22] Suzanne Pepper summarizes four reasons for the Nationalist government's rapid decline in prestige: the slowness of the government in disarming the Japanese and puppet troops, and in punishing Chinese collaborators (*hanjian*); the government officials' corrupt practices in taking over Japanese and puppet properties and organizations; inept economic and financial measures being carried out at the time; and the arrogant and condescending attitude of the officials toward the populace in formerly Japanese-controlled regions.[23] Effective CCP propaganda denouncing the GMD for its failure at the postwar takeover task, its widespread corruption and lack of discipline, and its harsh suppression of dissent also diminished the GMD's popularity. Moreover, the

Nationalists certainly could not rally the same patriotic loyalty in their military confrontation with the Communists as when the Japanese were the target.

As 1946 dragged on, the GMD appeared determined to reunify the country militarily, even though it meant running against the prevailing pro-peace mood at the time. At this stage, many intellectuals still held both the GMD and the CCP partly responsible for the internal strife. An open letter to Marshall, Chiang Kai-shek, and the CCP signed by 164 leading cultural and intellectual Chinese on June 8 requested all parties to work for peace for China's sake.[24]

On August 16, 1946, the American embassy in Nanjing received a copy of a declaration issued by a group of prominent Chinese Christian intellectuals, mostly Shanghai residents, regarding the political situation in China. Having checked the authenticity of the document, the embassy concluded that the signers of the document were indeed who they claimed to be. In the document, the intellectuals strongly urged a cessation of hostilities between the CCP and the GMD. They also called on both parties to forsake military measures in favor of peaceful and consultative means in the settlement of their differences. Asserting that "corruption, rottenness and inefficiency" characterized the Nationalist government, the signers demanded sweeping reforms.[25]

As the Civil War flared up in mid-1946, initial Chinese enthusiasm over Marshall's mission cooled down, and informed public opinion soon became divided over American material and physical assistance to one party in a two-party conflict. Many challenged the American claim of "noninterference" in Chinese domestic affairs, especially because of the American assistance in the transportation of Nationalist troops to Manchuria. Actually as early as late 1945, Zhang Dongsun, professor of philosophy at Yanjing University and chairman of North China Branch of the Democratic League, had signed a petition titled "To the People and Government of the United States." In it, Zhang voiced concerns about the grave consequences of a civil war and questioned American interference. He argued that "the painful lesson that we gained from recurrent civil wars during the past hundred years is that foreign interference, no matter how well-intentioned, does not have the healing effect of making China a united nation." While expressing great indebtedness to the Americans for their splendid war effort in defeating the Axis powers, especially Japan, and emphasizing the Sino-American friendship, Zhang contended that the landing of marines in north China had created an anomalous situation, which would further aggravate and prolong China's civil conflict. He therefore demanded the withdrawal of American marines from China. "American forces on the allegation of assisting in disarming the Japanese are now 'involved' in a civil war of the most serious nature in Chinese history. This has aroused considerable misapprehension among the Chinese people."[26]

Zhang's observations were echoed by John King Fairbank, director of the U.S. Information Service. In a letter to the State Department on December 6, 1945, Fairbank mentioned that he had noted "a marked increase in anti-American feeling." He observed that its "expression has been open and vigorous in print." By "moving Nationalist troops about the country in connection with Japanese surrenders," many Chinese believed that the Americans "have in effect taken sides in the civil conflict." Even though "this is the Communist line," Fairbank cautioned that "it carries a lot of weight in popular opinion."[27]

In the turmoil of Chinese domestic conflict, the fact that the U.S. government continued to assist the Nationalist regime through the extension of loans and training of its army and navy led the war-weary Chinese to question American political motives. In May 1946, 20 professors in Kunming signed an open letter to General Marshall. The letter not only urged the Nationalist government to purge itself of "reactionary elements" intent upon setting up a fascist government in China, but also requested the U.S. government to stop transporting and supplying Nationalist troops and making further loans to the GMD government. According to the professors, these moves would simply result in the killing of more Chinese and would delay the establishment of a democratic government.[28]

Some radical intellectuals also concluded that the U.S. policy of supporting the GMD was essentially to minimize the Soviet influence in China. In an interview with an American diplomat in December 1946, Luo Longji, a politically active intellectual who had once studied in the United States and was head of the Democratic League at the time, provided a critical view of U.S. policy toward China. He believed that the U.S. government pursued two objectives in its China policies: first, to establish a strong China that could collaborate with the United States so as to counteract the influence of the Soviet Union and, if necessary, fight on the side of the United States against the Soviet Union; second, to push for a democratic China essentially after the Anglo-American model. In this way, China could turn into a united, peaceful, and prosperous country, and thus a good customer for American products and a stabilizing element in the international political situation. Luo further argued that it was the first objective, a strong China capable of offsetting Soviet influence, that was more important to the United States. According to Luo, this U.S. policy had incurred strong opposition "among liberal and educated groups in China." Consequently, "American policy in China has recently been severely criticized, and even attacked, not only by the Chinese Communists, but by Chinese liberals as well." Luo predicted that the opposition would only grow stronger.[29]

For obvious practical reasons of their own, the Communists likewise strongly demanded the termination of American interference in China's internal affairs and accused the GMD of compromising Chinese sovereign rights in return for American military intervention. In mid-1946, realizing that the United States would not deviate from its support of the Nationalist government, the disillusioned Communists resumed their "anti-imperialist" stance and started launching open verbal attacks on Marshall's mission. They challenged its impartiality and labeled Marshall as one of the American "reactionary elements." The August 14 editorial of *Jiefang ribao* (Liberation daily), the central organ of the CCP, published in Yan'an, asserted that not only had Marshall's effort failed, but the Chinese Civil War had also grown greater in scope and ruthlessness than seven and a half months before. The editorial charged that Marshall's mission was "mediation in name and assistance to Chiang in essence."[30]

By adopting a nationalistic and anti-imperialistic line, and vigorously demanding the termination of American military support to the GMD government, the

Communists made good propaganda. In the meantime, they could also obtain much-needed approval and support from politically articulate Chinese. The latter had come to view the postwar U.S. policies of transferring GMD troops and providing lend-lease extension to the GMD government as a barrier to the achievement of peace and democracy in China. These beliefs of the politically sensitive Chinese coincided with, and were inspired and reinforced by, Communist propaganda.

The GMD government also endeavored to exploit the issue of nationalism to counteract the Communist propaganda and to draw the support of the intellectual community. Its nationalist stand, however, was compromised by its accommodation to the American military presence and by its pursuit of U.S. aid in the war effort against the CCP. On the other hand, the GMD campaigned against the continuing stay and the raping and looting activities of Soviet troops in Manchuria, and emphasized the close relationship between the Soviets and the Chinese Communists. Starting on February 22 of 1946, pro-government and anti-Soviet student demonstrations broke out in Chongqing, later spreading to Shanghai. The demonstrators called for the departure of Soviet troops from Manchuria and for the return of control over the region to China, and urged the Chinese people to preserve intact China's sovereignty over the region. During the Chongqing student demonstrations, however, approximately 100 demonstrators attacked the offices of Communist *XinHua ribao* (New China daily) and the Democratic League's *Minzhu bao* (Democracy news) and injured several employees of the Communist newspaper. Evidence indicated that the rioting was officially instigated, and this revelation brought the demonstrations within the intellectual community to a quick end.[31]

Anti-Soviet activities as performed in the academic field, however, were not entirely GMD-inspired. Ready to condemn any threat to Chinese sovereignty, many students and intellectuals directed their patriotic indignation to the Soviet Union. When the full text of the Yalta Agreement was published in China in February 1946, many were embittered by its provisions requiring China to cede to the Soviet Union special rights and privileges in Manchuria. Meanwhile, the Soviet delay in evacuating Manchuria and suspicion of ulterior Russian motives there incited genuine hostile sentiments among some Chinese youths and provoked them to join the demonstrations.[32] To express their discontent with the Soviet occupation of Manchuria, over 100 professors from Lianda signed a petition on February 24 demanding that the Soviet troops withdraw from Manchuria.[33] Zhu Ziqing, a famous professor of literature, wrote in his diary on that day that he had agreed to sign the petition on the Manchurian problem for purely patriotic reasons.[34] However, the complete evacuation of Soviet troops from Manchuria by May 1946 and the lack of active Soviet material assistance to the CCP during China's Civil War limited the scale of anti-Soviet outbursts.

The CCP-Soviet relationship during the course of the Chinese Civil War was a complex and curious one. Although contingently providing material assistance to the Chinese Communists, especially in Manchuria, through turning over to them captured Japanese arms and communications equipment, Soviet leaders generally believed that the CCP was too weak to win the Civil War and were reluctant to squander scarce Soviet resources in the Chinese military conflict. Primarily concerned with staying out of the China quagmire that might trigger a direct Soviet confrontation with the United States, Moscow largely maintained a neutral stand although the GMD was decisively pro-American. Evidence suggests that even when the CCP troops had won crucial military victories in north and central China and were getting ready to cross the Yangzi River for a final military showdown with the crumbling GMD forces in early 1949, Moscow was still dubious of the military capacities of the CCP and advised against the move. On the other hand, even though Soviet leaders, especially Joseph Stalin, did not have much faith in a total CCP triumph in China, common ideological beliefs ensured cooperation between the two parties. The CCP leaders cultivated the link with Stalin and the Soviet Party, kept them informed of almost all of their important decisions, and shunned open disputes even when they disagreed with the Soviets. The relationship reached a new stage after the CCP victory in 1949.[35]

THE CALL OF NATIONALISTIC YOUTH AT LIANDA FOR PEACE: STUDENTS' RESPONSE

Feeling responsible for the fate of China in times of national crisis and carrying on the May Fourth tradition of active political commitment, many students shared the national mood for peace in the wake of the defeat of Japan. They sent appeals to the GMD government and to U.S. leaders, held parades and demonstrations opposing civil war, and demanded the departure of American troops. Students in some big cities also carried out sporadic "U.S. Quit China" campaigns.

Even though no coordinated nationwide student movement took place during late 1945 and most of 1946, an incident that occurred in Kunming on November 25, 1945, soon gave rise to the so-called December First Movement, which drew nationwide attention. On the evening of November 25, the Student Self-Governing Association at Kunming, composed of representatives from Lianda, Yunnan University, and two smaller Kunming colleges and controlled mainly by the underground Communist students, held a mass meeting on the campus of Lianda.[36] The purpose of the meeting was to protest the obvious drift toward renewed hostilities between the two major parties. Having learned of the Student Self-Governing Association's plans for this gathering, local GMD officials prohibited public gatherings of any kind. The meeting went ahead regardless.[37]

A number of professors of different political inclinations had been invited to address the assembly. While students were listening to speeches calling for the cessation of hostilities, withdrawal of American troops, and freedom of speech and assembly, they heard shots from outside the Lianda campus. As the speakers continued addressing the students, local police and soldiers, in an attempt to break up the rally, surrounded the campus and cut off electricity for the microphone and lights and fired shots over students' heads. When the meeting did break up, the students trying to return to town found that the gates of the university had been closed and streets blocked by the troops. They subsequently decided on a three-day protest strike and the formation of the Kunming Student Strike Committee, and demanded an official investigation of the case, public apologies for those who attended the meeting, and a removal of the ban on meetings.[38]

Having trekked long distances to this remote southwest town, the refugee students at Lianda had suffered not only emotionally, but also physically as they endured inadequate teaching and learning facilities and poor living conditions. Confronting the national crisis of the Japanese invasion, they had kept their morale as a result of their patriotic fervor. They thus felt keenly the outrage of a civil war, and also believed that the American meddling only exacerbated the situation. Therefore, in addition to issuing a message to the Chinese people, the Kunming Student Strike Committee also issued open letters to President Truman, the American people, and U.S. military personnel in China respectively. The letter to President Truman, bearing the seals of 30 schools as well as the seal of the Student Strike Committee, asserted that as a group of patriotic students, they had always believed that the United States with a democratic tradition must be a truthful friend of Chinese people. However, the American government was now carrying out policies in China detrimental to the interests of the Chinese people and to the establishment of a new and democratic China. It questioned the activities of American troops in north China and asserted that only the Chinese people had the right to deal with Chinese affairs and asked the American government to keep its promise of "noninterference." The open letters to the American people and troops stationed in China repeated similar themes.[39]

The student political activities, however, led to a raid on the Lianda campus on December 1 by GMD soldiers and plainclothesmen, who shot to death four young people. The four victims, including a high school teacher, two Lianda students, and one high school student, became known as the "Four Martyrs." The December First Incident evoked extensive press coverage, protest rallies and parades, and memorial services for the four victims in various cities. Condolence letters, funeral couplets, flower wreaths, and impassioned poems from all over the country reached Lianda.[40] While radical students used the occasion to demand an immediate withdrawal of American troops from China, the movement also served to discredit the legitimacy of the GMD rule in the eyes of many politically conscious students. As tension between the GMD government and radical students mounted in the next few years,[41] the United States, by virtue of its link with the GMD, grew increasingly unpopular. Moreover, through intervening unsuccessfully in China's political disputes, the U.S. government soon became the primary target of student patriotic nationalism. In time, many politically active students believed that the continuous presence of American forces in China not only helped to perpetuate China's domestic disorder, but also reflected unfavorably on China's status as an independent and sovereign nation. In the end, the incidents involving GIs and local Chinese took on a nationalist dimension and brought the student anti-American sentiment to a boiling point.

THE SHANGHAI PEACE DEMONSTRATION

In the midst of political uncertainties, a large-scale radical demonstration took place in Shanghai, the largest and most cosmopolitan city in China, on June 23,

1946. Around 50,000 people from universities, vocational and high schools, labor unions, cultural clubs, merchants' associations, and press and women's organizations participated in the demonstration.[42] This broad range of radical elements converged over the antiwar issue. Even though similar demonstrations had occurred in other parts of China, they could not compare to this one in terms of magnitude and the wide variety of supporters.

The event that triggered the demonstration was the celebration of the departure of a Peace Petition Brigade headed by Professor Ma Shulun to Nanjing. The Brigade was arranged by two groups, the Federation of Shanghai People's Organization (*Shanghai renmin tuanti lianhehui*) and the Federation of Shanghai Student Peace Promotion Organization (*Shanghai xuesheng zhengqu heping lianhehui*). These organizations came into existence as a consequence of widespread public discontent with the impending full-scale war between the CCP and GMD, and provided leadership for organized political actions.[43] The Peace Petition Brigade intended to express to General Marshall and representatives of the GMD and the CCP the nationwide urgent desire for a peaceful settlement of the internal discord. Members of the delegation, including the prominent educator Tao Xingzhi who was a popular figure in Shanghai's intellectual circles, addressed the rally before departing. They claimed that they represented no parties and welcomed the support of all who yearned for peace in China.

When the delegation left by train for Nanjing, the demonstrators, with university students in the vanguard, marched through Shanghai streets. The purpose of the June 23 demonstration was to impress not only the GMD and the CCP, but also General Marshall with the strong desire of organized public opinion in Shanghai for a peaceful and constructive settlement of China's internal crisis. While antiwar in nature, the parade focused special attention on the U.S. government's China policy, and questioned American activities in China. Students and workers made up the major part of the parade. The demonstrators carried banners and exhibited posters in Chinese and in English. Many posters, handbills, and slogans urged the American troops to leave China, and blamed American military assistance for perpetuating China's internal problem. Many cartoons depicted American involvement in an unfavorable light and satired the United States. The slogans directly related to American activities in China included "Oppose the United States for continuing to assist China with ammunition in waging civil war," "Stop lend-lease," and "Japanese robbers having been disarmed, dear American troops, 'now you can go home.'"[44] One American diplomatic officer present at the scene claimed that the situation reminded him of the anti-imperialist movements in the 1920s.[45] During the parade, a U.S. Army captain, just coming out of the Shanghai Metropolitan Hotel, tried to cut through the line, but was refused passage and had to retreat into the hotel. U.S. naval personnel in jeeps were also reportedly obstructed by the demonstrators.[46]

The demonstration, organized by a small segment of the educated elite, vividly presented the political crisis in front of the general public of Shanghai. The anti-American slogans, songs, and cartoons, by reducing the issues to the fundamentals, simplified as well as dramatized the situation to those who might have been puzzled by the political situation.

Radical anti–Civil War demonstrations, with an antigovernment and anti-U.S. overtone, were not the only ones that took place in 1946. Students who were loyal to the government battled with radical students for control of the streets and influence. On June 21, two days before the radical Anti–Civil War Demonstration, loyalist students launched the Anti–Civil Disturbance March, during which they sang songs, shouted out slogans, and distributed handbills. Contrary to the Anti–Civil War Demonstration that was anti-GMD and anti-American in nature, the Anti–Civil Disturbance demonstrators aimed to increase support for the government by focusing the public attention on CCP rebellion. If the radical students identified the GMD as being more responsible for the outbreak of the Civil War, the loyalists blamed the CCP for China's political instability and claimed that the breakup of the CCP would be the prerequisite for a return to peace. The polarization of the student movement constituted a salient feature of the Civil War period.[47]

HEATED RESPONSE TO THE SINO-AMERICAN COMMERCIAL TREATY

In the midst of Chinese disappointment over the political failure of the Marshall Mission and seething discontent with real or perceived misconduct of American servicemen, a campaign against American economic activities in China developed rapidly in late 1946. In postwar China, political and military crises further unsettled an already war-wracked economy and caused the bankruptcy of many factories and commercial companies. The inflow of American commodities therefore incited animosity and even stimulated the "Buy Chinese Movement" in some places.[48] On November 4, 1946, after over a year's negotiations, the Nationalist and U.S. governments signed a new treaty, the Treaty of Commerce, Navigation, and Friendship (generally called the Sino-American Commercial Treaty), which, however, aroused a political uproar in urban China. [49]

During the so-called age of unequal treaties, the Chinese government had had no power of jurisdiction over foreign companies doing business in the Chinese treaty ports. The treaties signed between the Chinese and American governments in early 1943, however, ended the privileges American economic enterprises had enjoyed in China and subjected them to Chinese rules and regulations. Meanwhile, the two countries also agreed to negotiate a new commercial treaty once the war ended.

Conflicts of views, however, characterized the lengthy process of negotiations for the treaty, which began in earnest in September 1945. The Chinese and American negotiators differed over both fundamental and specific economic policies. From the American viewpoint, a free trade economic system based on private enterprise with only limited central intervention would be the key solution to global economic stability and to China's economic development. From the standpoint of the Nationalist government, China was not ready yet for a full-blown system of free enterprise. The fledgling Chinese national economy was still in need of the guiding hand of and protection from the government. Thus, a limited planned economy with certain state-owned enterprises coexisting with private businesses while benefiting from moderate official protectionism would be the best way to lead China to industrialization and prosperity. In other words, China's transition to free trade should be gradual.[50]

More specifically, the two sides differed over such issues as national treatment and most-favored-nation (MFN) status, which the American negotiators insisted on including in the treaty. The accordance of national treatment to Americans doing business in China would allow them to enjoy the same treatment as their Chinese counterparts. The Chinese negotiators objected to the clause on the grounds that unconditional national treatment to American businesses in China would render the Chinese government powerless in regulating them and in issuing policies beneficial to Chinese economic development. Furthermore, only 107 Chinese could immigrate to the United States annually under the U.S. immigration law, which would severely limit the number of Chinese businessmen engaging in economic activities in the United States, while the Chinese immigration law set no quota for Americans.

With regard to the MFN status, American negotiators pushed for the provision of unconditional treatment, which meant that whatever rights or privileges that China accorded to one treaty nation would be automatically extended to other nations under treaty agreements with China. The Chinese negotiators rejected unconditional MFN treatment for economic and essentially political reasons. They argued that the MFN status could not entitle a Chinese company doing business in the United States to reciprocal privileges since it would not be free from individual state taxes. Besides, such a provision would smack strongly of the MFN clause in the abolished unequal treaties, thus suggesting a return to the age-long humiliating treaties that China had been subject to in the recent past. The Chinese negotiators therefore insisted on conditional MFN, which entailed that rights and privileges enjoyed by foreign countries would be subject to conditions and requirements of present and future Chinese laws.

In the end, the treaty did include national treatment and MFN status, but such words as "unconditional" or "unlimited" were omitted. Negotiating from a position of weakness, the Chinese government made concessions. China's need for American capital in economic development and the Nationalist government's desire to cultivate American goodwill in return for U.S. financial and political support compromised the Chinese position. On the other hand, the American negotiators also made some compromises such as accepting certain limitations to the provisions, removing translation copyright of American works and American trade labels in China, and not mentioning freedom of press in the treaty.[51]

Following the signing of the treaty, the U.S. government publicly hailed the commercial treaty as symbolizing China's entry into the international community on an equal footing. It claimed that the treaty was enacted to meet new economic conditions because the renunciation of the old unequal system in 1943 required a modern one to guide the changed relations between the two countries. With the introduction of the Commercial Treaty, it affirmed that China and the United States had begun a new relationship of equality.[52]

Principal Chinese newspapers viewed the Commercial Treaty as an event of major importance and published the treaty text in full. Unlike the unequal treaties that had subjected the Chinese to a century of humiliations, the new document declared that China and the United States should grant each other the same rights and privileges. However, instead of saluting the Commercial Treaty as a recognition of China's new status as an equal among nations, Chinese newspapers representing different political opinions reacted strongly and almost unanimously leveled criticism at it.[53]

The Chinese press in GMD-controlled urban regions was often subject to government control. With the end of the Sino-Japanese War, the Nationalist government repealed wartime censorship regulations, and the Chinese press enjoyed some degree of freedom for a short while. Journals and periodicals mushroomed. The onset of the Civil War, however, led the government to impose once again severe restrictions on the news published. Publications aspiring for peace and unity or reporting on social strife and student unrest were condemned as Communist-instigated. Liberal newspapers often received threatening letters or were suspended. The most frequently used pretext employed by the government officials to shut down a newspaper was its supposed failure to register.[54] Nevertheless, editors of major unofficial newspapers still managed to express their own political opinions to a certain extent. Also, because many newspapers were owned by different branches of the Nationalist government, political variations within the GMD sometimes made a limited range of diversified press views possible. Consequently, despite government censorship, leading Chinese newspapers, which articulated the various Chinese concerns in response to America's China policy, can still serve as a useful barometer to assess the evolving attitudes among educated Chinese. Furthermore, major newspapers of different political persuasions reacted quite uniformly to certain issues involving Sino-American relations, such as the Sino-U.S. Commercial Treaty. One can therefore measure the general concern toward these issues and draw relevant conclusions.

For many Chinese intellectuals as well as businessmen, the treaty was not concluded in China's best interests; they were especially unhappy with the MFN clause partially because of their resentment of that clause in old unequal treaties. They claimed that although the MFN clause was supposed to be reciprocal, as an economically weak country, China could not yet compete with the United States equally. To extend extensive commercial rights to such a formidable economic power would obviously place the Chinese economy at a disadvantage. It would entail unequal competition since fledgling Chinese industries were not capable of effectively challenging cheap American goods and superior American capital in China, let alone in the United States. He Shiyan, a writer and also the manager of Minsheng Shipping Company, compared the Sino-American Commercial Treaty to an agreement between an adult and a child to each carry a load of 20 pounds in a supposedly equal race.[55]

The editorial of *Shangwu ribao* (Business daily), politically affiliated with the Chinese Chamber of Commerce, asserted that the treaty had "only the outward appearance of equality and reciprocity," and urged the Legislative Yuan to veto the treaty.[56] The Catholic newspaper in Tianjin, *Yi shi bao* (Benevolence news), also complained about the infeasibility for native goods to compete with the steady influx of imported American ones.[57] *Xinwen bao* (The news), controlled by the right-wing CC Clique of the GMD, asserted that the treaty could be considered mutually beneficial and equal only when China became industrialized and its foreign trade was properly developed. Only then would China be able to take advantage of terms this treaty conferred on it.[58]

There certainly existed genuine Chinese apprehension concerning the fate of Chinese national industry and real consternation that the advent of American merchandise might cause further economic dislocation. Consequently, the slogan of "dumping the American goods" was constantly heard.[59] The notion of American goods flooding the Chinese market, thus driving native products out of business, was such a popular one that the cartoonist Zhang Leping even included such an image in his 1947 *Adventures of Sanmao*. Titled "American Goods Flood the Market," the cartoon features a puzzled Sanmao looking at a truckful of American powdered milk; a hungry Sanmao staring through the store window at piles of cans of powdered milk; an envious Sanmao eyeing well-dressed, well-fed Chinese carrying home armfuls of cans; and a chagrined Sanmao watching a sad and downtrodden Chinese seller of fresh dairy products closing down his shop and selling his now skeletal cow (see Figure 5). In a dramatic way, the cartoon presented a critical image of American economic activities in China to the general public.

Furthermore, many prominent civic and cultural figures were convinced that the new treaty once again jeopardized Chinese economic independence and national integrity. According to them, the Sino-American Commercial Treaty forced China to cede the economic autonomy supposedly returned to China with the end of extraterritoriality, since the Chinese government could not apply its own laws to regulate foreign companies in China, except in some specific cases as in inland navigation. Some even sensationally compared the treaty to a knife that would kill the Chinese economy without shedding blood (*sharen bujianxue de dao*).[60]

The treaty created an uproar among informed Chinese, including leading businessmen, industrialists, economists, and writers as well as local officials, and directed their attention to the political consequences of such a treaty. Li Guian, a member of the Chongqing City Council, thought that the Commercial Treaty smacked of "economic imperialism" on the part of the United States.[61] The editorial of *Minzhu bao* of the Democratic League affirmed angrily that "the Sino-American Commercial Treaty is a treaty that infringes on national rights and dishonors the status of China as an independent nation. We heartily oppose it. National rights belong to the people and the people should have the right to disapprove the final ratification of the treaty."[62] *Xinwen wanbao*, a popular evening paper, labeled "liberal" by the American embassy, claimed that even though the United States intended to make China its appendage, the Chinese government, depending on the American government politically and militarily, had no choice but to agree to it.[63]

The Commercial Treaty had serious political implications for the ongoing power struggle between the CCP and the GMD and for Sino-American relations. The GMD officials largely failed to impress the public with the strenuous efforts that they had exerted in negotiating the treaty. Not appreciative and probably not aware of the hard work on the part of Nationalist negotiators to obtain a fair treaty, many members of the Chinese business community and intellectual circles believed that the treaty had betrayed Chinese national economic and political interests. Their disillusionment rendered them critical of the Nationalist government for its perceived inability to protect the Chinese domestic economy against aggressive American competition and to uphold Chinese sovereignty, and for bowing to American demands. As influential members of urban China, they had been strong supporters of the Nationalist government prior to and during China's long war with Japan. The Sino-American Commercial Treaty, however, created a significant rift between them and the GMD regime.

Intent upon turning the Commercial Treaty into a powerful political weapon, Chinese Communists seized the moment to further foster the negative image of the U.S. government and its "running dog"— the GMD government— in the eyes of the informed public. Consequently, the Communist broadcasts from Yan'an were most virulent in attacking the treaty and compared it to the notorious and humiliating "21 Demands" that the Japanese presented to the Yuan Shikai government in 1915.[64] The editorial of the Communist-operated *Jiefang ribao* condemned the Commercial Treaty as "the most shameful treaty of betrayal in the Chinese history." It denounced Chiang Kai-shek and the GMD government for signing such a traitorous (*maiguo*) treaty in return for American aid to continue the one-party dictatorship and to wage civil war. Claiming that the treaty had "stirred up hornets' nests in every circle of Chinese society," the Communists proceeded to designate November 4, the day when the treaty was signed, as "National Humiliation Day" in the Communist territories.[65] The move was significant since May 7, the day when the Japanese presented Yuan Shikai with an ultimatum on the "21 Demands," had been marked annually as National Humiliation Day. By naming another humiliation day, the Communists had linked the United States with treacherous Japan, and Chiang Kai-shek with traitorous Yuan Shikai.

The Commercial Treaty constituted a significant element in the development of an anti-American atmosphere. Evaluating Chinese public opinion through a survey of the Chinese press, the American embassy was disturbed by the overwhelmingly unfavorable reaction to the treaty.[66] Countering the heated Chinese response to the provision of the MFN clause, Ambassador Stuart called the Chinese criticism "unfounded" and "preposterous." He retorted that the new treaty was simply there to fill the vacuum and was mutually beneficial. Nevertheless, he acknowledged that heightened Chinese sensitivity over national sovereignty played a major part in the stormy reaction. Confronting the widespread Chinese criticism of the treaty, Stuart issued a press statement in Shanghai, China's economic center, in an attempt to justify the treaty and to dispel Chinese misunderstanding.[67]

The pubic outcries against the treaty embarrassed the Nationalist government and placed it on the defensive. To calm the heated public reaction and to rectify the "unequal" situation in which the American embassy had initiated a press release explaining the nature of the treaty, the Chinese Ministry of Foreign Affairs felt compelled to publish a statement emphasizing the necessity of the treaty and the ways in which the treaty would promote mutual benefits and interests.[68] In response to the adverse repercussions aroused by the Commercial Treaty, Nationalist leader Chiang Kai-shek later lamented: "In the form of forums, parades and demonstrations held in Nanking [Nanjing], Shanghai, Chungking [Chongqing], Chengtu [Chengdu] and other places, the anti-American movement spread."[69]

Signed at a time when the Marshall Mission was failing and when public discontent with the conduct of American servicemen in China was mounting, the treaty elicited protests from leading citizens in major Chinese cities, such as Beijing, Shanghai, Tianjin, Chongqing, Wuhan, Nanjing, and Guangzhou, added one more element of friction, and deepened the existing public attitude of suspicion and hostility toward the United States.

The demonstration of increasing hostility toward the Americans among urban Chinese of a broad spectrum of political backgrounds alarmed some Americans in China. Confronting the Chinese anti-American trends, Nathaniel Peffer, professor of international relations at Columbia University who was doing research in China at the time, provided a sobering report and claimed that the United States was losing "moral prestige" and was under "both resentment and suspicion" in China. According to him, a variety of elements there were finding fault with American policy. Even supporters of the GMD blamed the United States for not providing enough active support to crush the Communists. Dr. Peffer further asserted:

A large class among business people, academic people, civil servants resent that we give the government just enough support to enable it to believe that it can act with impunity without putting on it enough pressure to make it change its spirit and its practices. The radicals but not Communists think that our support both makes civil war possible and entrenches the worst elements in power. The extreme left is resentful because it believes we are entrenching a fascist regime in return for its being a tool for our own purposes, which it deems to be imperialistic domination. The charges against us vary according to source; but they are charges. . . . [F]or the first time America begins to occupy a new role in Chinese thought, and it is a role that denotes a loss of moral prestige. It ranges from disillusionment to open anti-Americanism. And it should not be ignored or underestimated.[70]

The prevailing anti-American tendency, especially the "non-Communist" one, disturbed the American embassy. Claiming Dr. Peffer's testimony a timely warning, Ambassador Stuart attested that Chinese national consciousness of the last few decades harbored an antiforeign attitude, which was latent in individual Chinese and would actively demonstrate itself in mass movements or in hostile personal opinion whenever a foreign country provoked it.[71]

As 1946 drew to a close, a general sense of futility prevailed in China. On December 18, 1946, when President Truman issued another long statement on America's China policy while China was engaging in a full-fledged civil war, the nonofficial press in China greeted his words with hostility. In his statement, Truman announced the cutback of American forces in China to 12,000 from the previous year's peak number of 113,000. He reiterated the American intention of not interfering in Chinese internal affairs. He maintained that "while avoiding involvement in their civil strife, we will persevere with our policy of helping the Chinese people to bring about peace and economic recovery in their country."[72] His statement was ill received in China.

A number of newspapers accused Truman's statement of being full of meaningless words and phrases. Truman's comments on the accomplishments of American troops in China were attacked as a smoke screen to conceal the true reason for their presence, namely, to help maintain the GMD in power.[73] They sneered at Truman's emphasis on the noninterfering nature of American policy toward China, and viewed it as an indication of American hypocrisy.[74] In general, in the eyes of many radical urban Chinese, U.S. policy toward China simply attempted to break the political deadlock on the one hand and continued assistance to the Nationalist government on the other. In response to Truman's statement, major Chinese newspapers, whatever their political persuasions, all reflected a deep sense of frustration. The united China for which people had craved had not only failed to materialize, but it also did not seem likely to come to fruition with the two contending parties at loggerheads.

The Chinese response to the American involvement often took place within the context of the internal development in the country. In the face of China's domestic political struggles and uncertainties, many Chinese intellectuals' perceptions of the United States swayed between expectation and disappointment, and appreciation and resentment. World War II had enhanced nationalistic sentiment and fostered political aspirations among educated Chinese for an elevated international status for postwar China. While Chinese expectations were high in the wake of the Japanese defeat, the dreary political reality soon brought on great disillusionment. In the immediate postwar period, the warm feelings toward the United States as China's critical ally during World War II rapidly switched to resentment. As one historian asserts, "Whatever good will Americans had acquired in China could not compete with the dedication of Chinese to their own interests."[75]

Toward the end of 1946, while the CCP and many radical intellectuals intensified their anti-American propaganda efforts by building upon, and thus further broadening, the unfavorable public image of the United States, the Chinese press in general had turned more anti-American in tone, and was almost unanimously critical of the U.S. government on the issues of the conduct of American forces in China and the Sino-American Commercial treaty. The Chinese distrust of Americans developed, however, not at a personal level, but essentially out of suspicion of the American policy toward China and a heightened nationalistic sentiment.[76] Lack of national security and unity rendered many young Chinese intellectuals especially sensitive to real and imagined snubs by a foreign power. By the end of 1946, American political, military, and economic activities in China had incurred the growth of widespread anti-American sentiment. One cartoon of late 1946, titled "Importation and Exportation," captured vividly the critical Chinese mood at the time: while the American government exported military and economic supplies to the Chiang regime, it imported in return "anti-American sentiment" from China.[77] The stage was set, and it fell upon the articulate, educated urban youths to translate the simmering discontent into a wave of anti-American national protests.

NOTES

1. The New Fourth Army of the CCP grew out of the scattered guerrilla forces in central China in late 1937. However, the increasing strength of the New Fourth Army centered in the strategic and rich region of the Yangzi delta alarmed Chiang Kai-shek, who in 1940 ordered the Communist units active south of the Yangzi to move north. Clashes and skirmishes between the Nationalist and Communist forces occurred throughout 1940. In January 1941, a force of 9,000 Communist troops attached to the New Fourth Army headquarters were ambushed and destroyed in the mountains by Nationalist troops. The incident essentially signaled the end of the United Front. (See Conrad Brandt, Benjamin Schwartz, and John K. Fairbank, *A Documentary History of Chinese Communism* [Cambridge: Harvard University Press, 1952], 235; Tang Tsou, *America's Failure in China, 1941–1950* [Chicago: Chicago University Press, 1963], 137–39; and Jonathan D. Spence, *The Search for Modern China*, 2d ed. [New York: W.W. Norton, 1999], 436, 439–41.)

2. A principal reason for the American interest in a unified China under U.S. influence derived from the fear of the spread of Soviet influence in Manchuria as well as in China proper. Steven Levine maintains that Marshall's mission was primarily to prevent the Soviets from grabbing Manchuria by removing "China as a node of conflicts in Soviet-American relationship" and keeping "Soviet political influence there to a minimum." (See Steven I. Levine, *Anvil of Victory: The Communist Revolution in Manchuria, 1945–1948* [New York: Columbia University Press, 1987], 5.)

3. The United States did not initiate the negotiations between the two Chinese parties. In August 1942, Chiang informed the Communist representative in Chongqing, Zhou Enlai, that he wished to speak with Mao Zedong. Although Mao did not meet Chiang himself, the high-ranking Communist general, Lin Biao, reached Chongqing in October 1942 to start the negotiations. During the talks, the Communists demanded that the GMD government recognize the legal status of the CCP and permit the extension of the Communist forces to form armies of 12 divisions. The GMD insisted that the Communists have at most 8 divisions and that the CCP be made legal only after the reorganization of its troops. The negotiations lingered on fruitlessly for eight more months before coming to a halt. Both the Nationalists and Communists claimed that the negotiators simply indulged in empty talks. In September 1943, at the GMD 11th Plenary Session, Chiang announced his willingness to accept a political solution to the Communist problem. Consequently, in May 1944 both parties resumed talks, which again produced no concrete results. As before, the controversies centered on the issues of the GMD's recognition of the lawful status of the CCP and the GMD's requirements of the reorganization of the Communist armies and their incorporation into the Nationalist army. The negotiations once again reached an impasse. In fact, even before the inception of this round of talks, the GMD had decided to emphasize the propaganda effect of the negotiations and not to expect any results. Although Chiang now repeatedly claimed that he intended to solve the Communist problem through political means, he really meant the political and military subordination of the CCP to the GMD. For all these years, the GMD had never stopped accusing the Communists of establishing "a state within a state," of continuing their armed insurrection, and of refusing to obey the orders of the Nationalist government. Confronting the GMD charges, the Communists claimed that the GMD had broken its original promise of establishing a united front and that it practiced one-party dictatorship. The differences, therefore, were long standing and irreconcilable.

4. Michael Schaller, *The U.S. Crusade in China, 1938–1945* (New York: Columbia University Press, 1979), 147–229, 251–89.

5. Lyman P. Van Slyke, ed., *Marshall's Mission to China, December 1945–January 1947: The Report and Appended Documents* (Arlington, Va.: University Publications of America, 1976), 1:19–20.

6. Schaller, *U.S. Crusade in China*, 298; T. Christopher Jespersen, *American Images of China: 1931–1949* (Stanford: Stanford University Press, 1996).

7. The Marshall Mission is a well-studied topic. Some of the works on Marshall's mission include Michael Schaller, *The United States and China in the Twentieth Century* (New York: Oxford University Press, 1990), 114–16; Schaller, *U.S. Crusade in China*, 291–300; Larry I. Bland, ed., *George C. Marshall's Mediation Mission to China, December 1945–January 1947* (Lexington, Va.: George C. Washington Foundation, 1998); James Readon-Anderson, *Yenan and the Great Powers: The Origins of Chinese Communist Foreign Policy, 1944–1946* (New York: Columbia University Press, 1980), 132–59; William Stueck, "The Marshall and Wedemeyer Missions: A Quadrilateral Perspective," in *Sino-American Relations, 1945–1955: A Joint Reassessment of a Critical Decade*, ed. Harry Harding and Yuan Ming (Wilmington, Del.: Scholarly Resources, 1989), 96–118.

8. For a brief explanation of Chiang's views toward the Marshall Mission, see Odd Arne Westad, "Could the Chinese Civil War Have Been Avoided? An Exercise in Alternatives," in *George C. Marshall's Mediation Mission to China*, 506.

9. The end of the war against Japan found the CCP in an inferior position in manpower and weaponry vis-à-vis the GMD military power. Despite their growing strength, the Communists nevertheless looked weak and the Nationalists strong. While Chiang opted for exclusive American support since any diversion might undermine the authority of the GMD, Mao initially welcomed the American mediation effort. Eventually, the American mediation achieved little except for intensifying the Communist distrust of the "U.S. imperialists" and providing the Nationalists with one more reason to complain about the inconsistency of the American China policy.

10. U.S. Department of State, *The China White Paper: August 1949* (1949; reprint, Stanford: Stanford University Press, 1967), 607.

11. Prior to Marshall's arrival, about 80 student representatives from 32 universities and high schools in Shanghai established an organization on December 14, 1945, to prepare for "The Meeting to Welcome Special Envoy Marshall," as Marshall was to land at the Shanghai airport first before departing for Chongqing. The student representatives decided that while expressing gratitude and welcome to Marshall for his mediation efforts, they would submit letters to him requesting withdrawal of U.S. troops from China and uttering students' desire for peace. Upon Marshall's arrival, around 4,000 students, accompanied by a band playing patriotic songs, marched to the hotel where the GMD officials were entertaining Marshall with an elaborate welcoming banquet. The parade, however, was interrupted by a group of pro-government students. See Gongqingtuan Shanghai shiwei, *1945–1949: Shanghai xuesheng yundongshi* (1945–1949: A history of the Shanghai student movement) (Shanghai: Shanghai renmin chubanshe, 1983), 12–19; Jeffrey N. Wasserstrom, *Student Protests in Twentieth-Century China: The View From Shanghai* (Stanford: Stanford University Press, 1991), 242–43.

12. When China's defense against Japan collapsed in 1938, the nation's leading universities and research institutes, their faculty, staff, and students, followed the Nationalist retreat west. Students and teachers of Beijing, Qinghua, and Nankai Universities were evacuated from Beijing and Tianjin and joined together to set up Lianda in Kunming. In the summer of 1946, these refugee universities began to move back to their home campuses. For a study of Lianda's eight-year history (1938–1946), see John Is-

rael, *Lianda: A Chinese University in War and Revolution* (Stanford: Stanford University Press, 1998).

13. U.S. Department of State, *China White Paper*, 608.

14. Wen Liming, "Lun yier yi yundongzhongde daxue jiaoshou yu Lianda jiaoshouhui—Zhongguo sishi niandai de ziyouzhuyi kaocha zhiyi" (A discussion on the university professors and Lianda's faculty meetings during the December 1 movement: One of the examinations on China's liberalism during the forties) *Jindaishi yanjiu* (Modern history studies) 70 (July 1992): 207–8.

15. R. David Arkush, *Fei Xiaotong and Sociology in Revolutionary China* (Cambridge: Harvard University Press, 1981), 188.

16. *Dagong bao*, December 18, 1946. *Dagong bao* was a Tianjin daily long known for its high journalistic standards. It had branch offices in several major cities, such as Shanghai and Hong Kong.

17. Chinese liberals can be broadly defined as those who were influenced by Anglo-American political and educational ideas. See Israel, *Lianda*, ix.

18. Lincoln Li, *Student Nationalism in China, 1924–1949* (Albany: State University of New York Press, 1994), 124; Mary G. Mazur, "Intellectual Activism in China during the 1940s: Wu Han in the United Front and the Democratic League," *The China Quarterly* 133 (March 1993): 36; see also "The Emergence of the Chinese Democratic League: Typescript History, 1946," the Tseng Chao-lun collection, in Hoover Institution Archives Holdings on China. Developed out of the United National Reconstruction Comrades Association, the Democratic League came into being in 1941 and was composed of mainly intellectuals with liberal inclinations. Hoping to work as an arbitrator between the two contending political parties, its influence was largely over with the onslaught of the full-scale civil war in 1947. It then operated closely with the Communist Party, and was branded the front organization of and the spokesman for the Communists by the GMD and was ordered to disband in October 1947. The golden age of Chinese liberalism thus came to an end. For a study of the political outlooks of the Democratic League and its relation with the CCP and the GMD, see Edmund S.K. Fung, *In Search of Chinese Democracy: Civil Opposition in Nationalist China, 1929–1949* (Cambridge: Cambridge University Press, 2000), 230–62. In her article "The United Front Redefined for the Party-State: A Case Study of Transition and Legitimization," in *New Perspectives on State Socialism in China*, ed. Timothy Cheek and Tony Saich (Armonk, New York: M.E. Sharpe, 1997), pp. 51–75, Mary Mazur examines the adaptation of the United Front to the transitional period of the new state during 1948–53.

19. Fung, *In Search of Chinese Democracy*, 263.

20. Given its past experiences with Chiang Kai-shek and its ultimate goal to achieve supremacy in China, the CCP would never submit its armed forces to GMD control. The Communist leaders had learned that only the independence of their army would guarantee the existence and future of the Party. Why then did the CCP call for a coalition government? First, it would make useful propaganda. Furthermore, a coalition government under the Communist terms would deprive Chiang of a great part of his authority and render the Communists free to work on their organizational program. While they would not give up their hard-won power, the Communists would attempt every means to undermine the influence of the Nationalists. The ultimate goals mattered most. This meant, in Chinese terms, unswerving strategy with flexible tactics. For a study of the Communist political strategy between 1945–46, see Joseph K.S.Yick, "The Communist-Nationalist Political Struggle in Beijing during the Marshall Mission Period," in *George C. Marshall's Mediation Mission to China*, 358–60.

21. Joseph K.S. Yick, *Making Urban Revolution in China: The CCP-GMD Struggle for Beiping-Tianjin, 1945–1949* (Armonk, N.Y.: M.E. Sharpe, 1995), 359.

22. By confronting the Japanese aggression, China witnessed the awakening of its masses and a strong outpouring of their national emotions. However, despite the inspiring surge of nationalism, the spiritual resistance of the Nationalist army at the beginning stage of the war, and the guerrilla activities carried out by the Communists, the Japanese swiftly overran most of eastern China, forcing the Nationalist government to remove its capital from Nanjing to Wuhan and then to Chongqing, a city in the remote southwestern province of Sichuan. As the war dragged on, Chinese casualties became enormous. The Nationalist army experienced ineffective commands, a failure to carry out orders, poor intelligence, and a lack of morale.

23. Suzanne Pepper, *Civil War in China: The Political Struggle, 1945–1949* (Berkeley: University of California Press, 1978), 9. See also Yick's *Making Urban Revolution in China* for discussions on the problems that the GMD encountered and generated in urban China following the Japanese surrender, 45–46.

24. Wasserstrom, *Student Protests in Twentieth-Century China*, 254.

25. "Transmission of Declaration with Regard to Current Situation in China," from American Embassy to the Department of State, August 27, 1946, RG59, 893.00/8-2746, National Archives (hereafter NA).

26. U.S. Department of State, "Copy of Statement Presented to United States Military Authorities in North China," November 15, 1945, in *Records of the Office of Chinese Affairs, 1945–1955*, reel 10.

27. U.S. Department of State, "Summary of a Personal Letter from Mr. John Fairbank, December 6, 1945," memorandum by Vincent, Director of the Office of Far Eastern Affairs, January 14, 1946, in *Foreign Relations of the United States [FRUS], 1946, The Far East: China* (Washington, D.C.: Government Printing Office, 1972), 9:131.

28. Arkush, *Fei Xiaotong*, 188.

29. "Views of Dr. Lo Lung-chi [Luo Longji] on the Present Political Situation in China," from Ward, Shanghai to Butterworth, Nanjing, December 2, 1946, *Records of the Office of Chinese Affairs 1945–1955*, reel 10.

30. *Jiefang ribao*, August 14, 1946.

31. U.S. Department of State, *FRUS, 1946, The Far East: China*, 9:439–40; Pepper, *Civil War in China*, 214.

32. Wasserstrom provides a critical view of the complex nature of the anti-Soviet movements in cities such as Shanghai and Chongqing in *Student Protests in Twentieth-Century China*, 246–50.

33. Li, *Student Nationalism in China*, 129.

34. See Lu Zude, "Zhu Ziqing xiansheng de shengping shiji" (The life story of Mr. Zhu Ziqing) *Wenshi ziliao xuanbian* (A selected collection of cultural and historical materials), no. 6 (1980): 94.

35. Chen Jian, *China's Road to the Korean War: The Making of the Sino-American Confrontation* (New York: Columbia University Press, 1994), 67–68; Odd Arne Westad, ed., *Brothers in Arms: The Rise and Fall of the Sino-Soviet Alliance, 1945–1963* (Washington, D.C.: Woodrow Wilson Center Press, 1998), 7–9.

36. Lianda's CCP branch was founded in 1939 and was forced to retreat to the countryside in the aftermath of the New Fourth Army Incident. In the early 1940s, the small number of hardworking young underground Communist students at Lianda established a reputation as model students. They then extended their political activities from study clubs and wall newspapers to student government. Having won recognition first as

class and then department student leaders, they gained control of the Student Self-Governing Association in 1944. See Israel, *Lianda*, 371.

37. See Li, *Student Nationalism in China*, 124–27; also see "Strike of University and Middle School Students at Kunming," from Philip D. Sprouse, Kunming, to Secretary of State Byrnes, December 18, 1945, RG59, 893.00/12-1845, NA.

38. Arkush, *Fei Xiaotong*, 184–86; Sprouse to Byrnes, December 18, 1945, RG59, 893.00/12-1845, NA; for a detailed discussion, see also Yier yi yundongshi bianxiezu, eds., *Yier yi yundong shiliao xuanbian* (A selected collection of the historical materials on the December 1 movement) (Kunming: Yunnan renmin chubanshe, 1980).

39. Yier yi yundongshi, *Yier yi yundong*, 1:62–66.

40. For discussions of the December First Movement, see also Israel, *Lianda*, 369–75; Pepper, *Civil War in China*, 44–52. For the political uproar precipitated by the December First Incident among radical students in Shanghai, see Wasserstrom, *Student Protests in Twentieth-Century China*, 244–45.

41. In *The Politics of Depoliticization in Republican China: Guomindang Policy towards Student Political Activism, 1927–1949* (Berne, Germany: Peter Lang, 1996), Huang Jianli discusses how the ruling party, the GMD, viewed student political activism and how it formulated and implemented policies accordingly.

42. "Anti–Civil War Demonstration, Shanghai, June 23, 1946," memorandum by Julian R. Friedman, Labor Attaché of the American Consulate in Shanghai, July 8, 1946, RG59, 893.00/8-2946, NA.

43. "Anti–Civil War Demonstration," memorandum by Friedman, July 8, 1946, RG59, 893.00/8-2946, NA; Wasserstrom, *Student Protests in Twentieth-Century China*, 253.

44. "Anti–Civil War Demonstration," memorandum by Friedman, July 8, RG59, 893.00/8-2946, NA.

45. "Anti–Civil War Demonstration of June 23, 1946," memorandum by James E. Mchenna, American Consul in Shanghai, July 8, 1946, RG59, 893.00/8-2946, NA.

46. "Anti–Civil War Demonstration," memorandum by Friedman, July 8, 1946, RG59, 893.00/8-2946, NA.

47. In *Student Protests in Twentieth-Century China*, pp. 253–61, Wasserstrom discusses persuasively the power struggle between radical and loyalist youths for control of the political stage in Shanghai during the demonstrations of June 1946.

48. Based on Chinese customs statistics, imports from the United States in 1946 constituted 57 percent of China's total imports. See Yuan Ming, "The Failure of Perception: America's China Policy, 1949–50," in *Sino-American Relations, 1945–1955*, 143.

49. For more information on the process of negotiating the treaty and on the treaty itself, see Julia F. Cosgrove, *United States Foreign Economic Policy toward China, 1943–1946* (New York: Garland Publishing, 1987); Tao Wenzhao, "1946 ZhongMei shangyue: Zhanhou Meiguo duiHua zhengcezhong jingji yinsu ge'an yanjiu" (The 1946 Sino-American commercial treaty: A study of economic elements in U.S. China policy in the postwar period) *Jindaishi yanjiu*, no. 2 (March 1993): 236–58; and Simei Qing, "Visions of Free Trade and U.S.-China Commercial Treaty Negotiations, 1945–46," in *China and the United States: A New Cold War History*, ed. Xiaobing Li and Hongshan Li (Lanham, Md.: University Press of America, 1998): 119–52. For a general treatment of the Sino-American economic relationship in the 1940s, see C.X. George Wei, *Sino-American Economic Relations, 1944–1949* (Westport, Conn.: Greenwood Press, 1997).

50. Qing, "Visions of Free Trade," 146–47.

51. Wei, *Sino-American Economic Relations*, 97–105; Qing, "Visions of Free Trade," 135–40, 146–47.

52. See Cosgrove, *United States Foreign Economic Policy Toward China*, 194.

53. From Stuart to Secretary of State, November 15, 1946, NG59, 711.93211-1546, NA.

54. For details, see Lee-hsia Hsu Ting, *Government Control of the Press in Modern China, 1900–1949* (Cambridge: Harvard University Press, 1974), chapter 7. In the Communist-held areas, the CCP exercised strict control over publications. The chief purpose of the press was to propagate Communist policies and instructions and to influence public opinion.

55. *Dagong bao*, November 8, 1946.

56. *Shangwu ribao*, November 8, 1946.

57 *Yi shi bao*, November 14, 1946.

58. *Xinwen bao*, November 8, 1946.

59. Shanghai daxue et al., *Xinbian Zhongguo xiandaishi* (A new edition of modern Chinese history) (Nanchang: Jiangxi renmin chubanshe, 1987), 238.

60 *Dagong bao*, November 9, 1946.

61. Quoted from *Shangwu ribao*, November 8, 1946.

62 *Minzhu bao*, November 8, 1946.

63. *Xinwen wanbao*, November 16, 1946.

64. Yan'an Broadcast, November 14, December 8, 1946, in "Press Publication, 1945–1946," *Records of the Office of Chinese Affairs, 1945–1955*, reel 3.

65. *Jiefang ribao*, November 27, 1946.

66. Stuart to Secretary of State, November 15, 1946, RG59, 711.932/11-1546, NA.

67. Ibid., November 24, 1946, RG59, 711.932/11-2446, NA.

68. Ibid., November 29, 1946, RG59, 711.932/11-2946.

69. Chiang Kai-shek, *Soviet Russia in China: A Summary at Seventy* (New York: Farrar, Straus and Cubahy, 1957), 186.

70. Stuart to Byrnes, October 17, 1946, *FRUS, 1946, The Far East: China*, 10:388.

71. Ibid., 389. In his memoirs, Truman attributed the increasing anti-American propaganda, mass meetings, and demonstrations at the time to instigation by the GMD extremists and the Communists alike. See Harry S. Truman, *Memoirs of Harry S. Truman: Years of Trial and Hope* (New York: Doubleday Company, 1950), 2:81.

72. U.S. Department of State, *China White Paper*, 694.

73. See, for example, *Guomin gongbao*, December 20, 1946, and *Minzhu bao*, December 20, 1946.

74. *Guomin gongbao*, December 20, 1946.

75. Paul Varg, *The Closing of the Door: Sino-American Relations, 1936–1946* (East Lansing: Michigan State University Press, 1973), 52.

76. In fact, most of the open statements by Chinese intellectuals during this period criticizing America's China policy began with broad remarks alluding to the traditional friendly relations between the two peoples in general and to the great American contribution to the defeat of Japan in particular, and proceeded to attack postwar American policy toward China. For example, in an open letter to Chinese compatriots and fellow students, the Federation of the Student Peace Promotion Organization in Shanghai emphasized the close ties of friendship between the Chinese and American people and welcomed the introduction of American books, scientific instruments, and American machinery. Yet the letter also sharply criticized the stationing of American troops, the selling of American military materials, and "the large-scale smuggling and sale of

American goods" in China, which they believed had augmented Chinese economic and political crises. See *Wen hui bao*, October 7, 1946.

77. Wen Chuan, "Meiguo zhengfude cuowu luxian bixu gaibian," (The erroneous American policy must be changed) *Qunzhong* (The masses) 12 (August 1946). Quoted from Yang Yusheng, *Zhongguoren de Meiguoguan* (Chinese views of America) (Shanghai: Fudan dexue chubanshe, 1996), 221.

4

THE SHEN CHONG RAPE CASE AND THE *KANGBAO* (ANTI-BRUTALITY) MOVEMENT, 1946–1947

The sojourn of American GIs in the immediate postwar China served as the vital factor in arousing nationalist fervor among the young, urban, and educated Chinese, and inadvertently assisted in the Communist cause. The most significant case that occurred during the American troops' stay in China involved the alleged rape of a Chinese college student, Shen Chong, by an American marine. The so-called Beiping rape case became a political and cultural *cause célèbre* among politically conscious young Chinese intellectuals. In response, vehement student demonstrations broke out across the country "protesting the brutality of US troops" (*kangyi Meijun baoxing*) and vigorously demanding an immediate withdrawal of American troops from China. Major newspapers published articles condemning the "disgraceful" behavior of the marines. At the time, many educated youths of different political persuasions in China seemed to be united in condemning GI conduct.

The rape case assumed great symbolic significance and was elevated to the level of *guochi* (national shame) as the student protestors equated the rape of Shen Chong with the violation of China and looked upon the victimization of Shen as being representative of China's own plight. In the end, the uproar the incident provoked further complicated an already volatile political situation, created powerfully negative images of the United States, and figured significantly in the CCP's urban victory over the GMD and Communist China's subsequent military confrontation with the United States in Korea. To probe beneath the surface of the outburst of student demonstrations, however, will disclose the cultural and political tensions within the Chinese society and in Sino-American relations. The outburst of a nationwide student anti-American campaign therefore has to be understood in the broader contexts.[1]

THE SHEN CHONG *SHIJIAN* (INCIDENT)

The incident took place on Christmas Eve of 1946. At approximately 8:30 P.M., Shen Chong, a 19-year-old student from National Beijing University (Beida),[2] was returning from a movie in Pingan Theater in Dongdan to her cousin's house,[3] where she was staying. She was stopped by two drunken American marines, Corporal William G. Pierson and Private Warren T. Pritchard. Pierson and Pritchard had been drinking at the Manhattan Café since early afternoon, and were now on their way to another party at the Beijing Hotel. A Chinese army mechanic, Meng Zhaojie, spotted two marines dragging a crying Chinese girl to the Dongdan Drill Field nearby. Meng returned to the Motor Pool Repair Shop and informed his fellow workers what he had just witnessed. Then five of them went to the Drill Field. When they approached the three, the two marines drove them away with threatening words. The army mechanics then reported to two Chinese policemen that a crying girl in the company of two American marines was in need of help. When they returned to the scene with the policemen, they found only a pair of bloodstained GI gloves and a GI scarf on the ground. When they spotted the group at the other end of the Drill Field, the marines again chased them away.[4] They left to report the incident to Guan Dejun, a Chinese patrol policeman in charge of the Dongdan area, saying that "a U.S. marine was mistreating a Chinese girl on the Drill Ground." Guan went alone to the place to investigate, and found only one marine, William Pierson, "lying there on top of Shen." Warren Pritchard had already left for the Beijing Hotel. Pierson shouted some angry words to him. Guan left and summoned one more Chinese policeman to the scene. When they returned, they found that Pierson was still "on top of the girl." They arrested Pierson on the spot, and phoned the Joint Office of Sino-American Police.[5] By this time it was about 11:30, almost three hours after the two marines' initial encounter with Shen Chong. Since the Chinese policemen refused to let Pierson leave for the Beijing Hotel and intended to take him into custody, Pierson stepped to the main street and accosted a patrolling American MP.[6]

When a passing MP on duty, Alvin Goldsmith, saw the group, Pierson explained to him that he had "stepped in a hole, and tripped falling on his girl knocking her down." At this moment, the Chinese policemen came. One policeman hit him with a rifle, while another stuck a pistol in his stomach. They also took his "girl" away from him. The MP then took Pierson, Shen, and a newly arrived Chinese officer from the Joint Office of Sino-American Police to the Marine Military Police Office where Shen Chong registered and Pierson was taken into custody.

Shortly afterwards, the Chinese police officer took Shen Chong to the Chinese Central Police Station for questioning. He also phoned her relatives, and tried to calm her down and to dispel any possible suicidal thoughts in her. Meanwhile,

Shen had to go through a variety of procedures, including a physical examination at the Police Hospital. The Chinese doctor who examined Shen found evidence of sexual intercourse and minor vaginal injuries, but also stated that "it is hard to determine that this is really rape." Shen was taken back to the police station where she filed a charge of rape against Pierson, which was made known to the marine authorities in Beiping on the morning of December 25. It was not until 5:00 next morning that Shen's brother-in-law, Yang Zhenqing, was able to take her home. In the early afternoon, the marine investigators, together with interpreters and medical officers, arrived at the Yang residence and took Shen Chong to the French Hospital for a physical examination. Having examined Shen, the American doctor of the Navy Reserve, Lieutenant Percival Clark, concluded that "the only injuries to Miss Chung's [sic] person were small cuts in the posterior maidenly membrane at the lower parts." While finding evidence of sexual intercourse, he indicated that had Shen struggled harder in the process, more marks and bruises would show on the buttock and thigh regions.[7]

While investigating the incident, the Marine provost marshal collected written statements from Shen, Pierson, Pritchard, and the witnesses. According to Shen's statement, Pierson raped her twice while Pritchard pulled her down. Too weak to protect herself, she struggled in vain and was forced to keep quiet. Pritchard then left for the Beijing Hotel while Pierson stayed with her. Pierson then dragged Shen around the Dongdan Drill Field in an attempt to find a place away from passersby. At one point, he took Shen inside a wooden shack, and then decided it was too dirty. He continued dragging Shen around until he found a relatively safe place away from the main streets. He then raped Shen one more time on the ground. Shen claimed that she was forced to go along with Pierson since there was no one in sight. She had to wait for a chance to call out for help for fear that she might be killed otherwise. When she saw a man on a bicycle riding by, she waved her white underwear to him. The man stopped, took a look, and left. Shortly after, two Chinese policemen and some soldiers arrived on the scene.[8] Shen Chong stated in conclusion that the insult had inflicted immense damage to her body and reputation, and demanded severe punishment of the two marines. She claimed that she would be too ashamed to live otherwise.[9]

Pierson denied the rape charge. He was, however, not consistent in his two written statements. In the statement he made on December 25, Pierson did not admit any sexual misconduct, but insisted that he had fallen into a hole while walking across the Drill Field with a Chinese girl, and at that instant, two Chinese policemen arrived. Then in his statement of December 28, he indicated that Shen was actually a prostitute, asking for five dollars, but settling on three, and admitted having "intercourse" with her twice. Because they had been interrupted by the police, he maintained, he did not pay her the three dollars. However, Pierson was so intoxicated that evening that he stated he could not remember whether or not Pritchard had had sexual intercourse with Shen Chong. In his statement, Pritchard also indicated that Shen was a prostitute and "willingly went across the Polo Grounds [Drill Ground], and laid down with Pierson."[10]

Based on their preliminary investigations, the Marine provost marshal investigators reached several conclusions: (1) Pierson had indulged himself in intoxicants to such an extent on December 24 that he had only a hazy recollection of what had happened on that evening; (2) Shen Chong did not make a practice of consorting with American personnel; (3) Shen Chong did not struggle and protest as violently as would be expected in a rape case, but the report did recognize that "this reticence could have been the result of shock, fear, or intimidation"; (4) Warren Pritchard was physically present at the scene of the alleged rape, but did not engage in sexual intercourse with Shen; and (5) Pierson did, "either through threat, physical violence, or a promise of money," have sexual intercourse with Shen. In the end, the provost marshal investigators recommended disciplinary action for Pierson.[11] Little did they realize that this was just the beginning of the soon famous Shen Chong *shijian* (incident) and the triggering event of a nationwide anti-American student movement.

"IF THIS CAN BE TOLERATED, WHAT CANNOT?" BEIPING STUDENTS IN ACTION

Having learned of the incident from a press informant in the Beiping Police Station, the Yaguang News Agency reported it on December 25. On the same day, the official Central News Agency, urged by the Beiping chief of police, issued a statement to the local press to postpone releasing news related to the incident. The statement emphasized that the victim's family had asked that the event not be publicized for the sake of the girl's reputation and to avoid inflicting suicidal pressure on the girl.[12] On the following day, however, several newspapers in Beiping carried an account of the episode, although they did not reveal the name of the victim. *Xinmin bao,* a left-wing newspaper, embarrassed the local GMD authorities by publishing the official statement as well.[13]

The Beiping press comments immediately after the incident were somewhat moderate in tone. While affirming the guilt of the marines involved and expressing indignation, their comments largely adhered closely to the assault case itself with little deliberation on the political implications. Some suggested that the municipal government could soon work out appropriate procedures with the marine offices to punish the culprits.

Response to the alleged rape case, however, was not confined to the news coverage. The event sparked a nationwide student anti-American campaign, and played a significant role not only in the making of the urban Chinese images of the United States, but also in the political power struggle between the CCP and the GMD. While the students at Beida responded first to the rape case, politically active students in other universities in Beiping, especially Qinghua and Yanjing, helped spread and publicize the event by organizing and launching a citywide student demonstration.

Beida, the birthplace of the May Fourth Movement of 1919 and the hub of China's New Cultural Movement, had figured significantly in the Chinese student movement. The rape of a Beida student by an American soldier created a sensation on the Beida campus, and constituted the first major emotion-arousing political and cultural event after the return of the Beida students from their wartime exile in Kunming in the fall of 1946. Radical students at Beida took action first, and plastered protesting posters on the Red Building Wall, which served as the campus's main bulletin board. One of them contained such inflammatory verses as "China is not a brothel for foreigners; Chinese college girls are not comfort women for American soldiers."[14]

In the immediate aftermath of the Shen Chong case, some local and Beida officials endeavored vainly to gloss it over and not to let it grow out of control. However, their statements became the focal point of repeated verbal attacks by the angry students of Beida, who insisted that the officials had intentionally belittled Shen Chong's fine personal character, her prominent family background, and her undeniable status as a Beida student. For them, it was an indisputable fact that a rape of one of their fellow students by an American serviceman had occurred, and to claim otherwise or to degrade Shen in any way suggested ulterior motives. Therefore, they reprimanded Beiping's mayor, He Siyuan, for allegedly having stated that the medical result could not yet settle the case for a rape, and Chen Xueping, proctor of Beida, for suggesting that Shen might not be a student of Beida at all, and thus there was no need for overreaction.[15] Beida professor of law Yan Shutang showed open disapproval of the student actions, and was reported to have said, "Why didn't you react to the rape of a young girl committed by a Chinese? Why do you respond so vehemently to the rape of a student by an American soldier?" The angry students immediately labeled his remarks as irresponsible, nonsensical, and ridiculous.[16] This was not the first time that Yan had enraged student progressives. He had long been known for his strong pro-GMD and anti-Communist stand. During the days of Lianda when Beida was part of the exile university in Kunming, Yan had urged a gradual move to constitutional government, opposed a coalition government, and attempted to absolve the GMD authorities of legal responsibilities for the death of four young people on the Lianda campus in the December First Incident.[17] Yan's remarks made immediately after the alleged rape incident certainly did not endear him to the radical students.

Underground CCP student organizers at Beida realized immediately the significance of the rape case for the Communist cause and moved quickly to capitalize on and augment the expression of student anti-American sentiment.[18] The leaders of the Student Committee of the Communist Underground Party concluded at an emergency meeting immediately after the Shen Chong Incident that they would use it to "hold high the flag of national dignity and inspire people's national indignation." They looked upon Beida as the key university in launching the movement because of the university's radical tradition and also because the rape victim was a student there. They decided that women students at Beida should take the initiative, as they could gain more sympathy.[19]

Following the suggestions made at the Communist Underground Party meeting, Liu Junying, president of the Beida Women Students' Association and an underground CCP member, helped organize a female student protest meeting on the afternoon of December 26. In response to the initiative taken by the women students, the Beida Historical Society called a meeting with student representatives of all the departments, school societies and clubs, and female students to discuss the possible courses of action. Those in attendance at the meeting, however, did not speak with one voice; they demonstrated a clash between what the historian Jeffrey Wasserstrom refers to as "radical" or "progressive" students and "loyalist" or "pro-government students." The pro-government students at the meeting opposed open agitation and contended that it was up to the Nationalist government to cope with the issue. Their voice, however, was the minority one at the meeting.

Through intense debate, the views of radical students prevailed. Having elected Liu Junying to chair the meeting, the participating radical students reached a series of resolutions. They included drafting petitions to President Chiang Kai-shek, the United Nations, and President Harry Truman regarding the atrocities committed by American servicemen in China; issuing declarations to Chinese students, the Chinese people, and the American people; holding classroom strikes; launching protest parades and rallies if possible, and collecting donations for the movement; and calling upon other universities to take uniform action. The radical students then made the following three demands: that the culprits and their immediate superiors be severely punished and a joint Sino-American open court be held in Beiping; that the highest authorities of the American troops in China publicly apologize for the rape case, and promise no more occurrences of similar unlawful events; and that American troops withdraw from China immediately. The meeting also resolved to organize a Beijing University Preparatory Committee Protesting the Brutality of American Soldiers in China, and to hold a class strike and a possible protest parade on December 30.[20] When the movement gained momentum and reached nationwide magnitude, similar committees mushroomed and became known simply as *kangbao* (anti-brutality) committees, and radical students often referred to the anti-American student movement as the *kangbao* movement.

The *kangbao* movement demonstrated most vividly the polarization of the student movement and the struggles between radical and loyalist students. The conflicts between these two student groups intensified during the Civil War years as they no longer faced the common Japanese enemy, and because of the deadly confrontation on the battlefield between the CCP and the GMD.[21] In the factional fight during the *kangbao* movement, the radical students were at a great advantage because they had on their side the emotionally appealing case: the Shen Chong Incident. Nevertheless, the struggle between the two groups lasted throughout the movement. At Beida, loyalist youths made serious attempts to thwart the protest activities.

Measures taken by the pro-government students to counteract the political efforts of the radical students, however, often had the opposite effect of pushing more politically neutral students to the latter's side. Shortly after the open clash between the two student groups, an eye-catching poster, titled "Information Network," appeared on the Beida bulletin board, accusing Shen Chong of being a Communist agent sent from the Communist headquarters, Yan'an, to deliberately seduce the American soldiers to instigate an anti-American movement.[22] The claim that the whole event was a Communist ruse of "bitter meat stratagem" (*kurou ji*) did generate some doubts among the Beida students about the nature of the incident. To refute the allegations, Liu Shiping, a Communist underground representative working for *Yi shi bao*, a local Catholic newspaper, succeeded in locating Shen's registration card at Beida, which stated: Shen Chong, nineteen years old; ancestral home from Minhou, Fujian Province; freshman at the Preparatory Class; permanent home address at Number 25, Gube Road, Shanghai.[23]

Meanwhile, Liu Junying managed to track down Shen Chong's home address in Beiping. Together with several other Beida women students, they visited Shen's home in the name of "offering condolence." They got to talk to Shen's cousin, Mrs. Yang, and were therefore able to realize the true purpose of their visit: verifying Shen's family background. Upon returning to Beida, Liu and others lost no time in posting on the bulletin board the interview content, emphasizing the prominence of the Shen family and identifying Shen Chong as a *mingmen guixiu* (a virtuous girl from a distinguished family). Almost immediately, information contained in the interview spread to other universities in Beiping, and then to universities in other cities.[24]

The posting of the student interview with Shen's cousin was intended to counter the rumor that the Shen Chong Incident was a Communist ploy and to spread the image of Shen as a virtuous and educated girl from a well-established upper-class family. It achieved the intended effect, as it "ignited instant flames of indignation" among the Beida students.[25] Many student posters emerged to condemn the "Information Network." Within days, the name of Shen Chong and her family background became national knowledge, and were used and reused for nationalistic and political purposes.

On the evening of December 29, the pro-government students in Beiping made another attempt to frustrate the planned street demonstration on the following day. While the Beida Preparatory *Kangbao* Committee was holding a meeting in preparation for the impending protest parade, pro-government students from such universities as Puren, Huabei, and Zhongguo arrived. The Communist sources claimed that they disturbed the meeting. Consequently, members of the Preparatory *Kangbao* Committee had to cancel the meeting. In the midst of chaos, fistfights ensued, and the pro-government students managed to break into the office of the Preparatory Committee, and destroyed the mimeograph machine as well as the anti-American written slogans and posters to be used at the next day's protest parade. They then held a conference of their own and passed several resolutions, which included supporting the government and protesting the atrocities of American soldiers; entrusting the government for a reasonable solution of the case; and focusing on studies and abstaining from parade and class strike activities. They also declared the establishment of the "Justice Association of Universities in Beiping."[26] This move on the part of the pro-government students did not succeed in calming the student agitation.

At this stage, the underground Communists were not yet certain whether the street demonstration could materialize. The pro-government student force still exercised considerable influence on the Beida campus. The protesting posters covering the Beida bulletin board had all been anonymous. Many Beida students still adopted a wait-and-see attitude. Less than one-third of the students had openly supported a protest parade on December 30. Eventually, the radical reactions of students at Qinghua University (Qinghua) and Yanjing University (Yanda) to the rape case encouraged the Beida students. Their joint efforts touched off the first large-scale nationwide student movement of the Civil War period, which profoundly influenced Sino-American relations and the power struggle between the CCP and the GMD.

The radical element at Qinghua proved to be stronger than that at Beida. On December 26, protesting posters started appearing on Qinghua's Democracy Wall, where diverse political views were often presented for public scrutiny.[27] On the next day, about 1,300 students, over one-third of the student body, signed a petition requesting that the Student Self-Governing Committee of Qinghua respond immediately to the Shen Chong Incident.[28] The committee then convened and voted to endorse the Three Demands advanced by Beida students, to hold a class strike on the twenty-ninth, and to contact the Student Self-Governing Association of the American-founded Christian university, Yanda, for a joint march on December 30.[29]

At Yanda, many students reacted vehemently to the rape case when the Beida women students' interview with Shen Chong's cousin was posted on the campus bulletin board. Immediately, the campus walls were covered with inflammatory posters and slogans condemning the GIs. The Yanda Student Self-Governing Association also convened and passed resolutions similar to those of Beida and Qinghua. In the early hours of December 30, it resolved to hold a joint protest parade with Qinghua upon being informed of the Qinghua Student Self-Governing Association's decision and made some hasty preparations for the parade, which was going to start in just a few hours. Student representatives of Qinghua and Yanda then informed Beida of their decision. [30]

Many students on the Qinghua campus spent a sleepless night preparing for the protest parade. The Student Self-Governing Association was busy organizing propaganda and picket teams. Some students were preparing written slogans, cartoons, and posters to be pasted on walls and vehicles and composing *kangbao* poems and songs, while some others were making small pennants with anti-brutality content written on them so that each student could wave one during the procession. The students responsible for composing songs found that the most effective and convenient way was to fill familiar and inspiring tunes with new *kangbao* words. This would render the learning and teaching of these songs effortless, and yet the time-proven inspiring tunes would stimulate even stronger passions among the demonstrators.

The students were so exhausted that by the time the parade was supposed to start early next morning, only about 300 students showed up. Student organizers had to go to the dormitories to awaken the sleeping students and ask them to get to the point of assembly quickly. About 1,000 students were there by the time the procession took off in the harsh cold wind. They were then joined by the students from Yanda.[31]

Over 2,000 students from Qinghua and Yanda marched seven miles from their campuses outside the city to Xizhimen, the northwest gate of the city.[32] Around 500 students from Huabei and Zhongfa Universities had already gathered inside the gate, reportedly organized by the Beiping GMD director to obstruct the passage of Yanjing and Qinghua students. A serious conflict was averted when General Li Zongren, head of the Nationalist government's Beiping office, learned of this situation and notified the Party director and the police chief to refrain from interfering with the student parade. The demonstrators from Qinghua and Yanjing then joined with the students from Beida and other institutions, including even some high schools, inside the city walls.[33]

The huge parade followed the planned route and wound through the main streets of the city in an orderly fashion. Their first major stop was the Executive Headquarters, the mediating agency of the now failing Marshall Mission; their second major stop was the Dongdan Drill Field where the alleged rape had taken place; and their final major stop was the Beiping GMD office where the student representatives would present petitions. Throughout the parade, student protesters distributed handbills and shouted slogans, but essentially "limited themselves to noise."[34] The six slogans students shouted were all predetermined. They included: "Protest the Atrocities of American Soldiers"; "Severe Punishment to the Criminals"; "American Troops Withdraw from China"; "United States Should Change Its China Policy At Once"; "Maintain Sovereignty and Independence"; and "Long Live a New Democratic China." The handbills bore such titles as "A True Picture of American Brutalities" and "Americans, Get Out of China." A great number of sidewalk writers covered walls with slogans, including "Our Chinese Daughters Are Not To Be Insulted" and "China Is Not a Colony of the United States."[35] The gate and walls of the Executive Headquarters compound were pasted with English slogans. Together with the marine billets near the Dongdan Drill Field, they served as the focal points of student protesters and received the largest number of written slogans.[36]

When the protest parade marched to the alleged assault site, Dongdan Drill Field, the students held a mass rally. Several students delivered emotional speeches. In a tearful voice, one woman student related a passionate version of the "beastly" behavior of the two American soldiers on the night of December 24.[37] Another woman student from Beida read a harshly worded piece titled "To the Victim." It was critical not only of the Americans, but also of the Nationalist government for being "boneless" and failing to protect Chinese people's interests. Typical of the tone of the *kangbao* movement, the speech asserted that Shen Chong's misfortune and shame were not hers alone, but symbolized the fate of China and the weakness of its government. Hence, Shen should not resort to the well-traveled road that women of her experience had often taken: committing suicide. "It is not you who should feel ashamed or commit suicide," the young girl declared, "but the lackeys who fawningly wait upon their foreign masters."[38] Emotional speeches delivered by tearful female students during the protest parade were a familiar sight throughout the *kangbao* movement.

American military personnel had been instructed to stay in their quarters and to avoid contact with student demonstrators. Other Americans were also cautioned to stay off the streets.[39] One jeep full of marines, while passing through the assault site where students were holding a protest rally, was immediately pasted with slogans. Americans working for the Executive Headquarters ate bread inside their office instead of venturing out into restaurants or home for lunch.[40]

The total number of participating students was estimated variously at 4,000 to 10,000. The Nationalist sources, conservative in nature, claimed the number of protesting students to be around 4,000, while the student and Communist sources, which favor round numbers, especially *wan* (10,000), claimed a probably somewhat inflated number of over 10,000.[41] Between 1947 and 1948, 18,332 students were enrolled in universities and colleges in Beiping. Even based on the conservative Nationalist estimate, almost one out of every four students participated in the *kangbao* protest parade, which demonstrates its magnitude.[42]

Students from Beida, Qinghua, and Yanda, the most prestigious universities in Beiping, formed the core of the protests. There were 11 universities and colleges in Beiping at the time.[43] About one-third of the Beiping college students were enrolled in the 3 universities. During the Civil War era, the Communist underground students were also most active in these 3 universities, which served as the center of the Communist student movement not only in Beiping, but also in north China.[44]

In the aftermath of the rape case, Shen Chong's background, her status as a student of the most prestigious university in China, her personality and behavior all assumed tremendous significance. Political, cultural, social, and moral issues intertwined with one another, highlighted the significance of the Shen Chong case, and served as the powerful motivation for the *kangbao* movement. The student account of the event emphasized that Shen was a *mingmen guixiu*. Shen Chong did come from a distinguished gentry family in Fujian Province, as claimed by the students. Her great-grandfather, Shen Baozhen, had once been the well-known governor general of Guangdong and Guangxi for the Qing dynasty, and her great-grandmother was the daughter of the famous anti-opium imperial commissioner, Lin Zexu. One of her close relatives was the late Lin Shu, one of the most illustrious literary figures in China around the turn of the century.[45] Her father, Shen Shao, was an official in charge of the transportation section in the Nanjing government. Shen Chong had been living in Shanghai before enrolling in the preparatory class at Beida and was then staying in the house of her cousin, whose husband was also a government official.[46]

Shen Chong's prominent family background distinguished her from girls of low birth, thus dismissing in the Chinese minds the possibility that she might be a prostitute. A student reporter from Yanta, who had a glimpse of Shen during a rare interview with her relative, Mrs. Yang, helped spread the image of Shen as a *mingmen guixiu*. In the article issued by *Yanjing Xinwen* (Yanjing news), a student journal, the reporter accentuated the differences in appearance and behavior between a well-brought-up girl and a girl from a common family. The article focused especially on Shen's demeanor rather than her looks, prompted by the idea that a woman's good demeanor and manners reflected her inner worth, her moral strength and proper upbringing, while her looks were naturally endowed and had little to do with good nurturing, and were thus irrelevant to a case where personal character or inner qualities weighed importantly. According to the reporter, Shen was "pale and expressionless," but looked "calm, quiet and serious." She appeared strikingly different from a girl of ordinary birth, who would be utterly confused and lost after such a shocking and terrible experience. The reporter thus asserted that Shen's calmness was beyond the reach of ordinary people, and that her composure was due entirely to her uncommon family background. Meanwhile, Shen's outward calmness and her relatives' assertion that she was a gentle girl devoted to her studies dissociated her from the group of frivolous, fun-loving "jeep girls" seen openly with the American servicemen and who were often viewed in the eyes of many Chinese as no better than prostitutes.

While drawing a sharp line between Shen Chong and girls of common or lower social background, the student article also presented Shen in a way that male college students could easily recognize and female students could readily identify with. Shen Chong looked every bit a typical college girl. Dressed in "blue-clothed *qipao* and cloth shoes" (the common attire of female college students at the time), Shen Chong was "completely free of extravagance and superficiality that characterized many girls nowadays." The article ended by raising the Shen Chong rape case to a new level and asserted that it symbolized the insult, damage, and sacrifice China had been suffering due to its weak foreign policy.[47]

In a recent article, Louise Edwards discusses the prominent role of gender in the class-based nationalist discourse in Republican China and the preoccupation of reform-minded intellectuals with the moral attributes of modern women. In traditional China, women were often accorded the responsibility for either saving or destroying the country. Many folktales have a ruler fall under the spell of a beauty at the expense of state affairs, which would cause the ruin of a kingdom or a dynasty. The intellectual class in the twentieth century thus made natural use of "the new woman as a symbol of national survival."[48] In the eyes of the largely male student body in Republican China, an ideal Chinese woman was supposed to manifest modernity (being well-educated, independent, and politically aware), yet adhere to the old moral codes (being chaste, virtuous, and modest). She was therefore paradoxically conceived to be a "new woman with new thinking, but old values," someone who was modern but not radically modern. Shen Chong symbolized in every way a modern woman of substance and of "intellectual and moral superiority."[49] Consequently, the rape of such a "superior" woman by a drunken, low-class American soldier[50] acquired new political and nationalist meanings, since it pushed to the fore the conjoining elements of gender, class, ethnicity, and national survival.[51] The sexual violation of a *mingmen quixiu* was seen as the violation of the essence of China, equal to the subordination of a struggling nation to a foreign power. Consequently, students asserted, "If this can be tolerated, what cannot?" (*Shi keren, shu bukeren?*)

In their propaganda endeavors, student leaders presented an image of Shen Chong as a virtuous, quiet, simply dressed, and educated modern woman with inner strength, and as representative of the most ideal type of young modern Chinese women. Several student accounts emphasized that Shen had gone to see the movie *Supremacy of Nationalism* (*minzu zhishang*) on that eventful night,[52] which suggested that she was by no means a frivolous girl, but one who was politically aware and concerned with the fate of the nation. Thus the image of Shen Chong as a chaste and well-brought-up upper-class modern girl spread, and her rape induced male students to "bristle with anger" (*nufa chongguan*) and filled female students with a strong sense of shame and grief over the fate of Shen Chong and especially that of China. In this sense, the Shen Chong Incident not only provoked a nationalist outcry, but also afforded a largely male student body a chance to reassert their role as China's "moral guardians."[53]

Gender and ethnicity took on a new significance when compounded by class. The combination of the three produced political thunder throughout urban China. The Chinese Nationalist authorities, the Communist underground, and American diplomats in China all immediately realized the powerful political implications of the incident. Chinese newspapers had been reporting rape cases committed by the GIs for over a year now, but they had failed to elicit much heated responses from the college students, since the alleged victims had been mostly working-class women from poor families. However, the Shen Chong Incident constituted an "intolerable" act and provoked the students' sense of indignity and mission, because Shen Chong was not just any woman, but a modern, well-educated *mingmen guixiu*, whose chastity was violated by an American "sex wolf"(*selang*).[54] As one scholar claims, since the nation is at stake, the crime of rape acquires special significance only when it is committed by foreign intruders.[55]

For the radical students in Beiping, the tainted reputation of American servicemen in China and Shen Chong's social background all rendered it unthinkable to doubt Shen Chong's version of events. Considering the location of the occurrence, Shen Chong's family and personal status, the tremendous importance the Chinese traditionally attached to chastity, as well as the inconsistency of Pierson's story, the event did smack of an assault. It was simply inexplicable that an 18-year-old college coed from the most prestigious university in China would willingly lose her highly valued virginity to a strange drunken foreign soldier on a bitterly cold night in the open field while another soldier witnessed the incident. In the larger context, however, the incident itself was not as significant as the profound political repercussions it provoked.

THE NATIONWIDE STUDENT *KANGBAO* MOVEMENT

Universities in China had served as storm centers for nationalist ferment ever since the founding of the Republic of China. The *kangbao* movement occupied a significant place in the history of the Chinese student movement. The Shen Chong case intensified anti-American sentiment among a large number of students, principally in the GMD-controlled cities, and led to the first nationwide student anti-American movement. During the *kangbao* movement, radical students, working as political actors, transformed the major Chinese streets into an effective political stage. The sexual attack upon one of their own rapidly sparked the organization of mass demonstrations. While students in Beiping initiated the campaign, the rape case soon precipitated student demonstrations nationwide to protest the conduct of U.S. marines and to demand an immediate withdrawal of American troops from China. Meanwhile, many campuses organized *kangbao* associations. The cases regarding the deaths of the rickshaw puller Zang Dayaozi and the high school teacher Xu Zhendong, and other cases involving the raping, beating, injuring, and even killing of Chinese civilians, all resurfaced and were forcefully reiterated during the student protests. Nevertheless, for the students, the rape of a college student from one of the most prominent universities by an American solider represented the "most galling and humiliating" (*qichi daru*) act.

In Shanghai, students at Jinan University took the leading role in organizing protests. The *kangbao* movement spread rapidly and soon involved almost all the local universities, colleges, and even quite a few high schools. On December 30, student representatives from 17 schools in Shanghai held a joint meeting, which led to the establishment of the Joint Committee of Shanghai Students Protesting American Brutality. On New Year's Day, about 3,000 college and high school youth from over 20 educational institutions marched in a massive parade. The protesting students also played out a drastic tableau, with two students acting as drunken marines. They were tied up with ropes and were pushed forward by women students.[56] Since early January local street urchins had begun to sing a little anti-American rhyme, "Meiguolao, zhen buhao!" (American hoods are really no good.)[57]

Also on New Year's Day, Nankai University and Beiyang University in Tianjin held a class strike and organized a protest parade, joined by students from other local universities and high schools. The demonstrators distributed posters along the roads and pasted them on walls, cars, trucks, and buses. About 2,000 students participated in the parade. They carried placards in both English and Chinese, with such slogans as "Marines Go Home," "China Is Not a U.S. Colony," "We Want Mutual Respect," "What Would You Think if Your Mother and Sister Were Raped?" and "Stop Your Brutal Acts." As a result of the student demonstration, the mayor of Tianjin had to cancel his New Year's reception for foreign diplomats. As the parade stopped outside the municipal government building, the deputy mayor addressed the students, asserting that the Beiping incident would come to a reasonable and lawful settlement, and that only the Nationalist government could deal with the issue regarding the departure of American forces from China, while a municipal government could do nothing about it.[58]

Tianjin at the time quartered the largest number of marines. On that New Year's Day, the marines were instructed to stay inside their billets to avoid conflict with the demonstrating students. Some marines obviously could make little sense out of all this anti-American commotion and actually found it somewhat entertaining. As student marchers were passing by a foreign-run bank, about 20 marines rushed out toward them. Holding their thumbs up, they shouted "*dinghao, dinghao*" (very good, very good). One of them asked the students to paste a poster on his back. When the parade approached the marine billets, a number of marines came out with their cameras. Having taken some pictures of the student procession, they then peeled off a big wall poster with the prominent English words "U.S. Troops Go Home Now" written on it and took several group pictures holding the poster in front of them. No conflict occurred between the students and the marines, although the students must have found the marines' behavior puzzling if not amusing.

The demonstrations held in Nanjing, the capital of Nationalist China, were also revealing of genuine indignation on the part of student demonstrators, because a large number of them came from the official Zhongyang (Central) University. Receiving official stipends, they were also supposed to follow the dictates of the government. Sharp divisions of opinion did present themselves in the initial meeting of the Student Committee of Zhongyang University on New Year's Day. While some students objected to the whole idea of public demonstrations, some others claimed that student demonstrators should protest the unruly behavior of Russian troops on Chinese soil as well. Nevertheless, the majority of the student representatives considered the Russian issue a matter for "separate consideration." These differences of opinion prevented the meeting from reaching an agreement. In the end, the Student Committee decided to let students from Zhongyang University join the upcoming demonstration on an individual basis, and not in the name of the university.[59]

On January 2, university students in Nanjing rushed onto the streets led by a propaganda truck, on top of which some students from the National Academy of Dramatic Arts enacted tableaux. In GI clothes and with big cardboard noses, one student actor beat a "Chinese peasant," while another aimed a gun at a "Chinese worker." A couple of others were playing out the "scene of the rape" with a "marine" holding a bottle of whiskey in one hand and dragging around a female student with the other.[60]

When the protesters arrived at the American embassy, Ambassador Stuart happened to be out. The student representatives then presented the embassy staff with a petition demanding punishment of the marines involved, compensation for Shen Chong, and withdrawal of U.S. forces. The wall of the embassy compound was plastered with slogans, such as "GIs Get Out" and "Mayor of Beiping, Don't You Have a Daughter?"[61]

On the evening of January 2, the Student Committee of Zhongyang University held another meeting and the majority of the student representatives agreed to carry out another parade on the next day; this time students would participate in the name of their university.[62] The demonstration thus continued on the following day with about 3,000 students, headed mainly by a large delegation from Zhongyang University.[63] This demonstration was better prepared and larger in scale than the previous one. Student demonstrators plastered vehicles and storefronts with written slogans and posters, held banners, and distributed handbills issued from a mimeograph machine on a propaganda truck. The leaders conducted a well-orchestrated and prominent shouting of slogans. Some pamphlets declared that the Beiping incident was only one of the "numerous outrages" committed by American troops in China, while others claimed that the ammunitions and weapons supplied to the Nationalist government by the United States had contributed to the killing of millions of Chinese.[64]

Rocks were thrown at some American automobiles along the way on the January 3 march, and Chinese policemen apparently intervened. John Melby, an American foreign service officer in Nanjing, recorded the two parades in his diary: "Like the rains, the riots came." He continued: "In Nanking [Nanjing] they were a little earthier, as usual. One was fairly orderly, but the other came to rock throwing and was broken up when the local gendarmes moved in swinging their belts. The brass buckles have a distinctive and sickening thud when they come in contact with a living skull." The anti-American slogans must have irritated him, as he wrote bitterly: "Both riots were rich demonstrations of the Chinese gift for foul invective—this subject lending itself admirably to a particular segment of the vernacular anyway."[65]

The student demonstrators first stopped outside the gate of the Nationalist government building, shouting slogans and pasting posters and cartoons on the gate. They then submitted four demands to the authorities, with the immediate withdrawal of American troops heading the list. Besides the already familiar student demands for severe punishment of the culprits and a guarantee of no more such happenings before the departure of American armed forces, the students also asked the government to report the atrocities committed by American soldiers to the Security Council of the United Nations.

When the parade stopped outside the embassy compound, a delegation of five students along with 30 newspaper reporters entered the compound and conferred with Ambassador Stuart. While expressing their appreciation of American assistance in the Chinese War of Resistance against Japan and in repatriating the Japanese soldiers, the student representatives denounced the Beiping assault and argued that recurrent incidents created by American soldiers had severely impaired bilateral relations. They then submitted three demands similar to the ones made by the students at Beida. Stuart expressed sympathy with the student wrath over the rape and with their patriotic spirit, and claimed that he was sorry to see Sino-American relations suffer such a setback. After assurances from Stuart of a full investigation of the Beiping case and a proper and just trial of the accused, the student delegates reported Stuart's responses to the waiting crowd outside, thus ending the day's demonstration.[66]

The *kangbao* movement spread rapidly geographically. From the end of December 1946 to the early months of 1947, students from more than 25 cities and towns, as far north as Harbin and Changchun and as far south as Guangzhou, Kunming, and even Taiwan, surged through the streets. As the students in leading cities were launching demonstrations, staging mass rallies, and going on strikes, the anti-American movement became more coordinated. Beiping student representatives established the Beiping Student Anti-Brutality Alliance.[67] Similar organizations soon came into existence in other large cities. In March 1947, the Federation of Associations in Protest against Brutality by American Troops in China was established with its headquarters in Shanghai to coordinate nationwide student anti-American activities.[68] Because of the explosive nature of the Shen Chong Incident, the Nationalist government largely refrained from interfering forcefully with the student demonstrators, and in some cases, surprisingly used its local police force to help maintain order and direct traffic. In his report to Nanjing, Mayor He Siyuan of Beiping recommended that the Nationalist authorities leave the student demonstrators alone because of the popularity of the movement.[69]

Almost all the *kangbao* demonstrations included such propagandistic activities as shouting slogans, distributing handbills, delivering street-side lectures, plastering walls and vehicles with anti-American slogans and posters, and presenting petitions. In their efforts to reach as many people as possible, including illiterates, students sometimes employed dramatic means such as staging didactic plays or creating tableaux. Some better-prepared protest parades also included bicycle corps and propaganda trucks covered with anti-American cartoons and equipped with loudspeakers. A very significant component of every protest parade was collectively singing familiar songs such as "The March of the Volunteers"[70] and newly composed *kangbao* songs. Sometimes, the students would simply use the tune of a well-known song and fill it with anti-American words. Group singing had assumed great prominence during the December Ninth Movement of 1935 when patriotic students took to the streets protesting against Japanese aggression against China. It remained an essential program of the student political rallies and demonstrations during the Civil War period. It took on a new significance as spectators often joined the student singing and turned it into a "multi-class group singing movement." In this way, songs "provided a valuable medium for spreading ideas and embedding slogans in the mind of the general population, and collective singing became an important way of expressing national and/or class solidarity."[71]

Student protest demonstrations, mass rallies, slogan shouting, singing, and distributing handbills were so effective that many college professors made public statements in support of the student efforts. Yanda students passed resolutions for launching a movement to boycott American goods and demanding a suspension of accommodations for American students on campus who had relatives in the military service in China pending a satisfactory settlement of the Shen Chong case by the marine authorities. In response, 13 Yanda professors, including two Americans, signed a letter of support.[72] On December 30, 48 Beida professors addressed a letter to Ambassador Stuart protesting the "infamous" actions by American servicemen.[73] Thirty-eight professors from Shanghai soon followed suit.[74] Xiangda, a history professor at Beida, allegedly asserted that it was inconceivable that having won the war against Japan, China's fate was worse than Japan's.[75] According to the Self-Governing Association of Qinghua, 99 percent of the professors at the university approved of the December 30 strike, and 90 percent supported the protest parade.[76] The president and the provost of Qinghua asserted that the Nationalist authorities should not prevent students from demonstrating and should protect their safety. Lu Zhiwei, who was in charge of Yanda at the time, openly supported the student demand for American troops to withdraw from China.[77]

Besides college professors, a broad spectrum of prominent Chinese, including writers, businessmen, cultural figures, and even some government officials, responded to the Shen Chong Incident. The national branch and some local branches of the China Women's Association issued statements expressing sympathy to Shen Chong and denouncing the "disgraceful" behavior of the American marines.[78] In the immediate aftermath of the Shen Chong event, the column of "Letters from the People" in the American-run *China Weekly Review* based in Shanghai was bombarded with angry protests from the Chinese readers against the rape case.[79] Even Beiping mayor He Siyuan, an alumnus of Beida, allegedly said later that if he were a young man, he would have participated in the movement.[80] The student fervor also affected common people on the street. In Shanghai, for example, some rickshaw pullers offered free rides to the student demonstrators; one rickshaw puller said that he supported the student protests because the students were demanding justice for Chinese victims, including the Shanghai rickshaw puller, Zang Dayaozi.[81] Hence, the movement was spreading not only horizontally among the students, but also vertically, across the social boundaries.

THE OFFICIAL CHINESE RESPONSE

As Wasserstrom argues, the Chinese authorities of whatever political leanings viewed youth political activism with skepticism if not open hostility throughout the twentieth century. However, they also treated college and university students as a significant social group worthy of special attention.[82] As a political party that grew increasingly conservative in nature and nervous about radical approaches to the nation's social and political problems, the GMD authorities were suspicious of student political activities for fear of their connections with and use by the CCP. Consequently, the GMD's advice to college students was to focus on schoolwork, stay away from politics, and refrain from *jiewai shengzhi* (raising new issues to complicate the existing situation).

The Shen Chong rape case greatly alarmed the Nationalist authorities, who realized immediately the political implications of the incident. Possible student agitation and Communist exploitation of the event at the expense of the GMD constituted their major concerns. Therefore, the Nanjing government repeatedly sent urgent telegrams to the Beiping mayor urging him to take all necessary precautions to prevent Communist instigation.[83] Meanwhile, probably suspicious of foul play, the Nationalist government was most anxious to find out the exact details concerning the rape case, including the background of Shen Chong, the reaction of Shen Chong's family to the incident, whether the rape had truly occurred, and the student mood in Beiping.[84]

On the other hand, the central government in Nanjing repeatedly requested the Beiping officials to keep the event under control. On December 30, the Ministry of Foreign Affairs instructed the Beiping government to seek a "quick and appropriate settlement" of the Beiping rape case, and to prevent it from affecting Chinese-American friendship.[85] On December 31, the Ministry of Education telegraphed the presidents of Beida, Qinghua, Beiping Teachers' College, and Beiping College of Railroad Management. The telegram revealed the official apprehension about the political consequences of the incident. It urged the school authorities to prevent the Communists from using it as a pretext to instigate student unrest. A few days later, on January 4, Zhu Jianhua, the minister of education, sent a directive to Hu Shi and Mei Yiqi, presidents of Beida and Qinghua, claiming that certain people were trying to whip up an antigovernment, anti-American movement using the Beiping incident as a pretext. Zhu maintained that the government had been paying close attention to the rape case and had urged the American marine authorities to proceed with the court martial as early as possible. On January 5, the Ministry of Education issued a directive to the university authorities in Beiping. According to it, the students should be reminded of the generous assistance the United States had afforded China, and should not "take the recent incident as a pretext to mar and insult the dignity of a friendly ally."[86]

In the immediate aftermath of the rape incident, Mayor He of Beiping was preoccupied with composing telegrams to Chiang Kai-shek, the minister of education, and the minister of foreign affairs; issuing memoranda to presidents of universities in Beiping to monitor the mood of the students and to keep the situation under control; and issuing letters of protest and memoranda to the American embassy in Nanjing. Based on the medical-examination results and the eyewitness accounts, the Beiping officials did believe Shen Chong's statement that she had been sexually assaulted. In the secret communications sent out to the Nationalist government and Chiang Kai-shek, Mayor He repeatedly claimed that the investigation results proved that Shen Chong had been a virgin with a "clean personal and family record," and that she was indeed raped by one marine with the assistance of another.[87]

Upon learning from a local newspaper in Nanjing that the victim of the Beiping rape case was his daughter, Shen Chong's father, Shen Shao, a government official, wrote a personal letter to Mayor He (it is not clear why Shen Shao did not receive the bad news from his family first). In his letter, Shen Shao highlighted three points: Shen Chong's family background, his own ties with the United States and Americans, and his strong wish to see justice done. He thus emphasized the fact that his daughter came from a prominent southern family and was well brought up. It would be pure malicious slander if the American defendant attempted to smear Shen Chong's moral character. As for himself, he had been educated in the United States, and had been working in the field of transportation for the past 20 years. During wartime, he had worked closely with the American military personnel in building airports in southwestern China. Having enjoyed a good relationship with the Americans, he certainly held no anti-American feelings. In the end, Shen Shao demanded that the "unlawful act" of the implicated American soldier receive severe punishment to "compensate a little for the immeasurable suffering and damage done to Shen Chong." He also requested his letter to remain confidential.[88] Mayor He was apparently pleased with the wording of Shen Shao's letter, since it emphasized that the event be resolved through legal means, which was in accord with the official view. Besides writing Shen Shao a reply letter complimenting him on his "sensible attitude," Mayor He also received him in private.[89]

Confronting the large-scale student *kangbao* demonstrations, the GMD officials also endeavored not to allow the event to affect adversely the official Sino-American relationship. Thus, when Foreign Minister Wang Shijie was wrongly informed that Hu Shi, president of Beida, intended to act as a witness in the court martial, he immediately telegraphed Hu Shi and urged him to reconsider his decision. Wang suggested to Hu that his decision might further aggravate the Americans because of his official position as president of Beida and because the Americans at the moment were already "mollified and exasperated." Hu replied that he was not qualified to be a witness, but that he was to be present during the trial.[90]

The Nationalist officials also tried to assuage possible American irritation over the development of the student movement through official channels. On January 2, in a talk with John R. Beal, an American correspondent serving as an adviser to the Nationalist government at the time, Peng Xuepei, Chinese minister of information, explained his efforts to dilute the repercussions of the Shen Chong Incident. He maintained that he had issued a circular to the GMD newspapers asking them to downplay the importance of student demonstrations and to emphasize the fact that as an individual matter, the case should not impair Sino-American relations. The newspapers, according to him, seemed reluctant to comply, as readers loved this kind of "American-baiting" news.[91]

Meanwhile, Cui Cunlin, counselor of the Chinese embassy in the United States, expressed deep regret to Washington on behalf of the Chinese government about the student protests and their demand for the complete withdrawal of American troops from China. Blaming the Chinese press for misrepresenting the protests, Cui maintained that irresponsible people working against "the best interest of the two governments" instigated those who participated in the movement and that the Chinese government was very much concerned "lest the American public should interpret these protests as representative of Chinese public opinion."[92]

The student anti-American movement placed the Nationalist government in an awkward position. To back the public in denouncing the Americans would risk losing important U.S. support the Nationalists needed. However, to exonerate the Americans would weaken the GMD's political stand in the eyes of the students. Government officials therefore endeavored to treat the rape incident as an isolated incident, to discourage any political complications, and to seek a prompt and satisfactory legal settlement. The official view was that the Shen Chong Incident had resulted from the poor personal conduct of the marines, who should be duly punished by law. The incident should not damage Chinese-American friendship and be used as a pretext to discredit China's ally and the American people. Consequently, the GMD officials repeatedly urged that the issue be settled through legal means and that politics not be allowed to compound the situation.

The editorial line of the official press expressed outrage toward the Beiping incident, but emphasized that it was a matter of legal adjudication, in which the Americans would do full justice, and that the behaviors of one or two men should not besmirch all the American military forces in China. Mayor He of Beiping likewise claimed that the personal behavior of the individual marines should not damage the Sino-American friendship.[93] Wu Zhuren, director of the GMD Beiping Municipal Party Bureau, warned the local press "not to give undue prominence to the affair, which involved a legal procedure, and not to associate it with politics."[94] Hu Shi, president of Beida, also urged that the assault case be treated as an isolated issue, free from political implications. In a press interview, he claimed that the essential difficulty was a cultural one as "the Americans did not attach as much significance to chastity as did the Chinese." He believed, though, that justice would prevail in the court martial.[95]

Nevertheless, the gravity of the situation prompted Nationalist officials, especially He Siyuan and Hu Shi, to take immediate action. Believing that the most effective way to pacify the student agitation was to seek a satisfactory settlement of the case, they exerted great efforts in reaching that end. Hu Shi himself acted as Shen Chong's guardian and invited three professors of law, Yan Shutang, Li Shitong, and Cai Ouheng from Beida, and Zhao Fengjie, chair of the Department of Law from Qinghua, to serve as the legal advisers for the case. Hu also asked Li Shitong and Zhao Fengjie to be Shen Chong's legal counsels and to act as her lawyers at the trial. To his disappointment, Hu found out later that Shen could only speak as a witness at the trial, while her legal counsels could only audit the trial.[96]

Meanwhile, the Beiping municipal government also issued a formal letter of protest and a memorandum to the marine authorities in Beiping. The protest letter was accompanied by a list of demands: (1) the marines involved should be punished; (2) the victim had suffered tremendous damage physically, mentally and socially resulting from horror and violation. The American authorities should offer a written apology and compensate for the loss suffered by the victim and be responsible for her living cost caused by the violation (the implication here is that Shen could no longer live a normal life after the rape), and the highest marine authorities in Beiping should pay the victim a personal visit; (3) the marine authorities in Beiping should exercise strong discipline upon their subordinates and strictly restrain their behavior from harming Chinese citizens and causing Sino-American incidents, and promise no more such occurrences in the future; and (4) the Chinese and American governments should further consolidate their cooperation to preserve their traditional friendship.[97] Although the official demands shared similar terms with the ones issued by the students, the difference was also salient. While the students insisted on an immediate withdrawal of all the American military forces in China, the official tone was more conciliatory, and called for closer Sino-American cooperation.

In the aftermath of the Shen Chong rape case, the GMD officials' attempt to keep the incident out of the press and the students off the street backfired. The Nationalist government appeared to have been incapable of protecting the interests of Chinese citizens, and therefore incurred open criticism from the students. The GMD not only failed to turn a volatile student movement to its own advantage, but also grew more suspicious of organized intellectual activism. Its secret police in Beiping went into action against "radical" elements in mid-February. In the name of conducting a "census check," they broke into homes and arrested about 2,000 people. Most of the arrested were prominent for their liberal political views. The mass arrests, however, served to unite the intellectuals. Thirteen well-known professors from Beida and Qinghua, who had so far avoided political activity, released to the press a sharply worded protest against the arrests. Upon learning that a student from Qinghua was also arrested, Qinghua students first went on strike, followed by students from Beida. Student organizations in Beiping then put forth the slogan: "Protect Our Human Rights!"[98] The GMD actions therefore further alienated the educated.

A COMMUNIST RUSE?

Communist sources credit the CCP with a leadership role in almost every major student movement during the Republican era, including the *kangbao* movement. The Shen Chong Incident indeed served as a strong and timely stimulus to the Communist urban revolution, as the CCP found in the incident an excellent opportunity to attack openly the GMD and the U.S. government through student demonstrations. Student demands for the withdrawal of American forces in China and for a stop to American interference in Chinese affairs coincided with the Communist line and certainly worked to the benefit of the CCP.

The CCP had been carrying out a propaganda war against the American military presence in China for months now. According to an anti-American directive issued by the Communist Beiping Urban Work Committee on July 1, 1946, the Communists should work on informing the public of the "atrocities" committed by the Americans, including the numerous accidents caused by military vehicles and the insulting of Chinese women.[99] The Shen Chong Incident provided the right fuse to ignite a large-scale anti-American campaign. The political opportunities presented by the Shen Chong Incident must have so excited the Communist underground workers in urban China that the Central Committee cautioned them not to be carried away and to use a "tone of deep sorrow," instead of one of "exhilaration" in its lines of propaganda, with a view to gaining wider sympathy.[100] The incident seemed to serve the Communist cause so well that rumors emerged after the incident that it was a "beauty trap" (*meiren ji*), a Communist ruse to ensnare the American marines for political gains.

In the immediate aftermath of the rape case, the CCP Central Committee provided guidelines to the Communist Underground Party. On December 31, it issued a directive to the Communists working in the GMD-controlled cities on how to respond to the Beiping student movement. It called on them to work among the students, to try to win over students with neutral political stands, and to help organize the demonstrations, which should be directed at isolating the United States and Chiang Kai-shek and denouncing the American intention to colonize China.[101]

In another report issued a few days later to the underground Communist representatives in various large cities, the Central Committee emphasized again the great significance of the student anti-American activities and instructed the representatives to work for the complete evacuation of American forces, the abolition of the Sino-American Commercial Treaty, and the boycott of American goods. It also informed them of the CCP's decision to designate November 4, the day when the Sino-American Commercial Treaty was signed, as "National Humiliation Day" in the Communist-controlled area.[102]

A student protest movement focusing only on the behavior of American soldiers and on their immediate departure could only partially serve the Communist goals. The CCP wished to push the movement further and to highlight the "blood relationship" between the GMD and the U.S. government. Consequently, in their lines of propaganda, the Communists endeavored to combine patriotic nationalism with attacks on the Chiang regime and to demonstrate "the inseparability between the American interference and the

Chinese Civil War."[103] Following the party line, the editorials of the Communist *XinHua ribao* made vociferous comments on the Shen Chong case. The Communists emphasized in exaggerated terms the undesirability of American troops in China. One editorial accused Chiang Kai-shek of acting as "a legal accessory to the American marines' criminal assaults." It went on to maintain:

Welcomed by the GMD government, and with no regard for the strong objection of Chinese people and just international opinion, the troops of American imperialists are forcefully stationed in China. Acting as evil and powerful conquerors of a colony, they have committed countless brutal acts violating Chinese lives and properties. China's international status and the dignity of the Chinese nation have been completely abused by the obsequious and traitorous policy of the Nationalist government and the criminal actions of the American troops. . . . Now the American soldiers in Beiping have committed the most heinous crime of raping Miss Shen, a student from Beijing University, which is a heavy blow to the national self-respect of every Chinese! Our hearts are filled with immense sorrow and indignation when we relate this event.[104]

While the CCP and GMD were engaging in a deadly military struggle for supremacy in China, the New Year's editorial of *Jiefang ribao* in Yan'an abandoned the last trace of caution in anti-American remarks. It berated American imperialism and its "running dogs" and asserted that an imperialist United States had replaced the fascists of Germany, Italy, and Japan as a new world aggressor.[105]

To prove the righteousness and popularity of the Communist cause and to underscore the CCP's role as the champion of anti-imperialism, Communist historians tend to highlight the role of the CCP in the student anti-American activities.[106] On the other hand, the Nationalists and American diplomats in the late forties were also eager to ascribe these activities to Communist agitation and manipulation, and blamed the CCP for the anti-American shift of urban Chinese opinion.

Both the CCP and the GMD acknowledged the vital role the Communist underground students played in the *kangbao* movement, and both claimed that the Communists were the ones who initiated the movement. For the GMD, however, most students who participated in the movement were politically innocent, but the malicious Communist instigators working among them whipped up their emotions against the interests of the government.

During the late 1940s, underground CCP representatives in urban China indeed worked hard among the educated elite, especially the students, to inspire their feelings of discontent with the American government. They strove to mobilize intellectual support by attacking the "imperialistic policy" of the United States. However, probably both the Communist writers and contemporary GMD officials and American observers exaggerated Communist influence. The Chinese anti-American phenomenon of the late 1940s occurred essentially in the major cities still under the GMD control. At a time when the Communist influence in the cities was still much weaker than that of the GMD and when the Nationalist authorities were reckless in suppressing dissent, the demonstrated youth antagonism toward the American government cannot be dismissed simply as Communist propaganda. Many student protesters themselves emphatically denied any claim that their opposition to U.S. China policy was anything other than spontaneous. Confronting the constant danger of suppression and persecution inflicted by the GMD police, many Chinese youths nevertheless lobbied on behalf of China's need for peace, unity, and independence. The rapid spread of the movement even stunned the underground CCP students; as a key underground leader, Qian Ying, claimed, "the swift development and the magnitude of the *kangbao* movement far exceeded our expectations."[107]

The vehement student response to the Shen Chong Incident was triggered essentially by moralistic, cultural, social, and nationalistic impulses. The movement reached a nationwide scale quickly mainly because the Shen Chong rape case, an emotion-arousing event, struck an immediate responsive chord among the students. As Wasserstrom suggests, although one should recognize the significant role individual Communists played in the student movement, one ought to remember that "the struggle had an independent life of its own."[108]

In the aftermath of the Shen Chong event, Charles J. Canning, a reporter for *The China Weekly Review*, refuted the claims that the anti-American demonstrations were "instigated" by the Communists. According to Canning, the assertions that the Communists ignited an instant nationwide anti-American movement were to credit them with far too much influence among the intellectual community:

To attribute the anti-American strikes and demonstrations to the Communists is paying the Communists too great a compliment. Can any one imagine that the Chinese Communists are so powerful that they were able to "instigate" in a few days a nation-wide mass movement, which had the participation and backing of the majority of Chinese students and intellectuals and a certain section of industrialists and businessmen?[109]

The editorial of the influential *Dagong bao* also questioned the validity of the allegation that "unscrupulous political elements" provoked the student movement. "If the Communists were capable of instigating so many college students to launch the demonstrations," affirmed the editorial, "then the motive and rallying point of this instigation merit serious consideration."[110]

In an attempt to capture the popular mood at the time, Robert Smyth, the American counsel general in Tianjin, inferred that while the Communists undoubtedly utilized the Beiping incident for their own purposes, the student reaction seemed to represent largely the general feeling among many Chinese. He believed that he sensed the common desire for the departure of American forces although the Chinese he met on social and official occasions were discreet enough not to allude to the matter.[111] Arch Steele, a correspondent for the *New York Herald Tribune* in China during the period, also noticed a strong anti-American feeling developing in the Beiping-Tianjin area. He suggested that the continued presence of American forces, American servicemen's recurrent frictions with the local populace, as well as the natural Chinese resentment against foreign forces were largely responsible for the tensions.[112]

The *kangbao* movement occupies a prominent place in the history of the Communist urban revolution. The Communist sources have attached great significance to the movement, and have claimed that over five hundred thousand (*wushi wan*) students participated in the movement. In the late 1940s, the charges of American imperialism and of Chiang Kai-shek's fawning subservience to it served as powerful propaganda for the Communist cause. The CCP therefore hoped to sustain the movement beyond its initial stage of explosion of emotions and to enlist the support of other recruits including "workers, clerks, women, poor city dwellers, industrialists, and even Chinese overseas" in its political battle against the United States and the GMD.[113]

PIERSON'S TRIAL

On January 17, 1947, an American court martial of the First Marine Division began to try Corporal Pierson in the Shen Chong case in Beiping. Immediately before and during the days of the trial, the Beiping Anti-Brutality Alliance was most active in issuing statements denouncing the fact that Pierson was going to be tried in a U.S. court martial instead of a Sino-U.S. court. At the trial, Shen Chong went to the court and testified as a witness. The audience was limited to Shen Chong's father, her legal advisers, Hu Shi, a number of GMD officials, and newspaper reporters. Pierson faced five charges: (1) assault, (2) coercion in attempting rape, (3) fornication, (4) behavior prejudicial to good conduct and military discipline, and (5) offense against decency. Pierson pleaded guilty only to fornication, and denied the rest of the charges.[114] Twenty-seven Chinese and American witnesses testified before a panel of seven American military judges. The Chinese army mechanics and policemen testified that they had heard Shen Chong cry and seen the accused on top of Shen, but had failed to come to her rescue initially because of the threats from the marines. The MP who found the group on the night of the alleged rape also testified that Pierson was "intoxicated." The American and the Chinese doctors who examined Shen shortly after the alleged rape testified that the examinations revealed minor injuries to her private parts and demonstrated that she had not had much or probably had had no previous sexual experience, although the minor bruises and cuts could also result from consensual sexual intercourse.

Pierson's counsel, Lieutenant Colonel John Masters, could not establish Shen Chong as a prostitute, but he did argue long and hard that Shen had consented to sexual intercourse with Pierson. Masters claimed that the place where the alleged rape had taken place was usually heavily traveled. Had Shen cried louder for help, more people would have come to her rescue sooner. Masters also argued that had Shen struggled hard as would be expected in a rape, she would have sustained more bruises and injuries to her private parts, while the lack of evidence of strong physical resistance suggested consensual sexual intercourse. Regarding the fact that Shen Chong had pressed a rape charge at the police station, Masters claimed that Shen did so only because she was caught in the act of fornication, and thus found it expedient to call it rape.

Ironically, although the counsel for Pierson was most unlikely to have read the stringent Rape Code of the Qing dynasty, where stiff evidential stipulations placed heavy burden of proof on the victim, his arguments ran along similar lines. Based on the Qing Rape Code, to establish a rape crime, the victim had to supply proof that she had fought against her attacker throughout the whole ordeal. "Such evidence must include: (1) witnesses, either eyewitnesses or people who had heard the victim's cry for help; (2) bruises and lacerations on her body; and (3) torn clothing." If the woman had stopped struggling in the course of sexual attack, then the case must be considered "illicit intercourse by mutual consent." In other words, as one scholar suggests, only severe physical injury, if not her death, could convince judicial officials of the genuineness of her rape charge.[115] In the case of Shen Chong, she actually met the three traditional Chinese criteria for rape, although Masters argued that she should have had more bruises and cried louder for her rape case to be established.

The prosecution, conducted by Lieutenant Colonel Paul Fitzgerald, argued the debilitating effect of the overpowering physical presence of the two marines (Pierson was a six-foot young man with "large and powerful" hands) on a 125-pound, 18-year-old college girl. Fitzgerald further contended that the law did not require a girl to do more than "her age, strength, the surrounding facts, and all attending circumstances make it reasonable for her to do, in order to manifest her opposition." He concluded that it was most difficult to explain why a young, educated girl from an excellent family would willingly spend three hours on a bitterly cold night in an open field with a drunken man she had just accidentally run into. The only explanation was that she stayed because she had no other choice.[116]

The trial ended on January 22. The flimsy arguments made by Masters failed to convince the military judges. Pierson was found guilty of all charges, demoted to the rank of private, and sentenced to 15 years' imprisonment. Pritchard was then tried in a separate court martial that opened on January 30. He was convicted of assault and sentenced to a bad conduct discharge and 10 months in prison.[117]

On March 5, General Samuel Howard, Commander of the First Division of the U.S. Marines stationed in China, ratified the court-martial sentence, which, however, was still subject to final approval by the Secretary of the Navy in Washington. In mid-June of 1947, the Judge Advocate-General of the Navy recommended releasing Pierson from confinement and reinstating him as corporal on the ground of insufficient evidence.[118]

By then the anti-American demonstrations related to the Shen Chong case had cooled off appreciably and the students had become preoccupied with the anti-hunger, anti–civil war movement.[119] This piece of news again aroused some fury in the press, and led to student petitions and protest manifestos. For the Chinese, that Pierson was guilty of rape was beyond any doubt and Washington's exoneration of his heinous crime further suggested the American disregard of justice. *Dagong bao*, an influential newspaper, while suggesting that "black sheep" among American servicemen had adversely affected the reputation of American forces in China, nevertheless asserted that "if an American serviceman who has raped a Chinese girl can be considered not guilty, then what kind of people will the Chinese be in the eyes of Americans?"[120]

The news about the Pierson case also caused consternation on the part of the GMD authorities, and led to another round of frenzied exchanges of telegrams between Beiping and Nanjing. Meanwhile, the Chinese foreign ministry also dispatched a letter of protest to the American embassy in Nanjing demanding that the original sentence of Pierson be maintained.[121]

Hu Shi, who had exerted much effort in securing a legal settlement that could pacify the students, found to his dismay that the court-martial ruling was rejected. Upon learning the news from a local Chinese newspaper, Hu Shi immediately telegraphed Stuart in Nanjing. He stated his grave concern and shock at the news, and warned Stuart of possible political repercussions among students because this news would "greatly inflame anti-American agitation." In the end, he strongly appealed to Stuart's serious consideration of the issue. Shortly after, Hu Shi read a more detailed account on the Pierson case from an American newspaper and realized that the recommendations made by the Judge Advocate-General had to await final approval by the Secretary of the Navy. He immediately sent another telegram marked "urgent" to Stuart strongly urging him to make the American government realize that the Pierson case was "most anxiously watched" by the whole Chinese nation as a "test of American justice." Hu flatly refuted the claim made by the American report that Pierson was convicted "in the midst of nationwide student demonstrations." He asked Stuart to recall that the student demonstrations took place on December 30, 1946, while the court martial was opened on January 17, 1947, and Pierson was convicted on January 22.[122]

Upon learning about the news related to the Pierson case, Shen Chong's father, Shen Shao, sent a strongly worded letter to Hu Shi condemning the American disregard of justice. He asserted that to reverse the sentence of Pierson's well-established criminal act would result in the complete dissipation of the Chinese admiration for American adherence to law. He implored Hu Shi to urge the Chinese government to interfere on behalf of his daughter to see justice done.[123]

The Department of the Navy then announced that the case was still under investigation, which worked to quench the renewed excitement. In mid-August, however, Secretary of the Navy John Sullivan declared a reversal of the verdict based on lack of evidence, and Secretary of Defense James Forrestal signed the final order.[124] This piece of important news came out when Chinese colleges and universities were in summer recess. When the fall semester began in September, the *kangbao* leaders found it difficult to regenerate the fervor of the previous semester.

IMPLICATIONS OF THE SHEN CHONG INCIDENT

Beiping had not witnessed any large-scale student demonstrations for over a decade. The last major student political activity prior to the *kangbao* movement was the patriotic December 9 demonstration targeting Japanese aggression in China in 1935. The sensational Shen Chong Incident, however, sent first the students in Beiping and then students in other major cities to the streets demonstrating. The incident was instrumental in crystallizing student anti-American sentiment. Why had this particular incident politicized such a large section of young Chinese intellectuals? What lay behind their anti-American agitation? The belief in the intellectuals' special social status certainly constituted the immediate cause. The "violent and rough rape" of a "pure and chaste" college student from a distinguished family by an American soldier suggested a monstrous, unpardonable, and intolerable act. Inherent in the outburst of anger was the assumption that university students belonged to a distinctive social class; therefore, they ought to be immune to molestation. In an interview with an articulate student concerning the anti-American demonstrations, an American diplomat asked him whether Chinese soldiers were not as rowdy as, if not more rowdy than, American soldiers; the student replied that Chinese soldiers molested only the peasants, not the intellectuals.[125] Although this was not necessarily an accurate statement, it did reflect the class bias and snobbery inherent in elite thinking.

The Shen Chong Incident also revealed a close link between class, gender, and nationalism. The illustrious family background, the sheltered upbringing, and the prominent status as a student of Beida set Shen Chong apart from women of low classes. The violation of female chastity easily assumed the magnitude of the violation of national dignity and honor when the woman violated was a college student and a *mingmen quixiu* and when the violator belonged to the already unwelcome and ill-reputed American troops. As a former underground Communist student organizer put it: "What distinguished the Shen Chong Incident was that an American had raped a Chinese and that the Chinese victim was a young college student."[126]

Ostensibly, the student protesters seemed to be overreacting. Yet, for them, this incident entailed not an isolated matter, but one with far-reaching significance. Student protesters were demanding not so much that justice be done to Shen Chong, but that justice be done to China. The rape of Shen Chong served as a symbol. Because of the assault upon a member of the Chinese elite, it appeared to many students that the Americans thought little of China as a sovereign state. The students repeatedly maintained therefore that the rape of one of their own comprised an affront to Chinese national dignity. When a wall poster appeared on the bulletin board at Zhejiang University, claiming that the rape of a Beida student by an American soldier should not be compared with the rapes of Chinese women by Japanese soldiers as the former was driven by sexual drive while the latter was encouraged by the Japanese government, it provoked angry responses.[127] Many claimed that this was not merely the rape of a Chinese woman, but the violation of the honor of the Chinese nation.[128] A manifesto titled "Students Strike in Protest against American Marines' Atrocious Act," issued by the Student Self-Governing Association of Qinghua, thus states sensationally that the "inhuman violation" of a Chinese student in a Chinese city by the American marine "was the biggest insult to the Chinese student community, the biggest menace to the safety of our fellow students, and the greatest slight to an independent nation."[129] Whereas any incident or event had the potential to provoke an outburst of anti-American demonstrations, the Shen Chong rape case, perceived by the students as a glaring manifestation of American disregard for Chinese prestige and honor and a demonstration of the American sense of racial superiority, provided the most ready catalyst for the outbreak of emotions. At the peak of the *kangbao* movement, Shen was metamorphosed into a "martyr," and a Chinese Joan of Arc.

For patriotic students in particular and for the public at large, the continued presence of U.S. troops in China served as an infringement upon China's autonomy. Over 6,000 American troops were stationed in Beiping toward the end of 1946. They operated the city's two airports and controlled the only rail transportation to the sea. American jeeps and trucks were everywhere on the streets.[130] The notion that American soldiers were treating China as a colony and Chinese people no better than "black slaves" emerged repeatedly during the student protests. The accumulation of incidents reminded the Chinese of their country's century-long humiliation at the hands of the Western powers. One historian suggests that following World War I, any foreign presence constantly pointing to the Chinese helplessness could have become a target of attack;[131] the Shen Chong event finally brought to the surface smoldering anti-American sentiments.

The fact that American soldiers in China enjoyed special privileges and were subject only to the U.S. judiciary seemed reminiscent of extraterritoriality and of China's inferior international status, and symbolized the disproportional nature of the relationship between the two countries. For this reason, many students had insisted that the culprits of the Shen Chong case be tried in a joint Sino-American court. The protest statements made by the Beida students emphasized the gap between China's seemingly new position of independence and the reality of its continued unequal status. One statement claimed that having fought for eight years and having won national sovereignty, independence, and territorial integrity, the Chinese should have the right to try foreigners committing crimes in China.[132] The absence of true mutuality in bilateral relations frustrated the students: "Wherever the American soldiers have gone, the lives and safety of the Chinese people have suffered the most serious menace. This is not only a question of discipline of the American soldiers, but is a psychological reaction expressed by the marines who look down upon the Chinese people and who consider China to be a colony of the United States of America."[133] Some of the student proclamations and statements were milder in tone, and alluded to the past American-Chinese friendship and to the U.S. assistance in defeating the "common enemy" of Japan, but insisted that the feeling of appreciation was now turning into resentment.[134]

Meanwhile, the American troops' continuous stay in China reminded many Chinese students of American occupation forces in defeated Germany and Japan. Some even claimed that the Americans had simply replaced the Japanese as the new "enslavers" of the Chinese. It is interesting to note that while politically engaged students were busy slashing at the Americans, their memory of the Japanese atrocities in China paled in comparison for the time being. Students' manifestos and statements made repeated comparisons of American and Japanese atrocities, and questioned in grossly exaggerated terms how an ally could behave as badly as, if not worse than, Japanese troops in the Chinese territories. In Shanghai, a rally in memory of the fifteenth anniversary of the bloody Japanese incursion into the city turned into an anti-American gathering. *Wen hui bao*, a Shanghai newspaper that had significantly expanded its circulation by reporting on the prevailing anti-American situation, maintained that while the meeting was intended to be anti-Japanese, yet "in the minds of the Chinese people, the United States has taken the place of Japan and has become the object of hate and disgust."[135] A number of propaganda pamphlets issued by the students compared American servicemen's behavior in defeated Japan and Germany with their behavior in China and concluded bitterly that they treated the Chinese the worst.[136]

While the students perceived the Shen Chong case as an imperialist outrage, and youth demonstrations identified the United States as the symbol of Western imperialism, national political crisis also constituted an important element of the whole trend of the protests. By the time the Shen Chong Incident occurred, the Marshall Mission to bring about a coalition government in China collapsed and Marshall was about to return to the United States. Even with the abolition of the unequal treaties, the victory over Japan, and the seeming elevation of China to the status of world power, "greatness" still seemed to be an illusion. Far from playing an active role in the postwar world, China was falling apart politically. Continued Chinese weakness had filled many Chinese intellectuals with a deep sense of frustration.

The Sino-American Treaty of Friendship, Commerce, and Navigation signed on November 4, 1946, and President Truman's statement of December 20, 1946, on American policies in China, created in urban China an atmosphere of suspicion and distrust toward American intentions. As discussed in the previous chapter, the Sino-American Commercial Treaty had agitated business and intellectual circles and been condemned by a large section of the Chinese press as an economic encroachment on China. A number of student *kangbao* alliances picked up the issue and charged the United States with economic invasion. The Student Self-Governing Associations of Wuhan University and Yanjing University, for example, reached the decision to push for a movement to boycott American goods.[137]

Despite the inevitability of the showdown between the GMD and the CCP, the fact that the United States continued to furnish the Nationalist government with arms and ammunitions induced politically conscious young Chinese to question American motives. Radical students were quick to point to the contradiction with the avowed purposes of the Marshall Mission and charged the United States with interfering in Chinese affairs. Many demonstrators contended that the Shen Chong case revealed a misleading American China policy, which contributed to China's continued disunity. They asserted that the stationing of American troops in China had complicated Chinese politics and helped push China into the pit of the Civil War.

In their frustration over China's bleak political prospect, the students demanded that the Chinese be left alone to settle their own affairs and blamed the U.S. government for the continuation of the Chinese Civil War. In a manifesto to students, the Student Self-Governing Association of Qinghua University declared that "as long as American troops do not withdraw from China, China's unity can never be realized, China's Civil War can never stop, the safety of Chinese people will be threatened, and we young students cannot study with ease."[138] Therefore the development of anti-American protests was accompanied by increasing censure of the U.S. government's China policy and the GMD government for inviting American support and for its weak foreign policy. In this sense the anti-American emotions among the students also served as an outlet for students' discontent with domestic affairs and for their frustrations about political instability in China. Thus, a U.S. marine's alleged attack on a female college student not only triggered an anti-American movement of nationwide proportion, but also resulted in intensified verbal attacks on the Nationalist government since the latter was identified as the client of the United States.[139] Nevertheless, not all student statements at this stage were harshly critical of Chiang Kai-shek and the Nationalist government. The petition to Chiang Kai-shek by the Beida students used a tone of conciliation and condemned only U.S. troops for China's marred equal status. The petition claimed that Chiang's "wise leadership," together with Chinese people's efforts, had helped China to defeat Japan and win both national sovereignty and territorial integrity. While the Chinese people yearned for peace and happiness under Chiang's leadership, American soldiers viewed China as a colony and persecuted Chinese people.[140] Although many Chinese intellectuals opposed the Civil War and blamed the government for economic mismanagement and for maintaining a one-party regime, they were not yet ready to accept Communists as the only alternative.[141]

The *kangbao* movement signified a turning point in the Communist urban revolution of the Civil War era. The Shen Chong Incident provided the Communists with powerful student allies, who turned the streets into an effective political stage to make their voices heard, elicit responses from urban people of various social backgrounds, and make national news. Like the other student political movements of the Republican era, the *kangbao* movement helped politicize the student body. It also represented a turning point in many students' perception of their own government, and served as a recruiting ground for the CCP since the active participants were recruited into the party. According to Communist student organizers, the *kangbao* movement marked a shift in urban Chinese sentiments from *qinMei* (pro-American) to *fanMei* (anti-American).[142]

The student resentment against the American servicemen had been building up all along; parading on the streets and shouting slogans functioned as a vehicle for the students to express their fury and as a political tool for them to mobilize public opinion and to call for public understanding and support. By taking the issue to the street and elevating the rape of Shen Chong to the level of *guochi* (national shame), the protesting students succeeded in creating a nationwide anti-American climate.

AMERICAN REACTIONS

The frequency of clashes between American troops and a considerable portion of the urban Chinese populace made the development of mutual antipathy inevitable. Even before the Beiping rape case some American diplomats in China had already become concerned over the repercussions of the continuous presence of U.S. soldiers in China and considered it "a source of adverse and growing criticism," which contributed to simmering anti-American feeling. They thus recommended a complete withdrawal of American troops from China since the latter had already accomplished the task of repatriating the Japanese and their insufficient numerical strength could not effect any significant changes in the GMD-CCP military position.[143]

Robert Smyth, the American consul general in Tianjin, reported on January 2 of 1947 that the welcome extended to the marines upon their arrival in 1945 after the Japanese surrender had worn very thin. He observed that the exacerbation arising from friction and incidents between the marines and the local population had greatly increased the Chinese resentment of the American presence. He sensed that the general desire of most local Chinese for the withdrawal of the marines had grown noticeably during the last few months, and concluded that the resentment could not be attributed simply to Communist propaganda, as publicly maintained by Chinese officials.[144]

In his insightful article, "Beiping Rape Case Has Deep Social, Political Background," written in the immediate aftermath of the Shen Chong event, Charles Canning observed a general decline of American prestige in China:

The "Ting Hao" [very good] days in Sino-American relations are no more. It is no secret that ever since V-J day, things have changed quite a lot and United States prestige and popularity in China have declined to an alarming extent—a comparison with the war days when every American and everything American was "Ting Hao." Chinese intellectuals and industrialists are getting more and more bitter and even hostile toward Uncle Sam.[145]

Nevertheless, the assertiveness and intensity of the student anti-American emotions surprised some Americans who believed in a special Sino-American relationship. Deploring the anti-American propaganda, *Time* magazine claimed that while China was in desperate need of American economic assistance, it needed American friendship above everything else, just as Americans also needed Chinese friendship.[146] Correspondent William Henry Chamberlin of the *Wall Street Journal* maintained that Americans were not "psychologically prepared" for the development of anti-American actions in China when wartime movies had depicted a most harmonious relationship. Therefore, "many Americans have rubbed their eyes with a sense of unpleasant surprise when they read accounts of milling hordes of Chinese students parading through the streets of Peking, Nanking and Shanghai."[147]

The nature of the *kangbao* movement rendered it impossible for Westerners, especially Americans, in China to sympathize with the student demonstrations. The importance the Chinese press attached to the Shen Chong Incident and the outburst of student emotions baffled or disturbed some Americans present in China at the time.[148] Henry Lieberman, a *New York Times* correspondent, asserted that "except in political terms, it seems difficult to understand the present indignation."[149] Suspicious of mass movements of this kind and disapproving of student motives, Ambassador Stuart argued that "when once swept by impassioned oratory or led into making commitments through skillful manipulations, even the most orderly and friendly students would join recklessly in these herd movements, and if not handled satisfactorily a hopeless crisis would be easily precipitated."[150]

The fact that many Americans were perplexed by the Chinese public reaction reveals that a perception gap existed between the two peoples. In his *Scratches on*

Our Minds, Harold Isaacs provides much insight into the conventional American views of American roles in China. Perceiving themselves as saviors, guardians, and teachers of China and the Chinese, Isaacs argues, a great many Americans believed that China was "a country we have always helped," and the Chinese were "a people to be helped," and expected nothing short of gratitude from the Chinese in return.[151]

In a rebuttal to Pearl Buck's assertion that Chinese resentment against American enlisted personnel in the late 1940s was a consequence of the numerous frictions between them and the Chinese populace, a reporter for *The China Monthly* wrote an article titled "China Does Not Hate Us" in June of 1946. Employing a paternalistic tone throughout, he argued that it was impossible for the Chinese to distrust and hate Americans after America had done so much to elevate China "from a weak, semi-colonial status to the role of one of the Big Four." He further claimed that the official career of Chinese diplomats such as Wellington Koo "reveals the story of China's march to world prestige under American tutelage." These diplomats had suffered international humiliations until "America put its shoulder to the wheel and helped lift China to the level of prestige now her sons so sagely grace." He extolled the generous American endeavors to extend to China "what we Americans think, feel and want for ourselves at home," or rather, "the American way of life." Finally, he contended that the vast interactions between the two countries made it "easy for the petty incidents of the careless jeep drivers to loom out of all proportion to the unaccountable aspects of the steady, helping hand we outstretch to China."[152]

The American belief that the Americans knew what was best for China grated on Chinese sensitivity. As early as the 1920s, when Chinese nationalistic feelings ran high, John Dewey, whose ideas on the importance of education influenced the leaders of the May Fourth Movement, discussed the potential danger in assuming a parental role in the relationship between nations. Dewey asserts that as a fast-growing nation, China would feel increasingly offended by any presumption of "parental tutelage even of a professedly benevolent kind." He claimed that politically, "the Chinese no longer wish for any foreign guardianship."[153]

Unable to comprehend the widespread Chinese anti-American protests, some Western observers simply attributed them to Chinese xenophobia. One of them claimed that "the Chinese man in the street has long been told, and is only too ready to believe, that all the troubles of his country are due to foreigners, and the sentiment engendered by this belief tends to be concentrated against the most conspicuous foreign nationality."[154] One American diplomat in China simply opined that the United States provided "an easy and vulnerable target" for Chinese propagandists and for "normally latent Chinese xenophobia."[155] Serving as the 1947 model of "arrogance," *Time* affirmed, "'American imperialism' had conveniently succeeded 'British imperialism' and 'Japanese imperialism' in the average Chinese intellectual's dictionary of opprobrium."[156] These observations, however, dismissed too quickly the genuine nationalistic feelings on the part of the Chinese.

College students took the rape case into their own hands and to the streets, transforming the personal misfortune of Shen Chong into a political and cultural matter of national shame. In this sense, the Shen Chong Incident transcended itself and became a symbol of Chinese weakness and American imperial behavior. Therefore, the students demanded not only moral justice for Shen Chong, but also national dignity for China. The incident provoked full-fledged nationwide student protests. The key components in the case were the image of Shen as a *mingmen quixiu*, a quiet, modest girl of excellent upbringing, from a prestigious university, and the fact that the rape was committed by an American soldier. The combination of these elements rendered the rape case intolerable, and provided the students with the opportunity to reassert their role as the "moral guardians" of the nation and spirited defenders of Chinese honor. The response to the incident revealed a pronounced growth of anti-American sentiment in the Chinese public, especially among young intellectuals. Although the students failed to realize their immediate demand for holding an open Sino-American court and the naval authorities in Washington eventually pronounced Pierson innocent, the demonstrations focused public attention on the stationing of American troops in particular and U.S. China policy in general. The marines had already begun evacuating China in the fall of 1946. Many more began to go home in early 1947. By September 1947, almost all had departed from China except for a company of marines who stayed on in Qingdao until 1949.[157] The student protests might have hastened the process of the withdrawal of American forces from China.

Legally, the GMD and radical students lost the battle as Washington eventually overturned the court-martial ruling on William Pierson and pronounced him innocent. Politically, however, radical students and the CCP scored a big victory. Prior to the Shen Chong Incident, the image of American soldiers as arrogant, drunken, and ill-behaved brutes had been confined essentially to the Chinese press coverage, Communist propaganda in Yan'an, and local populations in contact with the American servicemen. The *kangbao* movement, however, disseminated this image nationwide, especially among various prominent urban circles. The CCP propagandists then perpetuated and reinforced the negative image beyond the Communist triumph over the GMD in 1949. More significantly, the GMD and the U.S. government experienced immediate, yet far-reaching political losses as the *kangbao* movement created a powerfully negative image of a domineering and interfering American government that assisted a subservient, obsequious GMD regime in carrying on the Civil War. The fact that Pierson's verdict was rejected simply strengthened the negative perception.

If the GMD and the U.S. government were the losers and radical students and the CCP were the winners in the political struggle, the true victim was Shen Chong, whose personal humiliations provided a dramatic stage for a political play. Traditionally, a Chinese woman who had been physically violated often committed suicide under social pressure if the rape was made public, in order to redeem her name and that of her family,[158] or would be condemned to a life of loneliness. Since a woman's loss of chastity by rape, if made public, was almost tantamount to a death sentence, Shen Chong and her family had initially manifested little interest in turning the event into an anti-American crusade. However, the rape case, once made public, was out of the hands of Shen Chong and her relatives. Both those seeking a satisfying legal settlement and those engaging in fervent protests had "national" or "bigger" concerns on their minds. Thus, when the president of Beida and the Nationalist authorities found out that Washington had overturned the guilty verdict for Pierson, their immediate reaction did not concern the fate of Shen Chong per se, but was prompted by the fear that this piece of news might lead to a new round of anti-American student campaigning. Although women students actively participated in the *kangbao* movement and various women's organizations provided moral support for the movement, their outcries were also nationalistic and political in nature, and they often compared the rape of Shen Chong to the rape of the "soul" of China. In this sense, the political turmoil in the aftermath of the Shen Chong Incident was built on her alleged rape, but was not truly about it.

Throughout the *kangbao* movement, Shen Chong herself was out of public view and remained silent on the issue except for making a written statement and pressing a rape charge on the night of the event and appearing as a witness at the court martial. During the period of the student protests, even when occasionally a reporter was granted an interview, it was Shen Chong's relatives who did the talking. Shen Chong herself would be silent if she did make an appearance at the interview. After the stormy student protests over the event ended, Shen Chong seemed to have disappeared. A number of rumors concerning her whereabouts circulated. The most popular one was that she had become a Buddhist nun in the famous temple on the Wutai Mountain. The popularity of this rumor reflected the persistence of the traditional notion about the fate of a "defiled" woman. Although the political and cultural discourse of Republican China discredited the old aphorism that "it is a small matter to starve to death, but a serious matter to lose one's chastity," the sexual chastity ideology was so deeply entrenched that many still embraced it consciously or subconsciously. In an attempt not to expose the case to the public in the immediate aftermath of the Shen Chong Incident, the Nationalist authorities urged the local newspapers not to publish it under the pretext that Shen Chong might commit suicide out of "psychological pressure."

Despite the high-sounding student rhetoric that what had befallen Shen Chong was not (or not only) her personal misfortune but a national humiliation, in reality, many no longer expected her to live a normal life and continue her studies as a college student, given the fact that her rape was known all over China. Assuming that the violence committed against her had deprived her of the chance to live a normal life, people chose to believe that Shen Chong must have opted for the solution to live out the rest of her life in seclusion as a nun, a lonely fate that had befallen many "contaminated" women. However, Shen Chong did not seek suicide, the time-honored course for a woman whose humiliations had been made public, nor did she choose to become a nun, as many had chosen to believe. She did leave Beida after the incident and changed her name. As her given name contains a character from the Chinese phrase *chongshan junling* (mountain ridges), she chose another character, *jun*, from the phrase, and changed her name to Shen Jun. In the 1950s and early 1960s, she worked at the Office of Cultural Exchanges with Foreign Countries in Beijing, and was admitted into the Chinese Communist Party in 1960.[159]

Anti-Americanism, pushed to the fore through the student movement protesting the "atrocities" committed by American servicemen, constituted an important political issue in the course of the Chinese Civil War. The student demands for the immediate departure of American forces from China and no more American interference in China's internal affairs worked greatly to the advantage of the CCP. Soon after the Shen Chong Incident, the Communist leader Mao Zedong asserted that "the student movement in Peiping [Beiping], which began last December 30 as a result of the rape of a Chinese girl student, mark[s] a new upsurge in the struggle of the people in the Chiang Kai-shek areas."[160]

NOTES

1. The Shen Chong Incident has received little attention in the standard historical scholarship on Sino-American relations. Some studies of the student movement of the Civil War period, however, have discussed the incident to some extent. See, for example, Suzanne Pepper, *Civil War in China: The Political Struggle, 1945–1949* (Berkeley: University of California Press, 1978), 52–58; Jessie G. Lutz, "The Chinese Student Movement of 1945–1949," *Journal of Asian Studies* 31 (November 1971), 89–110; Joseph K.S. Yick, *Making Urban Revolution in China: The CCP-GMD Struggle for Beiping-Tianjin, 1945-1949* (Armonk, N.Y.: M.E. Sharpe, 1995), 92–103; Jeffrey N. Wasserstrom, *Student Protests in Twentieth-Century China: The View from Shanghai* (Stanford: Stanford University Press, 1991), 139–142, 261–263. This chapter examines the Shen Chong Incident from various perspectives and in the context of the shifting urban Chinese perceptions of the United States in the post–World War II period, and discusses its influence on Chinese-American relations at both the official and unofficial levels.

2. Shen Chong was born in 1928. According to Western calculations, she was only 18 years old at the time.

3. In her written statement, Shen maintained that she was living in the house of her brother-in-law, Yang Zhenqing. Yang had received an American education and was a government official, whose wife was Shen's cousin.

4. "Marine Provost Marshal Report on Investigation of Alleged Rape of Miss Shen Chung (Chong) by Corporal William G. Pierson (316637), U.S. Marine Corps, Weapons Company, Fifth Marines" from "Provost Marshal Investigators to the Provost Marshal, Peiping Area, 28 December 1946: Statement of Shen Chong, Statement of Mung Chao-chieh (Meng Zhaojie)," Marshall Mission File, National Archives (hereafter NA).

5. "Marine Provost Marshal Report: Statement of Kuan Te-tsung," Marshall Mission File, NA.

6. During the stay of U.S. military personnel in China in the immediate postwar years, MPs often patrolled the cities together with Chinese police to safeguard American property, cope with black market dealings, and handle Sino-American incidents.

7. "Marine Provost Marshal Report: Statement of Yu Ming-chian, Physician of Beiping Police Hospital and Statement of Lieutenant P. L. Clark III, U.S. Navy," Marshall Mission File, NA; Beijing dangan guan (Beijing archives), "Beiping shizhengfu youguan Shen Chong shijian laiwang handian xuanbian" (Selected documents and telegrams of the Beiping municipal government on the Shen Chong incident) (hereafter Shen Chong shijian), *Beijing dangan shiliao* (Archival materials on the history of Beijing) 33, no. 1 (1994): 13; Zhonggong Beijing shiwei dangshi yanjiushi, eds., *Kangyi Meijun zhuHua baoxing yundong ziliao huibian* (Collected materials on the movement

protesting the brutalities of U.S. troops in China) (Beijing: Beijing daxue chubanshe, 1989), 130.

8. "Marine Provost Marshal Report: Statement of Shen Chung," Marshall Mission File, NA; Beijing danan guan, "Shen Chong shijian," 13.

9. Beijing danan guan, "Shen Chong shijian," 13.

10. "Marine Provost Marshal Report: Statements of Pierson and Statement of Prit-chard," Marshall Mission File, NA.

11. "Marine Provost Marshal Report: The Marine Provost Marshal Investigation Re-port," Marshall Mission File, NA.

12. Beijing daxue lishixi, *Beijing daxue xuesheng yundong shi, 1919–1949* (A history of the student movement of Beijing university) (Beijing: Beijing chubanshe, 1979), 197; *Xin-min bao*, 26 December 1946.

13. See, for example, *Shijie ribao* and *Beiping ribao*.

14. Zhonggong Beijing shiwei, *Kangyi Meijun zhuHua baoxing*, 659.

15. Ibid., 192; Beijing daxue lishixi, *Beijing daxue xuesheng yundong shi*, 198; Zhou Chengen et al., *Beijing daxue xiaoshi* (A history of Beijing university) (Shanghai: Shanghai jiaoyu chubanshe, 1981), 274.

16. Beijing daxue yuanxi lianhehui, eds., *Beida yinian* (One year in Beida) (Beijing, 1947), 5; Aiguo yundong chubanshe, eds., *Meiguobing gun chuqu* (Roll out, American soldiers) (Beiping: Aiguo yundong chubanshe, 1947), 7.

17. John Israel, *Lianda: A Chinese University in War and Revolution* (Stanford: Stanford University Press, 1998), 183–84.

18. For discussions concerning the organizations and strategies of the Communist Underground Party, see Yick, *Making Urban Revolution in China*, 36–136.

19. Beijing Daxue lishixi, *Beijing daxue xuesheng yundong shi*; Qinghua daxue xiaoshi bianxiezu, *Qinghua daxue xiaoshigao* (A history of Qinghua university) (Beijing: Zhonghua shuju, 1981), 464; Zhonggong Beijing shiwei, *Kangyi Meijun zhuHua baoxing,* 685.

20. Wang Qing, "Meiguobing gunhuiqu!" (Roll back home, American soldiers), in *Qingnian yundong huiyilu* (Recollections of the youth movement), ed. Zhang Aiping and Xiao Hua et al. (Beijing: Zhongguo qingnian chubanshe, 1978), 1:216–17; Aiguo yundong chubanshe, *Meiguobing*, 11–12; and Zhou Cheng'en, *Beijing daxue xiaoshi*, 274–75.

21. For further discussions on the issue of the polarization of college students during the Civil War years, see Wasserstrom, *Student Protests in Twentieth-Century China*, 241–76.

22. Beijing daxue yuanxi lianhehui, *Beida yinian*, 5; Aiguo yundong chubanshe, *Meiguobing*, 6–7; Zhonggong Beijing shiwei, *Kangyi Meijun zhuHua baoxing*, 191, 687–88.

23. Zhonggong Beijing shiwei, *Kangyi Meijun zhuHua baoxing*, 688.

24. Ibid.

25. Ibid.

26. Ibid., 661–63.

27. Democracy Wall served as a place where students put their thoughts or protests onto paper to be read by all those who passed by. In the late 1970s, a Democracy Wall at another site in Beijing became especially famous, as a number of people began to put up posters on the wall demanding the introduction of true democratic freedom in China.

28. Xu Yurong and Zhang Fupei, who were heads of the Student Self-Governing Associations of Qinghua and Yangjing at the time, were underground CCP students. Some other active members of the *kangbao* movement were recruited to the CCP soon after the movement began. See Zhonggong Beijing shiwei, *Kangyi Meijun zhuHua baoxin*, 718.

29. Qinghua daxue xiaoshi bianxiezu, *Qinghua daxue xiaoshigao*, 464–65. The December Ninth Movement of 1935 against the Japanese aggression in China, the most significant student movement after the May Fourth Movement, began on the Yanjing campus. See Philip West, *Yenching University and Sino-American Relations, 1916–1952* (Cambridge: Harvard University Press, 1976), 90.

30. Zhonggong Beijing shiwei, *Kangyi Meijun zhuHua baoxing,* 664, 694–95.

31. Ibid., 691–93.

32. The Qinghua campus was about one mile from Yanjing University, and both were situated about five miles outside of Beiping's city walls.

33. "Anti-American Student Demonstration in Peiping on December 30 and 31, 1946, Precipitated by Alleged Rape of Chinese Student by Two American Marines," from Myers to Stuart, January 15, 1947, RG59, 811.22/1-1547, NA.

34. John F. Melby, *The Mandate of Heaven: Record of a Civil War, China 1945–49* (Toronto: University of Toronto Press, 1968), 176; Song Bai, *Beijing xiandai gemingshi* (A revolutionary history of modern Beijing) (Beijing: Zhongguo renmin daxue chubanshe, 1988), 203.

35. "Chinese Paraders Ask Marines to Go: Alleged Rape Causes Large Demonstrations in Peiping, Shanghai and Tientsin," *New York Times*, December 31, 1946; Song Bai, *Beijing xiandai gemingshi*, 203.

36. Zhonggong Beijing shiwei, *Kangyi Meijun zhuHua baoxing*, 700.

37. Ibid., 166.

38. Ibid., 669.

39. Henry Lieberman, "Chinese Students Again Assail US: Rape Case Against 2 Marines Causes Demonstrations in Shanghai and Peiping," *New York Times*, January 1, 1947.

40. Zhonggong Beijing shiwei, *Kangyi Meijun zhuHua baoxing*, 704.

41. "Anti-American Student Demonstration in Peiping on December 30 and 31, 1946, Precipitated by Alleged Rape of Chinese Student by Two American Marines," from Myers to Stuart, January 15, 1947, RG59, 811.22/1-1547, NA; Yanda xuesheng zizhihui, eds., "Da bi zhan qian hou" (Around the time of the big verbal fight), in *Yanda san nian* (Three years in Yanda) (Beiping: Yanda xuesheng zizhihui, 1948), 76. The reports from *The New York Times* correspondents suggested the numbers to be over 6,000 and 8,000 respectively.

42. Pepper, *Civil War in China*, 55.

43. Zhonggong Beijing shiwei, *Kangyi Meijun zhuhua baoxin*, 717.

44. Yick, *Making Urban Revolution in China*, 64.

45. For more information on Lin Shu, see chapter one.

46. Beijing dangan guan, "Shen Chong shijian," 17; Zhonggong Beijing shiwei, *Kangyi Meijun zhuHua baoxing*, 688; Wang Guohua, "Sheng Chong shijian shimo" (The whole story of the Sheng Chong incident), *Beijing wenshi ziliao* (Cultural and historical materials of Beijing) 51 (December 1995), 135.

47. Zhonggong Beijing shiwei, *Kangyi Meijun zhuHua baoxing*, 130–33; Liu Xiaoqing, "*Xianjing xinwen* zhuizong baodao: Sheng Chong shijian" (The pursuit of the Shen Chong incident by Yanjing news) *Minguo chunjiu* (The republican years) 84 (June 2000):18-19.

48. Louise Edwards, "Policing the Modern Woman in Republican China," *Modern China* 26 (April 2000), 125.

49. For discussions along this line, see Edwards, "Policing the Modern Woman," 124, 138–40.

50. In traditional China, soldiers were held in low esteem. A popular saying goes, "Good iron does not make nails, and good men do not become soldiers."

51. Articles in Tani E. Barlow, ed., *Gender Politics in Modern China* (Durham: Duke University Press, 1993), are an effort to grapple with the interplay of modernity and gender and class in China.

52. Aiguo yundong chubanshe, *Meiguobing*, 1; Zhonggong Beijing shiwei, *Kangyi Meijun zhuHua baoxing*, 129.

53. Edwards, "Policing the Modern Woman," 115–16.

54. In the article, "Penetration and Neocolonialism: The Shen Chong Rape Case and the Anti-American Student Movement of 1946–47," James A. Cook provides an essentially gender-conscious analysis and argues that the Shen Chong case provided the Chinese male students with "an opportunity to reassert traditional patriarchal roles as protectors and owners of female students." See *Republican China* 22 (November 1996), 68.

55. Lydia H. Liu, "The Female Body and Nationalist Discourse: Manchuria in Xiao Hong's *Field of Life and Death*," in *Body, Subject and Power in China*, ed. Angela Zito and Tani E. Barlow (Chicago: The University of Chicago Press, 1994), 161. In this article, Liu discusses the relationship between the female body and nationalism especially in the context of China's war of resistance against Japan.

56. Beijing dangan guan, "Hu shi danan zhong youguan Shen Chong shijian laiwang handian xuan" (Collected telegrams related to the Shen Chong incident in the Hu Shi file), *Beijing danan shiliao* (Archival materials on the history of Beijing) 34, no.2 (1994), 35; *Xinmin bao*, Shanghai, January 2, 1947; Gongqingtuan Shanghai shiwei, eds., *1945–1949: Shanghai xuesheng yundongshi* (1945-1949: A history of the Shanghai student movement) (Shanghai: Shanghai renmin chubanshe, 1983), 69; Chen Xiqing, "Shilun kangbao yundong jiqi yiyi" (A preliminary analysis of the anti-brutality movement and its significance) in *Jiefang zhanzheng shiqi xuesheng yundong lunwenji* (Essays on the student movement during the war of liberation], ed. Zheng Guang et al. (Shanghai: Tongji daxue chubanshe, 1988), 136.

57. William Gray, "Friendship Lost? How Stands US Prestige in China?" *Time* 49 (February 10, 1947): 22.

58. Memorandum by Smyth, January 27, 1947, RG59, 893.00/1-247, NA.

59. "Student Demonstrations in Nanking in Connection with Peiping Incident," memorandum by Butterworth, January 9, 1947, RG59, 893.00/1-947, NA; Zhang Ying, "Meiguobing gun chuqu!" (Roll out, American soldiers), *Xinhua ribao*, January 13, 1947.

60. "China: Nasty Words," *Newsweek* 29 (January 13, 1947): 40; Aiguo yundong chubanshe, *Meiguobing*, 67.

61. John Robinson Beal, *Marshall in China* (New York: Doubleday, 1970), 346.

62. Zhonggong Beijing shiwei, *Kangyi Meijun zhuHua baoxing*, 250–51.

63. One of the largest universities in China, Zhongyang University had a student enrollment of 4,500 around this time. One faculty member there suggested that despite the existence of leftist agitation on campus, students' feelings of outrage over the Beiping incident were sincere. See memorandum by Butterworth, January 9, 1947, RG59, 893.00/1-947, NA.

64. Memorandum by Butterworth, January 9, 1947, RG59, 893.00/1-947, NA; memorandum by Stuart, January 3, 1947, RG59, 893.00/1-347, NA.

65. Melby, *Mandate of Heaven*, 176.

66. Beal, *Marshall in China*, 346; memorandum by Stuart, January 3, 1947, RG59, 893.00/1-347, NA; Zhang Ying, "Meiguobing gun chuqu," *Xinhua ribao*, January 13, 1947. On January 6, students from six universities and colleges and members of the Student Union in Chongqing, the wartime capital, held an orderly mass demonstration. They first lined up on the street opposite to the U.S. consulate entrance, singing anti-American songs and shouting "scurrilous" anti-American slogans before parading through the city. See memo-

randum by Stuart, January 10, 1946, RG59, 893.00/1-1047, NA. Not long after the January 6 demonstration, students in Chongqing organized an "anti-brutality corps," which periodically staged small-scale demonstrations against the presence of American troops in China. The local police then dressed as plainclothesmen, mixed with student demonstrators, and beat them up. Riots ensued, resulting in numerous injuries. After this, student demonstrations in Chongqing diverted from anti-American issues. Students were again calling for strikes and holding meetings and demonstrations, but these were directed essentially at the local government. Memorandums by Stuart, February 12, 1947, RG59, 893.00/2-1247; February 15, 1947, RG59, 893.00/2-1547, NA.

67. Qinghua daxue xiaoshi bianxiezu, *Qinghua daxue xiaoshi*, 466.

68. Song Bai, *Beijing xiandai gemingshi*, 204; Chiang Kai-shek, *Soviet Russia in China*, 186.

69. Beijing dangan guan, "Shen Chong shijian," 17.

70. "The March of the Volunteers" was composed by Nie Er and written by Tian Han as a song to inspire the Chinese to rise up against the Japanese aggression. It has served as the national anthem for the People's Republic of China since 1949.

71. In *Student Protests in Twentieth-Century China*, Wasserstrom highlights the significant role group singing had played in student political activism, and provides a detailed and interesting study of the various techniques protesting students employed to publicize their issues and to gain the support of as many people as possible.

72. Zhonggong Beijing shiwei, *Kangyi Meijun zhuHua baoxing*, 764.

73. See *Xinmin bao*, December 31, 1946.

74. Zhonggong Beijing shiwei, *Kangyi Meijun zhuHua baoxing*, 393-94.

75. Ibid., 703.

76. *Yi shi bao*, December 30, 1946.

77. Zhonggong Beijing shiwei, *Kangyi Meijun zhuHua baoxing*, 703.

78. Zhonghua quanguo funu lianhehui funu yundong lishi yanjiushi, ed., *Zhongguo funu yundong lishi ziliao, 1945–1949* (Historical records on women's movement in China, 1945–1949) (Beijing: Zhongguo funu chubanshe, 1991), 218; Zhonggong Beijing shiwei, *Kangyi Meijun zhuHua baoxing*, 762; Thurston Griggs, *Americans in China: Some Chinese Views* (Washington, D.C.: Foundation of Foreign Affairs, 1948), 11. For statements made by prominent figures and organizations, see *Kangyi Meijun zhuHua baoxing*, 383–451.

79. *The China Weekly Review* was an influential English newspaper founded and run by the Americans in Shanghai. It was first established in 1917 in Shanghai by Thomas F. Millard from the United States. Its original name was *Millard's Review of the Far East* (Mileshi pinglun bao). J.B. Powell took it over in 1922, and renamed it *The China Weekly Review* in 1923, but kept its original Chinese name. *The Review* was forced to stop publication during the Pacific War. Powell's son, J.W. Powell, resumed its publication after the war was over.

80. Zhonggong Beijing shiwei, *Kangyi Meijun zhuhua baoxin*, 703.

81. Ibid., 238–39.

82. Wasserstrom, *Student Protests in Twentieth-Century China*, 22.

83. Beijing dangan guan, "Shen Chong shijian," 14–16; Beijing dangan guan, "Hu Shi dangan," 34–35.

84. Ibid., "Hu Shi dangan," 34.

85. Ibid., "Shen Chong shijian,"14.

86. "Anti-American Student Demonstration in Peiping [Beiping] on December 30, 31, 1946," from Myers to Stuart, January 15, 1947, RG59, 811.22/1-1547, NA; Zhonggong Beijing shiwei, *Kangyi Meijun zhuHua baoxing*, 766.

87. Beijing dangan guan, "Shen Chong shijian," 15–16.

88. Ibid., 17.

89. Ibid., 18.

90. Ibid., "Hu Shi dangan," 35.

91. Beal, *Marshall in China*, 345.

92. Discussion on "Anti-American Student Demonstration" between Cui Cunlin and Ringwalt, January 7, 1947, RG59, 893.00/1-747, NA.

93. Beijing daxue lishixi, *Beijing daxue xuesheng yundongshi*, 195; From Myers to the Secretary of State, December 30, 1946, in U.S. Department of State, *Foreign Relations of the United States [FRUS], 1947, The Far East: China* (Washington, D.C.: Government Printing Office, 1972), 7:3–4.

94. "Anti-American Student Demonstration in Peiping on December 30, 31, 1946," from Myers to Stuart, January 15, 1947, RG59, 811.22/1-1547, NA.

95. Zhonggong Beijing shiwei, *Kangyi Meijun zhuHua baoying*, 489.

96. Beijing dangan guan, "Shen Chong shijian," 16; Beijing dangan guan, "Hu Shi dangan," 35.

97. Beijing dangan guan, "Telegram by He Siyuan to Chiang Kai-shek" and "Telegram by He Siyuan to the Executive Yuan of the Nationalist Government," in "Shen Chong shijian," 15.

98. Beijing daxue xuesheng zizhihui, eds., *Beida 1946–1948* (Beiping, 1948), 5.

99. Yick, *Making Urban Revolution in China*, 101.

100. Zhonggong Beijing shiwei, *Kangyi Meijun zhuHua baoxing*, 3.

101. Ibid.

102. Ibid.

103. Ibid., 708.

104. *Xinhua ribao*, January 2, 1947.

105. *Jiefang ribao*, January 1, 1947.

106. See, for example, Zhongguo renmin zhengzhi xieshang huiyi Beijingshi weiyuanhui wenshi ziliao yanjiu weiyuanhui, eds., *Beiping dixiadang douzheng shiliao* (Historical materials on the struggles of the Beiping underground party) (Beijing: Beijing chubanshe, 1988); Wang Ping and Zhang Liyao, eds., *Zhongguo xiandai fengyunlu* (A turbulent history of modern China) (Shanghai: Tongji daxue chubanshe, 1988), 287–89; Shandong daxue bianxiezu, eds., *Zhongguo gemingshi lunwen jiyao* (Essays on the revolutionary history of China) (Beijing: Zhonggong dangshi ziliao chubanshe, 1987), 2:1016–1027.

107. Zhonggong Beijing shiwei, *Kangyi Meijun zhuHua baoxing*, 714.

108. Wasserstrom, *Student Protests in Twentieth-Century China*, 119.

109. Charles J. Canning, "Peiping Rape Case Has Deep Social, Political Background," *The China Weekly Review* (January 11, 1947): 166.

110. The editorial of *Dagong bao*, January 6, 1947.

111. Memorandum by Smyth, January 14, 1947, RG59, 711.93/1-1447, NA.

112. Memorandum by Smyth, January 14, 1947, RG59, 711.93/1-1447, NA.

113. Zhonggong Beijing shiwei, *Kangyi Meijun zhuHua baoxing*, 7.

114. Beijing dangan guan, "Shen Chong shijian," 18–19.

115. Vivian W. Ng, "Ideology and Sexuality: Rape Laws in Qing China," *Journal of Asian Studies* 46 (February 1987), 58–61.

116. "Records of Proceedings of a General Court Martial: Case of William G. Pierson" from Robert Shaffer, "A Rape in Beijing, December 1946: GIs, Nationalist Protests, and U.S. Foreign Policy," *Pacific Historical Review* 69 (February 2000), 58-59

117. The information source for the account of Pierson's trial is based on the confidential official reports in "Shen Chong shijian" and "Hu Shi dangan" from the Beijing archives; Zhonggong Beijing shiwei, *Kangyi Meijun zhuHua baoxing*, 635–54; and

"Records of Proceedings of a General Court Martial: Case of William G. Pierson" from Shaffer, "A Rape in Beijing," 56–60; and Xixiao Guo, "The Climax of Sino-American Relations, 1944–1947," (Ph.D. diss., University of Georgia, 1997), 288–91.

118. Griggs, *Americans in China*, 12–13; *Dagong bao*, Shanghai, June 25, 1947.

119. For discussions of this movement, see Pepper, *Civil War in China*, 58–93.

120. *Dagong bao*, June 25, 1947.

121. Beijing dangan guan, "Shen Chong shijian," 20.

122. Ibid., "Hu Shi dangan," 36.

123. Beijing dangan guan, "Hu Shi dangan," 36.

124. *Dagong bao*, June 25, 1947; Griggs, *Americans in China*, 13.

125. Memorandum by James P. Speer, January 15, 1947, RG59, 811.22/1-1547, NA.

126. Zhonggong Beijing shiwei, *Kangyi Meijun zhuHua baoxing*, 713.

127. *Wen hui bao*, January 6, 1947.

128. Zhonggong Beijing shiwei, *Kangyi Meijun zhuHua baoxing*, 147.

129. Ibid.

130. Griggs, *Americans in China*, 9.

131. West, *Yenching University and Sino-Western Relations*, 160.

132. Zhonggong Beijing shiwei, *Kangyi Meijun zhuHua baoxing*, 135.

133. Ibid., 146.

134. Ibid., 140.

135. Quoted from *Time* 49 (February 10, 1947): 22.

136. Zhonggong Beijing shiwei, *Kangyi Meijun zhuHua baoxing*, 157; 259.

137. Ibid., 281.

138. Ibid., 148.

139. Ibid.

140. Ibid., 141–42.

141. Stuart, *Fifty Years in China*, 189.

142. Zhonggong Beijing shiwei, *Kangyi Meijun zhuHua baoxing*, 675–76.

143. From Butterworth to General Marshall, November 20, 1946; RG59, 893.00/11-2046, NA.

144. "US Marines, Tientsin," from Smyth to Stuart, January 2, 1947, RG59, 893.00/1-0247, NA.

145. Canning, "Beiping Rape Case Has Deep Social, Political Background," 166.

146. Gray, "Friendship Lost? How Stands US Prestige in China?" 22.

147. William Henry Chamberlin, "Post War Ironies," *Wall Street Journal*, January 14, 1947. In his article, "A Rape in Beiping," Shaffer, through utilizing essentially English-language sources, looks especially at the American response to the Shen Chong case.

148. See, e.g., John Melby's diary on January 1, 1947, in *Mandate of Heaven*, 176.

149. *New York Times*, January 1, 1947.

150. Stuart, *Fifty Years in China*, 79.

151. Harold R. Isaacs, *Scratches on Our Minds: American Images of China and India* (New York: The John Day Company, 1958), 193.

152. John Goette, "China Does Not Hate Us," *The China Monthly* 7–8 (June 1946): 201–2.

153. John Dewey, "America and the Far East: The Issues of Pacific Policy," *Survey* 56 (May 1926): 188.

154. *The Economist*, December 20, 1947.

155. "Student Demonstrations at Peiping," from Butterworth to the Secretary of State, January 8, 1947, RG59, 893.00/1-847, NA.

156. Gray, "Friendship Lost? How Stands US Prestige in China?" 22.

157. Henry Aplington II, "China Revisited," *Marine Corps Gazette* 57 (July 1973): 31.

158. For a discussion of this issue, see Ng, "Ideology and Sexuality," 57–70.

159. According to one eyewitness account, some controversies arose among those who were in charge of Shen Jun's application. Some argued against Shen's application by claiming that she was arrogant and unapproachable. Some, however, argued on her behalf. Referring to the rape case, they maintained that Shen had once made a significant contribution to the Communist revolution. The fact that she was courageous enough to make public her humiliating rape by the American soldier, thus triggering a nation-wide anti-American campaign, was enough for her to be admitted into the Party. This latter opinion prevailed and Shen became a member of CCP. Meanwhile, she was married to a famous cartoonist.

160. Mao Tse-tung, "Greet the New High Tide of the Chinese Revolution," *Selected Works of Mao Tse-tung* (Peking: Foreign Languages Press, 1961), 4:120.

Figure 1. American GIs Featured Prominently in the Scene of "Chaos" in Shanghai. From Zhang Leping, *Adventures of Sanmao, the Orphan* (1947; reprint, Hong Kong: Joint Publishing Co., 1981), 154.

Figure 2. Sanmao Was "Clobbered" by a Drunken American Sailor. From Zhang Leping, *Adventures of Sanmao, the Orphan* (1947; reprint, Hong Kong: Joint Publishing Co., 1981), 153.

Figure 3. "There Is Always a Bigger Bully." From Zhang Leping, *Adventures of Sanmao, the Orphan* (1947; reprint, Hong Kong: Joint Publishing Co., 1981), 136.

Figure 4. "Damn You All"—Sanmao's Revenge Turned Out Only to Be a Dream. From Zhang Leping, *Adventures of Sanmao, the Orphan* (1947; reprint, Hong Kong: Joint Publishing Co., 1981), 137.

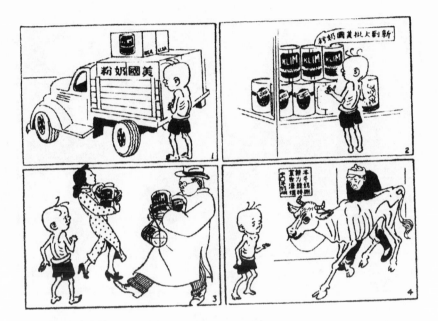

Figure 5. "American Goods Flood the Market."

2. New consignment direct from U.S.A.
4. Dairy business closing down —one cow for sale

From Zhang Leping, *Adventures of Sanmao, the Orphan* (1947; reprint, Hong Kong: Joint Publishing Co., 1981), 152.

Figure 6. The Culprit in the Shen Chong Incident Acquitted.

1. Dongdan Drill Field
2. American Laws
3. Acquitted
4. Chiang Kai-shek

From Li Cunsong et al., *Meijun baoxingtu* (*Atrocities of American troops in pictures*) (Beijing: Renshijian chubanshe, 1951), 1.

Figure 7. American Way of Life (I).

1. Republican Party
2. Democratic Party
3. Wall Street
4. American worker is oppressed
5. American workers on strike
6. Strike
7. Hungry American children look for food in a garbage can
8. Such is American culture
9. American children's education

From Zhongyang meishu xueyuan kangMei yuanChao weiyuanhui, eds., *Xuanchuanhua cankao ziliao* (Reference materials for propaganda posters), no. 3 (Beijing: Zhongyang meishu xueyuan, 1951), 14.

Figure 8. American Way of Life (II).

1. KKK members inflict violence on blacks
2. Robbers running wild in America
3. Severely oppressed American blacks
4. An unemployed American family on the street
5. Twenty-four hours in America
6. Murdering
7. Kidnapping
8. Poisoning
9. Highway robbery
10. Burglary
11. KKK—A Fascist organization in America: Truman was a member of the KKK

From Zhongyang meishu xueyuan kangMei yuanChao weiyuanhui, eds., *Xuanchuanhua cankao ziliao* (Reference materials for propaganda posters), no. 3 (Beijing: Zhongyang meishu xueyuan, 1951)., 15.

5

FAN MEIFURI: OPPOSING THE U.S. SUPPORT OF JAPAN, 1948

Growing student unrest marked the years 1947 and 1948 in China, where the political and economic situations provided fertile soil for political activities. The Civil War was devastating the economy with skyrocketing inflation. The degeneration of every aspect of student life, including the increasing cost of living, malnutrition, and a bleak future after graduation, all contributed to the sense of frustration and disillusionment. Besides economic distress, the Nationalist government's corruption and maladministration, the purge of student leaders, and the suppression of student political activities also worked to intensify swelling discontent with the GMD. Unsatisfactory living and learning conditions and deepening discouragement over the prospect of Chinese politics culminated in "Anti-Hunger and Anti–Civil War" demonstrations and strikes in numerous universities in the GMD-controlled territory in 1947 and led to the further radicalization of politically articulate Chinese.[1] Many student associations came into existence and matured during the various student campaigns. As the power struggle between the GMD and the CCP entered its final stage, Chinese intellectuals, especially the college students, became a potent political force. Although college and university campuses provided some protection from the turmoil from the outside world, they also served as the groundswell of active political activities.

While the nationwide student protests over the Shen Chong Incident gradually faded into the background, an undertone of anti-American sentiment persisted. Politically sensitive Chinese, although harboring little animosity toward individual Americans, nevertheless viewed the American government with grave suspicion or even open hostility. Their perception of the relationship between the U.S. government and the increasingly unpopular GMD as that of patron and client also served to tarnish the image of the United States. Anti-American tendencies emerged from radical student literature with a particular reference to "American imperialism."[2] Confronted with recurrent Chinese accusations, one editorial of the American-run *The China Weekly Review* attributed them to Communist propaganda. The editorial, however, elicited a number of agitated written responses from the readers, who claimed vehemently that the United States was indeed practicing an "imperialist" policy in China.[3]

Sensitive to any foreign action that seemed to compromise China's national integrity and unity, the increasingly radicalized Chinese youths resented any U.S. support given to the Nationalist government. Such aid, they believed, would only prolong the Civil War and prevent the GMD from making drastic reforms. They repeatedly asserted that China should be left alone to work out its own problems and protested against what they considered to be American government's intervention in China's domestic affairs. In the middle of the nationwide "Anti-Hunger and Anti–Civil War" campaign in May 1947, the student representatives of Nankai University in Tianjin presented to the American consul general, Robert Smyth, a letter addressed to the United States Congress. The letter urged that no more American loans be granted to the Nationalist government pending the termination of the Civil War and maintained that such aid would simply add fuel to the fire. "Any of your loans extended to China now are just drums of gasoline poured over the fire of the civil war," the letter declared. "Do you think that you are willing to see the fire of our civil war raging more fiercely?"[4]

In their vehement attacks on "American imperialism" and their self-claimed role as the champion of Chinese national independence, the CCP seemed to stand for the righteous cause. By repeatedly calling for China's independence from foreign influence in the propaganda campaign, the Chinese Communists drew strength from the reservoir of Chinese patriotism and appealed to the nationalist sentiment of Chinese students. In a study on the political attitudes of Chinese students in 1947, an American diplomat in Nanjing observed that "in denouncing the Americans the Communist shibboleth of 'imperialism' is ready at hand and is used uncritically."[5]

In April 1948, the United States Congress passed the China Aid Act providing economic and military aid to the Nationalist government in the amount of over $400 million.[6] The American military aid was quickly consumed by the flames of the Civil War. By 1948, military defeats suffered by the GMD troops convinced many educated Chinese that the Nationalist government's final collapse was merely a matter of time. Furthermore, GMD corruption and inefficiency meant that American economic aid could hardly relieve the economic distress Chinese people were suffering. Many radical Chinese therefore believed that the passage of the China Aid Act would only serve to extend Chinese miseries.[7] On the other hand, pro-GMD forces also found in American aid to China much to be dissatisfied with, complaining that the aid had served only as "a drop in the bucket." They protested that the United States still tenaciously continued its "Europe First and Asia Second" foreign policy.[8] Realizing the potential negative effect of aid to a government rapidly losing its viability, John K. Fairbank had warned in an article written a year before that such aid might boost the cause of the Chinese Communists, who, as a result, would claim themselves to be the defender of the people's cause and would "focus anti-foreign and anti-imperialist sentiment against the United States."[9]

The CCP and educated urban Chinese, especially radical college students, soon received another significant impetus in their anti-American activities. This time, however, the triggering issue was the American occupation policy in Japan. Stimulated by extensive Chinese press coverage of the U.S. postwar policy toward Japan, Chinese students again took to the streets and pushed anti-American sentiment to a new height. The stormy 1948 Chinese student demonstrations and protests constituted the last significant student movement prior to the Communist victory in 1949. It appealed to and received support from a broad spectrum of prominent Chinese, including educators, writers, businessmen, cultural figures, members of women's organizations, and even some government officials. The underground CCP students found in the renewed expressions of outrage against the U.S. government an excellent opportunity to gain wider political support for the Communist cause, and to further discredit the Chiang regime and the U.S. government. Furthermore, the last round of nationwide student anti-American activities before the Communist takeover further diminished the already badly damaged Chinese faith in the U.S. government.

THE SHIFT IN U.S. POLICY TOWARD JAPAN

Growing anti-American sentiment resulted from more than simply U.S. activities in China. International developments played an important role as well. A significant event took place in the spring of 1948, when Chinese students from major universities in the big cities took up the issue of U.S. policy toward Japan. During 1947 and 1948, the U.S. occupation of Japan underwent a major change in policy, with its emphasis shifting from essentially political and social reforms to programs for rapid economic recovery. Apart from the desire to make Japan less of a drain on American economic and financial resources, the world situation at the time dictated this shift. With the intensification of the Cold War in Europe and East Asia in 1947, the Truman administration and, gradually, General Douglas MacArthur, Supreme Commander for Allied Powers (SCAP) in Japan, decided to undertake a so-called reverse course, a term coined by the Japanese media to signify the drastic turn of occupation policy.[10]

The U.S. reversal of policy in Japan corresponded closely with the decline of the political stand of the GMD in China. Rocked by civil war, China no longer appeared capable of serving as a bastion against communism in Asia. The wartime American image of postwar East Asia, where the United States and a pro-American China would cooperate as partners to construct a new order, evaporated before a weak and war-torn China. Accordingly, Washington viewed a politically and economically stable Japan, the most modernized country in Asia, as a potential bulwark against Soviet expansion. This theme formed the central thesis of a speech titled "The Requirements of Reconstruction" delivered on May 8, 1947, by Undersecretary of State Dean Acheson.[11]

As the Cold War intensified, the image of Japan as a buffer came to dominate American thinking about Asia, and Japan's economic development began to assume particular significance. By early 1948 there appeared marked signs in U.S. occupation policy that Washington had come to view Japan in the general framework of containing communism. In January, Secretary of the Army Kenneth Royall publicly indicated the new direction of the U.S. policy. According to him, American efforts to demilitarize Japan might impede it from achieving economic independence; a weakened Japan would only be subject to more chaos and disorder.[12] Soon afterwards, a report prepared by Clifford Strike's Overseas Consultants Incorporated (the Strike Report) suggested halting the removal of most Japanese heavy industry as reparation and supplying funds for Japanese industrial revival.[13] Meanwhile, George F. Kennan, the architect of the containment policy, maintained that "the United States should devise policies toward Japan which would assume the security of that country from communist penetration and domination as well as from military attack by the Soviet Union and would permit Japan's economic potential to become once again an important force in the affairs of the area, conducive to peace and stability."[14]

In March, Undersecretary of the Army Major General William D. Draper, accompanied by prominent American businessmen Percy H. Johnston, Paul G. Huffman, and others, undertook a mission to Japan. The report of the Johnston Committee was the most authoritative in presenting the views of the Draper Mission. The Draper-Johnston Report urged a drastic decrease in reparations and an increase in Japanese industrial production that would be achieved by allowing Japan access to raw materials and markets in Asia. Advocating the eradication of any officially imposed barriers to Japanese foreign trade, the Draper Report suggested rebuilding the Japanese merchant marine and reopening Japan to foreign investments. It also endorsed retention of selected "primary war industries."[15] Aware of the deep hostility among Asian countries toward any signs of Japan's rehabilitation, the report argued that "we, in the United States, have been called upon to overcome deep and justifiable resentment in our attitude toward Japan. Neighboring nations have much to gain by the adoption of a new and more receptive attitude. The reciprocal advantages ensuing are unmistakable."[16] By 1948, the Japanese press openly informed its readers of the U.S. intention to rehabilitate Japan as a "protective wall" against the spread of communism in Asia.[17]

THE RESPONSE OF THE CHINESE PRESS TO THE "REVERSE COURSE"

U.S. policy toward Japan stimulated intense Chinese nationalistic opposition and resulted in exaggerated Chinese apprehension concerning the reemergence of Japan as a possible aggressor. For most Chinese, memories of the brutal war with Japan were still vivid. China had fought eight long years with Japan, lost more than 10 million lives, and was left with a completely devastated economy. Looking upon Japan as a dangerous economic rival and a potential invader, most Chinese could only view any signs of the former foe's revitalization with misgivings if not resentment.

In the eyes of many politically conscious Chinese, the American plan to restore Japan simply added insult to injury. They believed that the United States not only intended to rebuild Japan, thus threatening China, but also sought to make China's longtime enemy a potential ally. Concerned that China might become a pawn in a war between Russia and the United States, many Chinese nevertheless recoiled at the thought that Japan would become America's number one weapon against Russia in Asia. A letter to the editor of *North China Daily News,* a newspaper established by the British in Shanghai, summed up this concern: "America has been China's friend for many years. But unfortunately the condition has changed. America seems to be fixed in her policy of irreconcilable enmity towards Russia. She now loves China only to the extent that China can serve her as a weapon to fight Russia. And in that fight Japan will be her first and most important ally on this side of the world."[18]

Moreover, the revival of Japan would signify the evaporation of the Chinese hope for a predominant position in Asia. With the defeat of Japan in August 1945, many Chinese began to view their country as the rightful heir to the supreme economic and political position once occupied by Japan, and cherished the hope that China would eventually grow into a first-rate power. In 1948, however, China was deeply embroiled in the Civil War, and its hope of achieving economic and political strength in the near future became increasingly remote. While their own country was mired in political and economic crises, many urban Chinese were nevertheless bitter over the prospect of the rise of their former deadly enemy as the dominant economic power in Asia.

The Chinese press of diverse political leanings, including that controlled by the government, immediately denounced the new American attitude toward Japan. In fact, since the second half of 1946, major Chinese newspapers, such as *Dagong bao,* had begun to voice disapproval of the American occupation policy toward Japan. Criticizing the United States for acting unilaterally in designing the occupation policy, a number of newspapers expressed concerns over the "leniency" of SCAP's Japan policy. They claimed that American efforts to revitalize Japan's economy would lead to the revival of Japanese military ambitions.[19]

In the spring of 1947, a group of Chinese journalists visited Japan to inspect its postwar situation and returned with reports on rapid Japanese recovery and with the warning that Japan had not turned out to be as peaceful and democratic as China had wished to see. These reports resulted in further attacks on America's policy in Japan in the Chinese press. An article published by *The China Weekly Review* revealed the repercussions the American aid to Japan had aroused in the Chinese press. The article maintained that as the people who had suffered the most from the Japanese, the Chinese were raising their voices against the economic revival of Japan, "whether under the guise of making it pay for the occupation, securing a base against communism, financing food imports, or preserving 'a reasonable standard of living for the Japanese people.'" It concluded that the Chinese press was raising "a storm of protest, all shades of public opinion uniting on this issue."[20]

Viewing with alarm the measures the United States was taking to put Japan on its feet, many concerned Chinese feared that the reindustrialization of Japan would precede a revival of Japanese militarism. Major Chinese newspapers repeatedly referred to the Potsdam Declaration and claimed that recovery for Japan was equivalent to expansion of its war industry, a violation of the wartime agreement. They charged the United States with intending to increase Japan's war potential; implementing the concept of "a financial United States, an industrial Japan and an agricultural China"; and violating the stipulation of disarming Japanese arms by building up Japan as a bulwark against the Soviet Union. The Draper Proposal was especially condemned as constituting a U.S. plan to prepare Japan for war. The plan's recommendations of helping Japan achieve economic self-sufficiency were described as purely "ornamental words" to disguise its military aim in Japan.[21]

Wang Yunsheng, editor in chief of *Dagong bao*, was one of the most outspoken critics of the reversed American policy. Upon returning from his visit to Japan as a member of the Chinese delegation of journalists in spring 1947, he published 12 articles in *Dagong bao* under the general title of "Half a Month in Japan." His articles pointed to the danger of the new U.S. policy toward Japan.[22] In a subsequent letter to the editor of *Pacific Affairs*, Wang asserted that the United States was restoring Japan with the sole purpose of using Japan as a pawn in anti-Soviet activities. He argued that "American policy for controlling Japan, as General MacArthur represents it, is concerned neither with the reconstruction of Japan nor with the implementation of the Potsdam Declaration. Its root purpose is to utilize Japan as an instrument against Soviet Russia. What is aimed at is not the destruction of Japanese militarism, but preparation for a new war."[23]

Chinese sentiment regarding the "reverse course" for Japan was reported to Americans in the *New York Times*, in an article from Shanghai in late 1946 by an American journalist, Tillman Durdin. Durdin maintained that "the economic revival of Japan and the extent of the rapprochement between Japan and the United States" constituted a growing concern in China and led to "considerable resentment against the United States." The Japan issue was a significant ingredient in the development of anti-American emotions that pervaded "not only the Communists and their sympathizers in China, but also many others of different political complexions."[24]

SHANGHAI STUDENTS TAKE THE LEAD

The U.S. policy toward Japan continued to receive heated and emotional criticism from the major Chinese press up to 1948. Such press coverage provided a strong stimulus to the student anti-American movement. Spearheading the movement were the college students in Shanghai. In May 1948, Shanghai students launched a campaign denouncing U.S. economic plans for Japan. Protests soon reached nationwide proportions. College and high school students of major cities in the GMD-controlled regions again manifested their intense feelings by staging demonstrations and holding public meetings protesting America's Japan policy. The student movement of "Opposing the U.S. Support of Japan" (*fan MeifuRi*) in spring and summer of 1948 constituted the last significant campaign before the

Communist takeover. Its conduct suggests that anti-American attitudes, based on resurgent Chinese nationalism, extended well beyond the CCP and attracted the support of most Chinese moderates and even some elements of the GMD. In this sense, the estrangement between the United States and China after 1949 had more complex causes than merely the triumph of the Communists in the Chinese Civil War.

The CCP, however, benefited significantly from the political uproar created by the *fan MeifuRi* movement. Often working under the cover of Student Self-Governing Associations on campuses, underground Communist members put their organizational skills to work.[25] As the troops of the two rival political parties were engaged in the bloody war on the front, the CCP underground worked assiduously among the urban elite, especially the students, to build a "second front" in the GMD-controlled cities. Once seizing upon an issue with a popular appeal, the Communist propaganda machine began to move fast. Not surprisingly, the CCP directed ardent verbal attacks at U.S. policy in Japan. It denounced the American government as heir to German and Japanese imperialism. One of the CCP slogans for the International Labor Day of May 1, 1948, was "the working class and all the people of the country unite together to oppose America for its interference in China's internal affairs, its violation of Chinese sovereignty, and its support of the revival of the Japanese aggressive forces."[26] However, the fact that the Communists capitalized so readily on the Japan issue with a view to undermining the American image in China also demonstrated the issue's broad appeal.

Students in Shanghai transformed the *fan MeifuRi* sentiment in the press into powerful demonstrations and rallies on the street in May 1948. On the evening of the significant day of May 4, around 15,000 students from 120 universities and high schools gathered on the Democracy Square of Jiaotong University (or Jiaoda) for a bonfire rally denouncing the American policy of "building up" Japan. Meng Xianzhang, an economic specialist who had taken a strong interest in the shift in U.S. occupation policy, made a major speech titled "A Comprehensive Look at the American Policy of Building Up Japan." In his speech, Meng claimed that American aid to Japan was simply "indulging the tiger," which constituted a serious potential threat to China. He believed that Japan, like a rapidly growing tiger, would invade China again within the next 10 years. He predicted three courses of military actions that Japan could take in the future: (1) Japan would invade north China if war broke out between the United States and the Soviet Union; (2) the United States would send Japanese forces to China to fight the Communists when the latter's power grew overwhelmingly strong; and (3) the United States would use the Japanese against the Russians.[27] Though sounding sensational or propagandistic, Meng's views did point to the exaggerated Chinese fear that the U.S. policy of anticommunism could result in direct Japanese military action in China to stem the power of Chinese Communists, or in the dispatch of Japanese troops to China in the case of a war between the leading world powers.

The rally launched the Shanghai Student Association Opposing U.S. Support of Japan and Relieving the National Crisis (*Shanghaishi xuesheng fan MeifuRi, wanjiu minzu weiji lianhehui*) to coordinate the protest activities.[28] The newly established association subsequently initiated a "100,000-name petition drive" opposing U.S. aid to Japan. Students in several Shanghai universities founded a number of branch *fan MeifuRi* associations.[29]

At Fudan University, the *fan MeifuRi* Association held a *"fan MeifuRi* Week," during which around 400 students went into the Shanghai streets and lanes explaining to the general public the importance of opposing American efforts to rebuild Japan.[30] Meanwhile, students at Fudan also developed various other activities to publicize the issue. For example, they designated a Remembrance Day to recount the crimes the Japanese had committed during the wartime; a Correspondence Day to write to friends and relatives about the importance of *fan MeifuRi*; a Singing Day to learn *fan MeifuRi* songs; and an Exhibition Day to display *fan MeifuRi* posters.[31]

St. John's University, a missionary school founded and run by American Episcopal missionaries, figured prominently in the student *fan MeifuRi* movement, possibly because the police had largely refrained from intervening in student unrest there in the past and because the students were especially eager to dissociate themselves from their American linkage. In any case, on May 18, the Student Self-Governing Association of St. John's sponsored a joint student-professor meeting to discuss the Japan issue and concluded that the American policy of supporting Japan signified a new crisis for China. The fact that the Chinese professors in the institution openly criticized American policy in Japan disturbed the American faculty there, who believed that the speeches made by the professors only served to further provoke the students.[32]

On May 25, the Student Self-Governing Association of St. John's held a three-day *fan MeifuRi* exhibit. Anti-American posters featured, among other scenes, a figure representing the United States handing big bags of money over a fence to Japanese militarists, and offering ammunition and planes to the Japanese. It also showed General MacArthur placing a war helmet on the head of a huge ape representing Japan.[33] On May 29, at a press conference held on the campus by the Student Self-Governing Association, student representatives declared that, although St. John's was a university funded by American churches, the students were Chinese and they would never forget their own country. They insisted, however, that they were only against American policy of supporting Japan, and not against the American people.[34]

To broaden the basis of support for the movement, the Student Self-Governing Association of Jiaoda hosted a *fan MeifuRi* forum on June 3 and invited seven prominent figures from educational, industrial, and political circles as guest speakers. An estimated 3,500 people attended the forum. Wu Zhendong, chairman of the forum and head of Jiaoda's Student Self-Governing Association, made an opening speech in which he affirmed that Chinese youths, who always stood at the forefront of patriotic movements, would certainly stand up against the revitalization of "Japanese fascism" supported by "the American imperialists."

Shanghai mayor Wu Guozhen, who had surprisingly accepted the invitation and attended the forum, took the unpopular stand of defending American policy. He argued that the U.S. policy of building up Japan was to prevent the spread of communism, since the Japanese would turn to communism if they remained poor. He recommended appealing further to the United States for an increase in its aid to the Nationalist government to help eliminate the Communist menace in China. He then made the unpopular suggestion that students organize a rally in the name of "Requesting an Increase in American Aid to China to Relieve the National Crisis." Other panel members refuted Mayor Wu's claims.[35] Industrialist Zhang Chunbai spoke in a more sensational vein. The American policy would induce the Chinese people to be "the slaves of slaves," with the Chinese becoming subservient to the Japanese who in turn would be the slaves of the Americans. His speech drew warm responses from the audience.[36] In its report on the forum, *North China Daily News* also commented that the student movement opposing the U.S. support of Japan seemed to "gain momentum every day."[37]

Following the lead of Shanghai students' anti-American movement, around 2,000 students from 11 universities in Beiping held a *fan MeifuRi* rally on the Democracy Square of Beida in memory of the May Thirtieth Movement. This move linked a student movement targeting the Japanese and the British brutalities against the Chinese in the 1920s with the present student protests against the prospect of renewed Japanese imperialism assisted by the Americans.[38] Students from Yanjing University created a tableau depicting the "obsequious" gestures of the Japanese and the Nationalist leader Chiang Kai-shek in front of their American "masters."[39] By not taking a strong stand against the "reversed" American occupation in Japan, the GMD again appeared to have bowed to American influence and to have failed to protect Chinese national interests in the eyes of politically engaged Chinese.

The opposition to U.S. policy also received enthusiastic support from the intellectual community. For example, a group of 347 college presidents and professors from Shanghai universities sent a telegram to President Harry Truman and Secretary of State George Marshall in early June urging the United States to stop reviving Japan.[40] By this time, Chinese protest was too strong for Americans to ignore.

"DON'T BITE THE HAND THAT FEEDS YOU"

Chinese anti-American demonstrations in the postwar period often baffled and disturbed American observers, who failed to comprehend the nature of the intense Chinese responses to the American role in China. As a result, the responses of American officials in China tended to inflame rather than pacify Chinese nationalist sentiment. Confronted with widespread Chinese discontent over America's involvement, J. Leighton Stuart, American ambassador to China, stated in a memorandum to Washington in April 1947 that the generous American aid to the Chinese would certainly make Americans feel "a pained surprise at this apparent ingratitude." In an attempt to interpret the prevalent anti-Americanism, Stuart suggested that the most palpable explanation lay in American aid to China and the constant American proclamations of good intentions toward the Chinese people. These, he believed, had aroused high Chinese expectations. Inclined to rely on others, the Chinese had become accustomed to turning to Americans for help and invariably became anti-American when the Americans failed to meet their sense of need. As was the common practice of many American observers at the time, Stuart also conveniently attributed the intellectual opposition to the U.S. government to Communist engineering and manipulation.[41] American consul general John Cabot in Shanghai concluded in early 1948 that the Chinese had always blamed "foreigners for their troubles and the United States [had] become the number one whipping boy."[42]

In the face of the surging *fan MeifuRi* movement, some Americans in China, notably in Shanghai, grew uneasy and attempted to refute the charges made by Chinese intellectuals. The fact that St. John's, an institution founded and still largely funded by the Americans, assumed an eminent position in Shanghai students' protests especially dismayed the Americans in Shanghai. Consul General Cabot became the major spokesman rebutting the student accusations. On Memorial Day of 1948, he delivered a speech on the campus of St. John's in which he pointed to the unreasonableness of the student protests. Cabot asserted that those who received their education through the benevolence of the Americans, and whose daily food depended on the labor and the generosity of the American people, should not bite the hands that fed them. He believed that the students who took an anti-American stand were deceived by "sinister propaganda" employed by elements contriving to weaken the Sino-American relationship.[43]

Receiving wide coverage in local Chinese newspapers, Cabot's speech not surprisingly served only to arouse a tirade of bitter responses from the increasingly radicalized student circles. Most annoyed by Cabot's accusation of ingratitude and tone of condescension, some students at St. John's even pasted notices on campus walls requesting that the government nationalize the institution.[44] A pamphlet titled "The American Consul General Talks Nonsense" issued by the Federation of North China Students Opposing American Support of Japan and Resolving the National Crisis (hereafter, North China Student Association) vigorously attacked the speech. Most sensitive to Cabot's allusion to American "benevolence" and "righteousness" toward China, the pamphlet referred to the sale of American airplanes and gasoline to the "Japanese devils" while the Chinese were "spilling [their] blood" fighting against them during the early stage of the Sino-Japanese War. The pamphlet also reiterated the recent wrongs committed by American soldiers on the Chinese citizens. It concluded with a flourish of high sounding rhetoric: "Though the Chinese are poor, yet they still have pride. They will definitely not be the slaves of anyone."[45]

Considering "anti-American propaganda" to have "assumed alarming proportion" and to have been in danger of "getting beyond control," Ambassador Stuart then issued a long press statement on June 4 defending American policy in Japan and criticizing the growing antagonism in China toward the U.S. government. He maintained that as an old friend of Chinese intellectuals, he found the fact that academic circles formed "the core of anti-American agitation on the question of Japan" hard to accept. Stuart also suggested that it was ungrateful of Chinese students to launch an anti-American movement just when the United States had passed the China Aid Act. Warning that the student anti-American campaign might severely impair the traditional friendship between China and the United States and adversely affect U.S. aid to China, he argued that the charges of America's fostering Japanese military and economic imperialism were groundless.[46]

PUBLIC OPINION IN THE AFTERMATH OF STUART'S STATEMENT

As with Cabot's remarks, Stuart's public statement did more harm than good in terms of placating the *fan MeifuRi* sentiment. Stuart himself admitted that the verbal attacks leveled at him as a result of his statement had been "very widespread and violent, chiefly among editors, teachers and students."[47] His statement was widely quoted and commented upon in the unofficial Chinese press. He was especially reproved for adopting a "superior" attitude and a "menacing" tone and for lecturing to the Chinese. The newspaper of the General Labor Union, *Li bao*, issued a forthright editorial defending the students' anti-American movement. It argued that excessive American aid to "feudalistic forces in Japan," which constituted part of the U.S. national defense plan, endangered China's very existence. The paper censured Stuart for employing an "arrogant" tone and demanded to know how a small group of "instigators" could motivate a large number of students to take action.[48]

Apparently prompted by Cabot's speech and Stuart's statement, the influential *Dagong bao*, which had been a persistent critic of U.S. policy in Japan, published a lengthy editorial titled "An Analysis of the Anti-American Sentiment." The editorial argued that the student *fan MeifuRi* movement could not be provoked by "treacherous elements" or an act of impulsiveness for two reasons: the movement continued to grow and expand despite strong government discouragement, and the opposition to American policy of aiding Japan was not confined to the Chinese people alone. Asserting that Sino-American friendship should be built on "moral principles" instead of on "blind gratitude," the editorial suggested that the U.S. goverment's "generous acts" were often motivated by self-interest: "If the United States is aiding Japan simply out of concern for the Japanese people's livelihood, then from the humanitarian standpoint, the Chinese people would not have openly and firmly opposed it. However, the United States places national defense above everything else, and in all its international actions, it thinks only in terms of bases and strategies."[49]

According to the editorial, the United States' desire to maintain its status as the world leader led it to interfere, often unconsciously, in other nations' internal affairs. The article pointed especially to American nationalism and haughtiness. It quoted *Time* magazine as stating that "a century ago, when the world was girdled by the British Empire, the Englishman's voice sounded from the earth's far corners: 'I am a British subject.' Now, in the middle of the 20th century, the most arresting tones of history says something else: 'I am an American.'"[50]

In response to *Dagong bao*'s smoothly worded yet sharp criticism, the *Shanghai Evening Post and Mercury*, an English-language newspaper run by Americans, issued a harsh editorial titled "*Ta Kung Pao (Dagong bao)*: A Study in Decay." It claimed that *Dagong bao*'s editorial was "one of the cleverest and most persuasive pieces of apology for Chinese anti-Americanism" that had appeared, and expressed concern with the development of "a narrow, nationalistic jingoism" on the part of a newspaper that had enjoyed a reputation as moderate, independent, and one of the best in China. Regarding the reference to manifest American pride, the *Post* saw in it a revelation of the "inferiority complex" of *Dagong bao*'s editors. It harangued *Dagong bao*'s editors for inflaming anti-U.S. sentiment by erecting an "imaginary danger" regarding Japan, while distracting the Chinese from the real danger of the Soviet Union and the Chinese Communists. It charged that *Dagong bao* resorted to "anti-Japanese and anti-foreign jingoism" because it lacked courage to analyze domestic issues.[51]

Dagong bao did not respond to the *Post*'s rather harsh attack, but continued to publish editorials on events related to the question of Japan. It also published letters and statements from business and academic circles critical of Stuart's statement. For example, on June 9, *Dagong bao* printed two letters signed respectively by 14 and 19 readers in professional circles. Both letters criticized the "threatening tone" found in Stuart's statement as ill-befitting someone who held the position of ambassador and had spent years in China's educational field. The letters denied that the student movement was Communist instigated and declared that the students were essentially motivated by their conscience to fulfill their obligation to the nation of China and to the world. One letter charged that U.S. Japan policy was influenced by the American domestic need to relieve economic crisis and to serve the interests of "monopoly capitalists." It declared that China would not allow "a hungry tiger" to be reared beside it.[52]

Influential members from a broad spectrum of backgrounds responded to Stuart's statement. A group of 300 prominent women from educational and cultural circles made a public protest.[53] Two hundred eighty-eight Shanghai industrial, commercial, and educational leaders signed a statement of protest against American occupation policy in Japan. Meanwhile, 437 teachers from major universities in Beiping issued another statement addressed to Stuart. The teachers listed in great detail the "facts" involving American aid to Japan at the expense of Chinese national security and economic welfare. They claimed that Stuart had exposed his "true colors" by insulting and threatening the Chinese students for their patriotic movement.[54] An additional 88 faculty members of Qinghua University returned the rationing coupons for American relief food and signed the following declaration: "To oppose the American government's policy of building up Japan, to protest the slanders and insults inflicted on the Chinese people by American Consul Cabot in Shanghai and American Ambassador Stuart, and to demonstrate the Chinese people's dignity and integrity, we firmly refuse all relief materials supplied by America for the purpose of purchasing our souls."[55] Some students from Beida also smeared a paste made from relief flour on Democracy Wall and wrote on it "Chinese conscience cannot be purchased."[56]

Professor Zhu Ziqing of Qinghua University, a renowned literary figure and one of China's foremost essayists, died from disease and malnutrition on August 12, 1948. He reportedly asked his family immediately before his death not to purchase American relief flour since he had already signed the declaration.[57] During the Cold War era of the Chinese Communist confrontation with the United States, Zhu's story of "preferring death to taking American relief flour" became the content of Communist propaganda. He was repeatedly hailed as a national hero whose behavior demonstrated "national heroic integrity."

A "NEW HIGH TIDE" IN THE STUDENT ANTI-AMERICAN MOVEMENT

The student *fan MeifuRi* movement reached its peak in the aftermath of Stuart's statement. Infuriated by Stuart's singling out of student anti-American activity as "demonstrably false," student spokesmen pointed out that the Chinese press had been criticizing American policy in Japan for more than a year.[58] Regarding Stuart's remarks as another sign of American interference in China's internal affairs, an insult to Chinese national dignity, and a threat to the Chinese, student associations in various cities organized further demonstrations and protest meetings. The intense feelings against Stuart at Yanjing University, where he had previously served for many years as president, forced him to cancel his scheduled speech at its Commencement on June 29.[59]

A few days after Stuart's June 4 statement, the North China Student Association published a harsh message accusing Stuart of interfering with students' patriotic activities. It quoted figures proposed by various American groups, such as the Strike Committee and the Draper Mission, for raising the level of Japanese industrial production, and demanded reparations in the form of industrial equipment from Japan. The message maintained Chinese students' determination to oppose the alleged American policy of building up Japan at the expense of China, and claimed that no intimidation and suppression could stop students' patriotic movement.[60] Meanwhile, the North China Student Association also issued a sharply worded pamphlet that described Stuart's statement as deceitful, intimidating, and signaling "American imperialism's direct suppression of Chinese people's patriotic movement." The student leaders were especially sensitive to Stuart's emphasis on China's dependence upon American aid and to the perceived tone of arrogance and superiority in Stuart's statement.

To refute Stuart's suggestion that the anti-American movement was motivated by malicious intentions, the student leaders claimed emphatically that the movement arose out of the spontaneous expression of students' love for their country and world peace. They were particularly incensed by Stuart's warning that those who agitated against the United States on the issue of Japan ought to be prepared to "face the consequences" of their actions. "We do not know what 'consequences' are in Stuart's mind," the students wrote in the pamphlet. "Is it the stoppage of the so-called 'aid to China' so as to threaten the Chinese government into suppressing the students' patriotic movement?" According to the students, Stuart's statement simply signified the further intervention of "American imperialists" in the domestic affairs of China and their restraining of the Chinese patriotic movements.[61]

The North China Student Association also issued an open letter addressed "To Our American Friends." The letter emphasized traditional Chinese-American friendship and targeted U.S. aid to Japan. It read in part:

There has been a long traditional friendship between the peoples of China and America, and during the war the two peoples fought side by side against Japan. The Chinese people will never forget the aid and assistance from America in their resistance against Japan. Today in order to prevent the implementation of the erroneous peace threatening U.S. policy, to realize the Potsdam agreement, and to maintain world peace, we appeal to the peace loving people of China and America to urge the U.S. government to change its present policy toward Japan.[62]

On June 9, between 4,000 and 5,000 students from nine universities in Beiping held a *fan MeifuRi* demonstration. The North China Student Association and Beida's Students' Self-Governing Association distributed leaflets protesting American aid to Japan. One leaflet, with a large number of signatories, claimed vehemently that the United States was restoring Japan's military strength (in their vehement attacks on the U.S. occupation policy in Japan, the students seldom mentioned the "no-war" clause in Japan's Constitution of 1947). This pamphlet was also very particular in its indictments. It accused the United States of acting unilaterally and arbitrarily in making decisions regarding occupation policies and of implementing a dangerous, selfish, and mistaken Japan policy in obvious violation of the Potsdam Declaration. As a consequence of the new American policies, the pamphlet argued, Japan had established a "Sea Peace Preservation Department" in preparation for the reestablishment of the Navy Ministry, increased its police force, and renewed its insults upon the Chinese nationals in Japan. The pamphlet listed the Japanese police's firing on Taiwanese in the Shibuya Tragedy,[63] the closing of Chinese restaurants, the search of Chinese business establishments in Yokohama and Tokyo, the strict limitations placed on the luggage carried home by Chinese in Japan, the use of the demeaning term "Zhi Na" for China, and the use of the insulting term "Third National" in referring particularly to Chinese and Koreans.[64] The pamphlet argued that, as a victorious nation and one of the "Big Four," China could not permit such developments. The leaflet also accused the United States of turning the wartime Japanese-sponsored "Japan-Manchukuo-China" policy into an American-supported triangular relationship consisting of "America's dollars, Japan's factories and China's raw materials and markets." Consequently, it urged the Chinese people to unite and develop a powerful national diplomacy.

To further enliven and dramatize the demonstration and to make a stronger appeal to the common people, the demonstrating students also sang anti-American songs. One, titled *"Fan MeifuRi* March," ran as follows:

> March on! March on bravely!
> Fear not bayonets, fear not iron rods.
> Oppose firmly American support of Japan.
> For we have no wish to be slaves.

Another song, "Oppose U.S. Support of Japan," contained equally poignant wordings:

> Fellow country, with one heart
> Oppose the support of Japan.
> We must swear to death to oppose,
> To oppose the American support of the rise of Japan.
> Let us join together to form an iron wall
> To defeat the American and Japanese bandits,
> To attack the American and Japanese Fascist tyrants,
> To march on toward the path of new life.[65]

Slogans written in English issued for and shouted during this demonstration included: "Prevent a Second 'Marco Polo Bridge Incident'";[66] "The Peoples of China and America Stand Up Together to Protest U.S. Reviving Japanese Imperialism"; "Patriotic Chinese Stand Up to Overcome Our National Crisis"; "Long Live the Independence of Chinese Nation!"[67]

During the June 9 parade, members of the propaganda team wrote down slogans everywhere with chalk and even with pitch. They delivered emotional speeches to the people on the street reminding them of the menace of renewed Japanese militarism. A tableau was also created to attract the attention of more people. It featured Japanese soldiers beating the Chinese, with Americans standing by laughing and saying "tinghao, tinghao" (very good, very good). The work of the propaganda team appeared to have aroused the emotions of ordinary people on the street, who responded with remarks about how hard life was while Beiping was under Japanese control.[68] The student demonstrators eventually clashed with the local policemen, who fired shots into the air and attempted to hem the students in by beating them with belts.[69]

The Shanghai Student Association had planned a large-scale *fan MeifuRi* parade of 120 universities and high schools to be held on June 5. However, it failed to materialize because cordons of heavily armed police and troops had locked the campus gates of major universities, surrounded the universities, and forcefully confined the students to campuses.[70] Nonetheless, around 7,000 students still managed to gather in front of U.S. Naval Forces Headquarters. They were dispersed by police and troops, who arrested about 30 of the demonstrators.[71]

In the aftermath, the mayor of Shanghai, Wu Guozhen, started a campaign against the student leaders. Determined to uncover the organizers of the movement and bring them to trial, he targeted the Student Self-Governing Association of Jiaoda, the hotbed of the *fan MeifuRi* movement in Shanghai, using President Cheng Xiaogang as the intermediary. Consequently, student leaders at Jiaoda began a "war of nerves" (*shenjing zhan*) with Mayor Wu. The two parties engaged in a heated exchange of questions and answers regarding the *fan MeifuRi* movement, which was played up in the local press.

In response to Mayor Wu's charges, the students defended their positions on the grounds that they were patriotic gestures, motivated by grave concerns for the survival of the nation, and were not inspired by Communist elements. They claimed that Mayor Wu, in forcefully suppressing the movement, had not only violated the students' "human rights," but also acted contrary to the interests of the Chinese nation.[72]

Public opinion rallied on the side of the students. The local press described Mayor Wu's verbal contest with the students as "ridiculous." On June 21, Tang Wenzhi and Zhang Yuanji, presidents of Jiaoda 40 years before, published "An Open Letter to Mayor Wu Guozhen" in *Dagong bao*, in which they argued that "American support of Japan truly endangers the very existence of our nation economically and militarily. This action has enraged the people of the whole nation." The letter explained that the students held demonstrations to express their feelings out of pure patriotism and demanded that Mayor Wu cease his persecutions. Incensed by the whole incident, Nationalist leader Chiang Kai-shek immediately called the heads of the Shanghai Party Department and the City Council to his office in Nanjing. Chiang chided them for their failure at politics since the most respected GMD statesmen (in reference to Tang Wenzhi and Zhang Yuanji) had been won over by the "Communists," a clear indication of the Nationalists' losing the heart of the people.[73]

The resignation of President Cheng Xiaogang of Jiaoda at the peak of the "war of nerves" drastically advertised his discontent with Mayor Wu's behavior and testified to the erosion of any middle ground in the debates. The student leaders at Jiaota then organized a *fan MeifuRi* meeting and invited prominent figures of known leftist tendencies from cultural and educational circles, including Ma Yinchu, a well-known economist, and Xu Guangping, wife of the late literary giant Lu Xun, to make speeches in support of the student activities.[74] In this sense, Mayor Wu's "war of nerves" with the students at Jiaoda drew more public support to the side of the students.

After the rise of the student anti-American movement in Shanghai and Beiping, the movement quickly spread to other cities, including Guangzhou, Kunming, Nanjing, Qingdao, Fujian, Chengdu, Chongqing, Wuhan, and Changsha.[75] The *fan MeifuRi* student movement in Kunming was especially noteworthy since more than 10,000 college and high school students participated in the protest parade held in mid-June, which made the parade one of the largest in the *fan MeifuRi* movement. The subsequent mass arrests of the student protesters by the local authorities and the ensuing student protests against the arrests made the Kunming student movement the most polarized one of the nationwide *fan MeifuRi* movement.[76]

Concerned over the political situation in China and hoping to be of some service to the home country, the Chinese Students' Christian Association in North America sponsored a conference in July 1948. Over one hundred Chinese students from universities all over America and eastern Canada attended the conference and passed six resolutions. The general secretary of the association then sent a copy of the resolutions to Mrs. Eleanor Roosevelt to share with her their beliefs that the protesting students in China were "in neither political camp in the civil war." The resolutions reflected to a certain extent the political attitude of the students studying in North America at the time. They called for a coalition government, agrarian reform, disconnection of the Christian churches in China from repressive political forces, and better preparation by all Chinese students to make real contributions to the construction of China.

Moreover, the Chinese students in North America demanded that except for the aid directly benefiting the Chinese people, the United States should stop all military, financial, and economic aid, which served to stimulate the "corrupt and reactionary elements" in the Nationalist government and helped to prolong the Chinese Civil War. They opposed the shift in American occupation policy in Japan, refuted Stuart's statement, and proclaimed their support for the nationwide student protests in China. Stuart's statement, according to the student resolutions, "attempted to stifle democratic expression and intimidate our whole nation." It also called on Chinese students to help promote American friends' understanding of the true nature of the present struggle in China.[77]

By the second half of 1948, the peak of the student *fan MeifuRi* movement had passed. The students had effectively made their voices heard and in the process had helped radicalize non-Communist elements among the Chinese intellectual community, which by this point had joined the CCP in support of an anti-American, nationalistic foreign policy. The Chinese press, however, continued for some time more with published criticism of the "reverse course" and warnings about the danger of a resurgent Japan. On the third anniversary of Japan's surrender, most major Chinese newspapers simply increased attacks upon America's policy in Japan. Predicting the coming of another world war in view of tense international relations, many papers warned of the menace a revived Japan would pose to China. Some demanded the executions of Japanese war criminals because of the crimes they had committed in China and to eliminate the root of Japanese aggression.[78]

Unable to comprehend the depth of Chinese anti-Americanism, Ambassador Stuart puzzled over the fact that young educated Chinese made such a great cause out of America's building up of Japan, which was merely "a hypothetical fear in a far-away future." He wondered why they did not instead direct their patriotic efforts to the Soviet Union and alert "the nation to the immediate danger as dramatized by the loss of Outer Mongolia and the imminent loss of Inner Mongolia, the Northeast (Manchuria), etc." Stuart thus observed that reminding the students of Russian behavior in northern China stimulated "nothing but airy skepticism as to the facts or mute indifference." He nevertheless found the phenomenon significant. "It is a strange psychosis but one that must be reckoned with especially if—as has usually been the case—what the students are thinking now is an index of what the nation as a whole will soon be thinking."[79]

Stuart's bafflement over the less enthusiastic reaction of the educated Chinese toward Russian encroachment was shared by other American observers in China. Consul James Pilcher found it strange that "nationalistic feeling can be stirred up against the U.S. despite traditional friendship rather than against Soviet Russia, which had done so much more to offend Chinese nationalist sensibilities."[80] An editorial in *The China Press Review* also argued that Chinese students and intellectuals were stumbling into the "well-known pitfall" of ignoring the menace that the Russians posed to northern China yet being intensely critical of the role the U.S. played in China. Chinese students

yell about American encroachment in South and Central China, American influence with the present regime in Nanking, American interference with the nation's internal affairs by the granting of economic and monetary aid to Nanking and by the arming and training of Nanking's troops, but they never object to the extraterritorial privileges of the Russians in Dairen, nor of [*sic*] their dominant position in the railroad connecting China with Siberia. . . . This same "blind spot" is observable among many Chinese professors and other intellectuals who are actively opposed to the present Government.[81]

Marshall Carter, special assistant to the secretary of state, also believed that the political attention of the Chinese students should be directed to the Soviet Union.

Pointing to the fact that the students concentrated on attacking the United States to the exclusion of the Soviet Union, Carter suggested that students should pay more attention to the various special rights and privileges the Soviets enjoyed at Lushun and Dalian in Manchuria. The Soviet violations, Carter suggested, typified a kind of intervention in Chinese domestic affairs.[82]

The swelling anti-American sentiment among politically conscious Chinese was indeed not matched by their demonstrated anti-Russian feeling, which was much milder in comparison during this period. Deepening Chinese anti-American sentiment in 1948 resulted largely from the U.S. government's "interference" in China's internal affairs, and also from the unpopular American occupation policy in Japan. While the Soviet Union had certainly won its share of unpopularity among Chinese intellectuals through its actions in Manchuria, the Soviets did not play as conspicuous a role as the United States in China's domestic politics, and therefore did not incur large-scale intellectual protests.

THE OFFICIAL REACTION TO *FAN MEIFURI*

The official opposition to the *fan MeifuRi* movement had been lukewarm before Stuart's statement. The Nationalist government seemed to allow a certain degree of latitude as long as the turmoil did not directly target the GMD. Possibly sharing some of the feelings expressed forcibly by the students, the Nationalist government had largely refrained from arousing further public uproar by forcibly suppressing a movement based on nationalism. However, following Stuart's formal criticism of the student movement, the GMD officials grew more concerned over the possible adverse effect of anti-American activities on U.S. aid to China in particular and on U.S.-China relations at large. Meanwhile, the veiled and sometimes direct attacks on Chiang Kai-shek and the Nationalist regime during the student *fan MeifuRi* protests also enraged the authorities. Armed government police and troops began to forestall or break up student demonstrations with vigor and to keep students under surveillance, and many more student activists were thrown into prison. Chinese foreign minister Wang Shijie immediately declared in a public statement that, despite some Chinese apprehension concerning America's policy in Japan, the Chinese public held no ill feelings toward the United States. In a speech to the board of trustees of Nanjing University, a missionary-funded school, Vice Minister of Education Han Liwu emphasized traditional Chinese-American cultural ties and denounced the present agitation against America as unjustifiable.[83]

The GMD authorities also could not have failed to realize the importance of Japan's economic recovery for economic development and progress in China in particular and East Asia in general. Vice President Sun Fu commented in June 1947 that China ought to make early peace with Japan to guarantee that Japan would never rise again as an aggressor and that it would make proper contributions to peace and stability in East Asia. According to him, China should be prepared to resume commercial relations with Japan since each needed the goods and services that the other could provide.[84]

Meanwhile, the official newspapers also departed from their previous reproachful tone regarding U.S. policy toward Japan and in unison praised Stuart's statement. Together with the official *Zhongyang ribao, Xinwen bao, Shen bao,* and *Heping ribao* all suggested that professional students acting as Communist agents misled and misinformed industrial, commercial, and educational leaders. They found Stuart's statement to have been made with the "best intentions" and called it "moving." *Zhongyang ribao* claimed that Stuart's explanation would help to dispel Chinese misunderstandings. *Shen bao* explained that the purpose of American efforts to rebuild Japan was to contain communism, and that the anti-American movement inspired by Chinese Communists simply demonstrated the conflict of interests between Communists and Americans in Asia. Therefore, the United States should counter the student anti-American movement with more aid to China.[85] This change of attitude on the part of major conservative newspapers smacked of influence from or pressure exerted by the Nationalist government. Ironically, these actions only served to increase the intellectual perception of the GMD as a puppet of the U.S. government. In the end, the overwhelming public support for the movement forced the government to ease the direct attack on the activists for the time being and to try to bring the movement to a halt by ending the semester early and sending the students home.[86]

IMPLICATIONS OF THE *FAN MEIFURI* MOVEMENT

Stimulated by the extensive press coverage and by the marked signs of the American commitment to rebuilding Japan during the early months of 1948, a great number of Chinese students in Shanghai, Beiping, and other GMD-controlled cities reacted vehemently to the U.S. "reverse course" in Japan. Many feared that the reorientation of American occupation policy in Japan would lead to a revival of Japanese militarism. They resented the United States for aiding a country that had been a common foe not too long before, and responded readily to the rallying cries of *fan MeifuRi.* As the most outspoken political critics within the GMD-controlled cities, increasingly assertive radical students launched a movement that found verbal support from many prominent Chinese. Distinguished professors, scholars, businessmen, lawyers, cultural figures, and even government officials demonstrated concerns and indignation over the prospect of Japanese military recovery.

Furthermore, politically alert young Chinese found in the *fan MeifuRi* protests an effective outlet for their profound discontent with America's postwar policy. In his report to Washington in early 1948, Consul General Cabot of Shanghai described the hostile attitude toward the U.S. government as evinced in the non-Communist Chinese press, particularly in the Shanghai and Nanjing regions. According to Cabot, the Chinese press accused the United States of "economic imperialism, power politics, dollar diplomacy, ruthless expansion and monopolistic practices."[87] Although harboring genuine concerns about a militarily revived Japan, politically aware Chinese were increasingly frustrated with the bleak economic and political reality in GMD-controlled China and believed that the American involvement had simply prolonged their misery. In the midst of the seething Chinese discontent with the U.S. "interference" in Chinese affairs, the

American policy of reconstructing Japan served as a lightning rod for popular grievances. Through protesting the U.S. "reverse course" in Japan, many students vented their bitterness on a subject that had tremendous appeal.

The attack on American policy in Japan was as much a reproof of the Chiang regime as it was a vilification of the U.S. government. Already holding various grievances against the GMD, radical Chinese were further disillusioned with their government's weak stand toward U.S. occupation policy in Japan, for its failure to uphold Chinese interests and for its dependence upon the American support. For example, some posters at an antigovernment, anti-American exhibit organized by the students from Shanghai College of Law likened Chiang Kai-shek to Yuan Shikai, implying that Chiang acted as a traitor in acquiescing to U.S. policy toward Japan the same way that Yuan had accepted Japan's humiliating "21 Demands" three decades before.[88]

The nationwide student *fan MeifuRi* protests enjoyed even broader support than the *kangbao* movement of the previous year. This was partially due to the fact that the Nationalist goverment was rapidly losing credibility and the Civil War. The political climate created by the *fan MeifuRi* movement greatly benefited the CCP. It served as a kind of shield that prevented the GMD authorities from resorting too readily to high-handed measures and that allowed the underground Communists to merge more easily with the student protesters to protect themselves.[89] By working actively among the students and claiming to stand at the forefront of the movement, the CCP made effective alliance with influential members of Chinese society. Furthermore, the GMD inadvertently assisted the Communist cause by identifying the CCP with a popular movement. Accordingly, the CCP appeared to be the better defenders of Chinese national interests and garnered more credibility. In this sense, the *fan MeifuRi* movement featured prominently in paving the way for the ultimate Communist urban victory. The CCP used the movement to its advantage because of its wide appeal. However, the movement also revealed elements of student spontaneity; as Wasserstrom argues, "it is inaccurate to think of [student] protests in black and white terms, as either purely 'spontaneous' or purely 'orchestrated' affairs; most of them fall into the large gray area between these poles."[90]

Some American diplomats in China also admitted that the *fan MeifuRi* movement did not arise purely out of "Communist machinations." In a report to Washington, Consul General O. Edmund Clubb of Beiping suggested that "the propaganda voiced by the students in their present demonstrations is after all in general line with editorials which have been appearing recently in the columns of the various official press." While maintaining that "professional students" planted in the leading universities inspired and organized the student *fan MeifuRi* movement, he conceded that "they could not have created the prevalent mood."[91]

In early June, American vice consul Alfred Jenkins in Beiping undertook a study of the forces behind the *fan MeifuRi* student demonstrations. He interviewed a number of people who provided him with different explanations as to the causes of the movement. Besides the theory that it was Communist inspired, Jenkins also noted that some interviewees even believed the GMD was initially behind the movement because of its opposition to the "reverse course" and its dissatisfaction with the amount of American aid to the Nationalist government. Some claimed that the movement was spontaneous and represented true feelings among the students, while others asserted that many students who opposed the American aid to China found in *fan MeifuRi* a means to release their feelings, which they could not otherwise manifest as safely.[92]

The increasingly hostile students stood in the forefront of the new wave of the anti-American campaign. Obviously, it was beyond the power of Chinese youths to sway American policy-making decisions regarding Japan, but the student *fan MeifuRi* movement significantly influenced Chinese public opinion. The movement quickly gained force and assumed the form of a widespread popular opposition movement. An American diplomat reported to Washington in early June that the *fan MeifuRi* movement seemed to have aroused a previously dormant middle group or the third force, including politically neutral students and the general public, to action.[93] Significantly, many American policymakers, such as John Carter Vincent, had once described these moderates as the foundation of a democratic, pro-American China.

John Cabot considered the Chinese public opinion in the aftermath of Stuart's statement and his own Memorial Day speech as reaching a "hysterical state." He believed that distorted Communist propaganda was met with wide acceptance. "As a result," Cabot affirmed, "even some who are friendly to us feel that the statement and the speech were a mistake."[94] At the peak of the *fan MeifuRi* agitation, Cabot repeatedly urged Washington to send him factual information pertaining to the specific charges made by the Chinese.[95] Stuart again attempted to find the cause of anti-American demonstrations in Chinese psychology and attributed it to what he believed to be the Chinese habit of seeking a scapegoat in times of hopelessness.[96]

Increasingly perturbed by the uproar of protests in China and other Asian countries in response to U.S. "reversed" policy in Japan, officials in Washington launched a propaganda campaign to counteract the anti-American agitation. The campaign focused on emphasizing the need to restore the Japanese economy to ensure the economic stability of Asia and assuring the Asians that an economically prosperous Japan would not become a military menace to world peace again.[97]

In mid-June, Information Officer Allen Haden from the Office of the United States Political Adviser for Japan held a conversation with two members of the Chinese Military Mission to the Allied Council in Japan: Dr. Wu Wenzao, chief of the political section, and Major Qian Mingnian, public relations officer. The conversation focused on the Chinese press and student agitation against the United States and its policy in Japan. Both Wu and Qian emphasized that authentic public apprehensions regarding the reversed policy toward Japan should be distinguished from blind assaults on the United States. Wu reiterated the Chinese fear that a strengthened Japan as a bulwark against the Soviet Union could lead to renewed Japanese aggression against Asian neighbors and that a newly industrialized Japan would again dump cheap goods onto the China market. He suggested that if the United States could officially offer a promise of protection in the case of renewed Japanese aggression, Chinese public opinion would be mollified. Haden concluded from the meeting that although members of the China Mission might not be in accord with the general anti-American sentiment, they definitely sympathized with the Chinese agitation against the U.S. Japan policy.[98]

To find a means to address these concerns, Haden undertook a trip in late July to China and the Philippines where agitation against the economic revival of Japan was also strong. He subsequently produced his own evaluation of the situation and recommendations. He believed that a genuine fear of potential Japanese aggression and a sense of inferiority to Japanese capacity characterized Chinese and Filipino criticisms of SCAP. The fact that Japan was recovering rapidly alarmed public opinion in these countries. According to Haden, more publicity on Japan's economic recovery would serve no useful purpose. In the case of China, Haden recommended molding public opinion by confining publicity to information on the demilitarization of Japan, on reparations favorable to China, and on Chinese exports to Japan. All references to American magnanimity toward the Japanese should be avoided, and any news on "rehabilitation" and the word "rehabilitation" should be shunned.[99] By this stage, however, such cosmetic changes were too little, too late.

The *fan MeifuRi* movement was nationalistic in its inspiration and originated in the Chinese fear of a revival of Japanese economic and military aggression. It further discredited the U.S. government and its position in China in the eyes of many politically conscious Chinese. When Francis Styles, an American consul in Shanghai, suggested an increase in United States Information Service (USIS) materials at St John's to offset the "flood of Communist inspired propaganda there," the acting president of the university told him frankly that it would be of no use. According to the latter, USIS materials would definitely fail to "foster a more understanding and friendly attitude by the students toward the United States." Continued American intervention in China's affairs would doom any efforts in this regard. Consequently, "any American attempts, no matter how cautious, at political indoctrination would in all probability backfire."[100]

Upon seizing power in 1949, the CCP leadership, in order to maintain and heighten the momentum of the Chinese revolution, continued its self-claimed role as the anti-imperialist champion. In the early 1950s, the nationwide "Resist America, Aid Korea" campaign became an outstanding political cause. In staging the anti-American campaign, the Communist organizers made extensive use of the prominent anti-American issues developed in the late 1940s. The American occupation policy toward Japan assumed new significance and served as one of the flagrant examples of "American aggressions against the Chinese people."

NOTES

1. For a discussion of the movement, see Joseph K.S. Yick, *Making Urban Revolution in China: The CCP-GMD Struggle for Beiping-Tianjin, 1945–1949* (Armonk, N.Y.: M.E. Sharpe, 1995), 104–11.

2. From Clubb to the Secretary of State, April 6, 1948, in U.S. Department of State, *Foreign Relations of the United States [FRUS], 1948, The Far East: China* (Washington, D.C.: Government Printing Office, 1973), 7:184.

3. See *The China Weekly Review*, January 31, 1948.

4. "Students' Anti-Starvation–Anti-Civil War Activities in Tientsin," from Smyth to Stuart, June 3, 1947, RG59, 893.00/6-347, National Archives (hereafter NA).

5. "Political Attitude of Nanking Students," memorandum by American Public Affairs Officer, Josiah Bennett, October 17, 1947, RG59, 893.00/10-1747, NA. In his report, Bennett also claimed that emotion rather than objectivity characterized the students' anti-American feelings. According to him, Chinese students often failed to notice the American aversion to the inefficiency and corruption in the Nationalist government. They did not understand that much of the American aid to China had been motivated by "humanitarian motive rather than by sinister design." Fundamentally, Bennett argued, the students' frustration with the United States stemmed from the latter's support of a government from which the students had withdrawn loyalty.

6. For details on the China Aid Act, see U.S. Department of State, *The China White Paper: August 1949* (1949; reprint, Stanford: Stanford University Press, 1967), 991–93.

7. In a letter to *The China Weekly Review*, one Chinese wrote that despite the goodwill American taxpayers held for China, American aid, being one-sided, simply compounded the already complicated Chinese political situation, and therefore failed to win the people's goodwill. See *The China Weekly Review*, July 24, 1948.

8. See John Cabot to Secretary of State, October 22, 1948, RG59, 893.00/10-2248, NA.

9. John K. Fairbank, "China's Prospect and U.S. Policy," *Far Eastern Survey* 16 (July 2, 1947): 145. American Consul General John Cabot in Shanghai also recognized the less desirable effect of the American China aid program on Chinese public opinion. In a memo to Secretary of State Marshall, he warned that "unclarified aid" to the Nationalist government could have several ill effects: "(1) strengthening of far left groups; (2) indefinite continuation and extension of civil war; and (3) fostering of anti-Americanism in liberal groups through latter's claim of non-support and in reactionary groups by their claim of inadequate support." From Cabot to the Secretary of State, April 27, 1948, *FRUS, 1948, The Far East: China*, 7:211.

10. John D. Dower, *Embracing Defeat: Japan in the Wake of World War II* (New York: W.W. Norton, 1999), 526. Although the period from August 1945 to April 1952 when Japan was under foreign control was officially known as the Allied occupation of Japan, in reality, the United States dominated every aspect of the occupation. For discussions on U.S. occupation of Japan, see Michael Schaller, *The American Occupation of Japan: The Origins of the Cold War in Asia* (New York: Oxford University Press, 1985); Akira Iriye, *The Cold War in Asia* (Englewood Cliffs, N.J.: Prentice-Hall, 1974); Roger Buckley, *Occupation Diplomacy: Britain, the United States, and Japan, 1945–1952* (New York: Cambridge University Press, 1982); Theodore Cohen, *Remaking Japan: The American Occupation as New Deal* (New York: New Press, 1987); and Dower, *Embracing Defeat*.

11. Quoted from D.S. Holman, "Japan's Position in the Economy of the Far East," *Pacific Affairs* 20 (December 1947): 371.

12. See Samuel S. Stratton, "The Far Eastern Commission," *Far Eastern Survey* 16 (August 25, 1948): 191.

13. Schaller, *American Occupation of Japan*, 120.

14. Quoted from Iriye, *Cold War in Asia*, 173.

15. Schaller, *American Occupation of Japan*, 129–30.

16. See Jerome B. Cohen, "Japan: Reform vs. Recovery," *Far Eastern Survey* 17 (June 23, 1948): 141.

17. *New York Times*, August 9, 1948.

18. *North China Daily News*, June 7, 1948.

19. See, for example, *Lianhe ribao*, October 15; *Shen bao*, December 8; *Xinwen bao*,

December 8; *Dagong bao*, October 4.

20. *The China Weekly Review*, July 14, 1947.

21. See "Fandui Deleibe jihua" (Oppose the Draper plan), *Dagong bao*, May 28, 1948.

22. *Dagong bao*, Shanghai, March 22 to April 15, 1947.

23. Wang Yun-sheng, "Japan—Storm Center of Asia," *Pacific Affairs* 21 (June 1948): 195.

24. *New York Times*, November 2, 1946.

25. Books published in the People's Republic of China on the various student movements after the May Fourth Movement invariably emphasize the significant role played by the Communist activists in an effort to underscore the righteousness of the Communist cause. For a study of the Communist influence on the Student Self-Governing Association of Jiaoda, see Thomas D. Lutze, "New Democracy: Chinese Communist Relations with the Urban Middle Forces, 1931–1952" (Ph.D. diss., University of Wisconsin at Madison, 1996), 416–24.

26. Beijing daxue lishixi, *Beijing daxue xuesheng yundongshi*, 242.

27. For a full text of Meng Xianzhang's speech, see Qinghua daxue xuesheng zizhihui, *Qinghua yuekan* (Qinghua monthly) (May 28, 1948): 3–5.

28. Zhou Wangjian, "Huiyi Shanghai xuesheng fan MeifuRi yundong" (A recollection of the Shanghai student movement opposing the American support of Japan), in *Wenshi ziliao xuanji* (A selected collection of cultural and historical materials), 24 (1979): 155–57; Shanghai daxue et al., *Xinbian Zhongguo xiandaishi* (A new edition of modern Chinese history) (Nanchang: Jiangxi renmin chubanshe, 1987), 282; Gongqingtuan Shanghai shiwei, eds., *1945–1949: Shanghai xuesheng yundongshi* (1945–1949: A history of the Shanghai student movement) (Shanghai: Renmin chubanshe, 1983), 159–60.

29. Wang Niankun, *Xuesheng yundong shiyao jianghua* (An account of important historical events of student movements) (Shanghai: Shanghai chubanshe, 1951), 93; A Zhe, *Zhongguo xiandai xuesheng yundong jianshi* (A short history of modern Chinese student movements) (Hong Kong: Dasheng chubanshe, no date), 161–62.

30. Gongqingtuan Shanghai shiwei, *1945–1949*, 167.

31. Lutze, "New Democracy," 429.

32. From Cabot to the Secretary of State, May 27, 1948, RG59, 893.00/5-2748, NA.

33. Ibid., May 28, 1948, RG59, 893.00/5-2848, NA.

34. See *Dagong bao*, May 30, 1948; Gongqingtuan Shanghai shiwei, *1945–1949*, 171.

35. Gongqingtuan Shanghai shiwei, *1945–1949*, 171.

36. Ibid. See also Cabot to the Secretary of State, June 4, 1948, RG59, 893.00/6-448, NA.

37. *North China Daily News*, June 2, 1948.

38. The event that triggered the May Thirtieth Incident was the killing of a Chinese worker of a Japanese-owned textile mill by the Japanese guards. This led to student protest demonstrations, strikes by workers, and a number of arrests. On May 30, 1925, thousands of students and workers held a parade in the Shanghai International Settlement protesting the killing of the Chinese worker and demanding the release of the six students arrested by the British. They were fired upon by the police under the order of the British inspector and 11 were killed. (Janathan D. Spence, *The Search for Modern China*, 2d ed. (New York: W.W. Norton, 1999), 322–23.

39. See *Dagong bao*, May 30, 1948; Beijing daxue xuesheng zizhihui, eds., *Beida 1946–1948* (Beiping, 1948), 12–13; Beijing daxue lishixi, *Beijing daxue xuesheng yundongshi, 1919–1949* (A history of the student movement of Beijing University, 1919–1949) (Beijing: Beijing chubanshe, 1979), 243; Song Bai, *Beijing xiandai gemingshi* (A revolu-

tionary history of modern Beijing) (Beijing: Zhongguo renmin daxue chubanshe, 1988), 223.

40. From Cabot to the Secretary of State, June 24, 1948, RG59, 893.00/6-248, NA; Gongqingtuan Shanghai shiwei, *1945–1949,* 170.

41. "Anti-American Feeling in China," from Stuart to the Secretary of State, April 22, 1947, RG59, 711.93/4-2247, NA.

42. From Cabot to the Secretary of State, in *FRUS, 1948, The Far East: China,* 7:33.

43. Gongqingtuan Shanghai shiwei, *1945–1949,* 168; Beijing daxue lishixi, *Beijing daxue xuesheng yundongshi,* 243.

44. From Cabot to the Secretary of State, June 3, 1948, in *FRUS, 1948, The Far East: China,* 7:271.

45. "Anti-American Demonstration and Propaganda," from Clubb to Stuart, June 11, 1946, RG59, 893.00/6-1148, NA.

46. For Stuart's full text, see *U.S. Department of State, The China White Paper,* 869–71.

47. From Stuart to the Secretary of State, June 30, 1948, *FRUS, 1948, The Far East: China,* 7:328.

48. Translation of the article was included in Consul Pilcher's memorandum to the Secretary of State, June 9, 1948, RG59, 893.00/6-948, NA.

49. *Dagong bao,* June 7, 1948.

50. Ibid.

51. *The Shanghai Evening Post and Mercury,* June 8, 1948.

52. *Dagong bao,* June 9, 1948.

53. Zhonghua quanguo funu lianhehui funu yundong lishi yanjiushi, eds., *Zhongguo funu yundong lishi ziliao, 1945–1949* (Historical records on women's movement in China, 1945–1949) (Beijing: Zhongguo funu chubanshe, 1991), 218.

54. *Dagong bao,* June 14, 1948.

55. Qinghua daxue xiaoshi bianxiezu, *Qinghua daxue xiaoshigao* (The history of Qinghua University) (Beijing: Zhonghua shuju, 1981), 485.

56. Xiao Chaoran et al., *Beijing daxue xiaoshi, 1898–1949* (The history of Beijing University, 1898–1949) (Shanghai: Shanghai jiaoyu chubanshe, 1981), 297.

57. See Qinghua daxue, *Qinghua daxue xiaoshigao,* 485; A Zhe, *Zhongguo xiandai xuesheng yundong jianshi,* 163.

58. *New York Times,* June 8, 1948.

59. From Stuart to the Secretary of State, June 30, 1948, *FRUS, 1948, The Far East: China,* 7: 328.

60. Xiao Chaoran, *Beijing daxue xiaoshi,* 296.

61. "Anti-American Demonstration and Propaganda," from Clubb to the Secretary of State, June 1, 1948, RG59, 893.00/6-148, NA.

62. From Clubb to the Secretary of State, June 9, 1948, RG59, 893.00/6-948, NA.

63. For an account of the incident, see "The Shibuya Case" in *The China Weekly Review* (8 March 1947): 46–47.

64. With regard to the term "Third National," the special reporter of *Dagong bao* in Tokyo even sent back a report titled "Third National! Third National!" with a view of denouncing the revival of Japanese racism. A Third National, according to the reporter, referred to a Chinese or a Korean who had lived in Japan since before the war. While describing in detail an incident involving only the Japanese and the Koreans in Japan, the author aimed to expose Japanese racist attitudes. See *Dagong bao,* Tianjin, May 19, 1948.

65. "Anti-American Demonstration and Propaganda," Clubb to the Secretary of State, June 11, 1948, RG59, 893.00/6-1148, NA.

66. The Marco Polo Bridge Incident triggered the outbreak of the Sino-Japanese War in 1937.

67. From Clubb to the Secretary of State, June 9, 1948, *FRUS, 1948, The Far East: China*, 7:280–81; Beijing daxue lishixi, *Beijing daxue xuesheng yundongshi*, 245.

68. Beijing daxue lishixi, *Beijing daxue xuesheng yundongshi*, 245–47.

69. *New York Times*, June 10, 1948; Xiao Chaoran, *Beijing daxue xiaoshi*, 297. Following the example of the Shanghai students, students in Beiping also started a "fan MeifuRi 100,000 Name Petition Movement." See Xiao Chaoran, *Beijing daxue xiaoshi*, 297.

70. From Pilcher to the Secretary of State, June 5, 1948, *FRUS, 1948, The Far East: China*, 7:275–76.

71. "China Acts to End Anti-U.S. Agitation," *New York Times*, June 6, 1948; Wang Niankun, *Xuesheng yundong shiyao jianghua*, 94–95.

72. From Pilcher to the Secretary of State, June 12, 1948, RG59, 893.00/6-1248, NA.

73. He Jiliang and Lu Jing, "Jiefang zhanzheng shiqi Shanghai gaoxiaode jiaoyun he xueyun" (Educational and student movements of Shanghai colleges and universities during the war of liberation) in Zheng Guang et al., ed. *Jiefang zhanzheng shiqi xuesheng yundong lunwenji* (Essays on the student movement during the war of liberation) (Shanghai: Tongji daxue chubanshe, 1988), 200.

74. For details, see Cabot to the Secretary of State, "Decline in Mayor K.C. Wu's Prestige with Shanghai Students," July 16, 1948, RG59, 893.00/7-1648, NA; see also Gongqingtuan Shanghai shiwei, *1945–1949*, 177–85.

75. In Guangzhou, student pamphlets, characterized by anti-American hostility and emotionalism, received wide distribution in early June. Student leaders from Sun Zhongshan University issued a pamphlet, in the name of the 2,857 students of the university, titled "Message to the Public in Connection with Our Opposition to the United States Support of Japan and Relieving Our Nation from the Present Crisis." It proclaimed that the "imperialistic U.S. policy of aiding Japan toward recovery" constituted a serious national crisis. The pamphlet denounced MacArthur as "the agent of the monopolistic capitalists of Wall Street. " It also accused the United States of raising Japanese industrial production to a level higher than it was in the years from 1931 to 1934 and of aiding Japan toward reestablishing its heavy war industry, its Sea Peace Preservation Office, its military schools, and naval and air bases. The pamphlet asserted that the United States aimed to build up Japanese industry through obtaining raw materials from China in order to eventually manipulate China. Weak Chinese industry and commerce would then face a tragic fate. The pamphlet affirmed in exaggerated detail the threat of a rearmed Japan to China. See "Anti-American Pamphlet," memorandum by Boucher, June 29, 1948, RG59, 893.00/6-2948, NA.

76. For a large collection of materials on the student *fan MeifuRi* movement in Kunming and especially on the active Communist role in the movement, see Zhonggong Kunmingshi dangshiban and Yunnansheng danganguan, eds., *1948 nian kunming "fan MeifuRi" yundong* (The 1948 *fan MeifuRi* movement in Kunming) (Kunming: Yunnan renmin chubanshe, 1989).

77. From Paul T.K. Lin to Mrs. Roosevelt, July 6, 1948, RG59, 893.00/7-648, NA.

78. See Stuart to the Secretary of State, August 31, 1948, RG59, 893.00/8-3148, NA. *Dagong bao* remained the most persistent critic of U.S. policy toward Japan. The editors continued to blame an "over-lenient" SCAP for "protecting and cultivating a militaristic Japan," for monopolizing the trials of Japanese war criminals, and for reducing the Potsdam declaration to merely "a scrap of paper." The paper accused the United States of planning to turn Japan into the "arsenal" and the 'anti-Communist bulwark" of East Asia, and deplored SCAP's failure to live up to the ideals set up by President Roosevelt. See the editorials of *Dagong bao* in August and September of 1948.

79. From Stuart to the Secretary of State, June 30, 1948, *FRUS, 1948, The Far East: China,* 328–29.

80. From Pilcher to the Secretary of State, January 19, 1948, RG59, 893.00/1-1948, NA.

81. *The China Press Review* (7 June 1948): 10.

82. From Marshall Carter to Mrs. Roosevelt, July 10, 1948, RG59, 893.00/7-1048, NA.

83. See *New York Times,* June 6, 1948.

84. Memorandum by the American Embassy, July 11, 1947, RG59, 893.00/7-1147, NA. The Nationalist government's decision to resume trade with Japan in the summer of 1947, however, provoked nationwide protests from industrialists, professors, students, and even government officials.

85. See Pilcher to the Secretary of State, June 7, 1948, RG59, 893.00/6-748, NA.

86. Lutze, "New Democracy," 446.

87. From Cabot to the Secretary of State, January 12, 1948, *FRUS, 1948, The Far East: China,* 7:32.

88. Ibid., June 1, 1948, *FRUS, 1948, The Far East: China,* 7:268–69.

89. As the Communist troops were winning the war on the battlefield, the CCP leaders began to think more about urban takeover work. The urban underground Communist organizers would be indispensable in helping the victorious Party consolidate its urban control. Confronting the GMD's repressive measures in late 1948, the CCP Central Committee issued strict orders to the underground organizers to keep a low profile, avoid confronting the GMD directly, and shun any kind of "adventurous" activities. They were instructed to conserve their strength and await the arrival of the People's Liberation Army. See the directive written by Zhou Enlai in August 1948 for the CCP Central Committee, titled "Chiang guan qu douzheng yaoyou qingxing tounao he linghuo celue" (Keep a clear head and employ flexible strategies for struggles in Chiang-controlled regions), in *1948 Kunming fan MeifuRi yundong,* 48–50.

90. Jeffrey N. Wasserstrom, *Student Protests in Twentieth-Century China: The View from Shanghai* (Stanford: Stanford University Press, 1991), 119.

91. From Clubb to the Secretary of State, June 11, 1948, *FRUS, 1948, The Far East: China,* 7:293–94.

92. "Anti-American Student Demonstrations," from Clubb to the Secretary of State, June 14, 1948, RG59, 893.00/6-1448, NA.

93. From Pilcher to the Secretary of State, June 5, 1948, RG59, 893.00/6-548, NA.

94. From Cabot to Butterworth, July 14, 1948, RG59, 893.00/7-1448, NA.

95. Pilcher to the Secretary of State, June 7, 1948, *FRUS, 1948, The Far East: China,* 7:279.

96. From Stuart to the Secretary of State, June 11, 1948, RG59, 893.00/6-1148, NA.

97. "News of the Week," *The China Weekly Review,* June 19, 1948.

98. From W.J. Sebald, Editorial and Information Specialist from the Office of the U.S. Political Adviser for Japan to the Secretary of State on "Comments by Members of the Chinese Mission in Japan Regarding the Anti-American Agitation in China," June 17, 1948, RG59, 893.00/6-1748, NA.

99. From Sebald to the Secretary of State on "Criticism of United States Policy in China and the Philippine Islands," August 19, 1948, RG59, 711.93/8-1948, NA.

100. From Consul Francis Styles of Shanghai to the Secretary of State, October 8, 1948, *FRUS, 1948, The Far East: China,* 7:489.

6

KANGMEI YUANCHAO: THE "RESIST AMERICA, AID KOREA" MOVEMENT, 1950–1953

Anti-American sentiments among politically conscious Chinese intellectuals were fully exploited by the Chinese Communists during not only China's Civil War but also Beijing's confrontation with Washington in the Korean War. In 1950, the Chinese Communists, fresh from a bitter war with the Chinese Nationalists, faced the urgent task of consolidating their political control, reconstructing a war-wrecked economy, and finishing the reunification of the country. However, China was soon embroiled in a war fought on foreign soil. North Korea's military initiative against South Korea in June 1950 pushed Communist China into its first international crisis.[1] Entanglement in another major war was the last thing the newly established government needed. At first, the Beijing leadership offered verbal support of the North Korean effort and verbal attacks on the United States following the American entry into the war under the auspices of the United Nations. Also, the war was initially in the favor of the North Korean forces as they drove enemy forces to the southern end of the Korean peninsula. However, the situation drastically reversed itself in the fall, as the American counterattacks pushed the North Korean troops all the way back and continued pressing on northward to the Yalu River, the Chinese-Korean border separating Manchuria from Korea.

China's decision to intervene in the Korean War in late 1950 has received much scholarly attention and sophisticated analyses. For example, in his pioneering book, *China Crosses the Yalu*, Allen Whiting argues that the Chinese military intervention resulted primarily from Beijing's strong belief in a clear and impending threat to China's physical security. Using recently declassified Chinese sources, another scholar, Chen Jian, provides a new perspective to the studies of the origins of CCP foreign policies. He maintains that the CCP leaders, especially Mao Zedong, intent upon perpetuating the inner dynamics of the Chinese revolution, perceived advantages in military intervention in the Korean War. By meeting successfully the challenge posed by the Korean crisis, China would not only safeguard its physical security, but would also greatly enhance its international position, perpetuate its revolutionary momentum, and serve as an inspiration for revolutionary movements elsewhere in the world. In *Mao's Military Romanticism*, Zhang Shu Guang further sheds light on the mentality of the Beijing authorities, and takes into account Mao Zedong's firm conviction in the invincibility of the people's war in tackling the Korean crisis.[2] An analysis of the CCP's decision-making process is, however, beyond the scope of this study, as this chapter focuses mainly on the propaganda war on the home front and on its role in the making of Chinese images of America.

Once the decision to fight America was made in October 1950, the Chinese government lost no time in shaping public opinion in support of the war effort. The Communist leadership's decision to fight an American-led coalition in Korea ushered in a massive domestic political campaign and a nationwide effort to expunge American influence. Uncertain about the prospect of receiving full support from a war-weary people, and intent upon convincing people of the righteousness of China's cause and the invincibility of the Chinese troops, the Communist leaders saw the need for launching a large-scale political movement to rekindle Chinese people's patriotic emotions and to dispel any lingering "fear-America" or "worship-America" mentality. To mobilize broad support for the war effort and to further generate people's indignation toward the United States, Party propagandists capitalized on the repertoire of recent emotion-arousing anti-American issues and themes.

Furthermore, the CCP leadership used the anti-American political campaign to stimulate other activities and score political points domestically. Momentum was gained, for example, through appealing to people's patriotic love for China and hatred for America, collecting donations for purchasing war-related materials, having people sign patriotic pacts to pledge their support for the Korean War, providing relief and aid to military personnel and their families, and campaigning for greater economic production.[3]

Meanwhile, direct Chinese involvement in the Korean War raised serious domestic repercussions. Confronting open hostilities abroad, domestic political tensions increased greatly in late 1950. The new government significantly tightened domestic control by intensifying the campaigns of suppressing domestic "counterrevolutionaries," of extirpating foreign missionary influences from China, of attacking corruption, waste, and bureaucracy among government officials (the so-called Three-Antis), and of expunging such vices as bribery, tax evasion, theft of state assets, fraud, and stealing of state economic secrets among businessmen and capitalists (the so-called Five-Antis).

China's entry into the war also led to a hardening of attitudes toward Westerners, especially Americans, and a nationwide hunt for spies and enemy agents. Despite their continued verbal attacks on the U.S. government upon assuming power in

1949, the Communists had not demonstrated much open hostility toward individual Americans in China, who could still enjoy a modicum of freedom of action. With the outbreak of the Korean War, however, the contingent of Americans, including businessmen, educators, and missionaries, increasingly found themselves under surveillance and strong suspicion, and soon had to depart from China in the midst of fervent nationalist passions stirred up by the war.[4] With tensions generated by the Chinese-American military confrontation, it was no longer permissible to differentiate between the U.S. government and individual Americans as had been the case with the previous anti-American movements. Western missionaries came under severe attack. Horrifying stories were told of children killed in orphanages run by foreign nuns and of missionaries living in great comfort in huge mansions while their yards were littered with death pits for Chinese children. The spread of stories of this nature dated back to the antimissionary activities of the 1860s and 1870s. Appalling stories related to missionaries also accompanied antiforeign, anti-Christian activities of the Boxer period. The charges that emerged in the early 1950s were the latest round of earlier precedents, which nevertheless fanned new flames.[5] Meanwhile, a number of Americans who had chosen to stay were now accused of engaging themselves in antirevolutionary activities. Some were arrested on the charge of espionage. In one of the plays written in 1951, an American clergyman who had remained after the defeat of the Nationalists was charged with carrying out clandestine activities against the new regime. After his arrest, he was harangued by a revolutionary:

> You [Americans] failed to conquer the Chinese people with your billions of dollars and thousand upon thousand tons of artillery. Now no matter how many sugar-coated bullets you employ, you won't be able to prevent the defeat of the bandit army of Jiang Jieshi [Chiang Kai-shek], and the complete failure of your policy of invading China. The Chinese people will not allow you to continue dominating us. Your crimes will be punished.[6]

Many Westerners had already left China when or soon after the Communists took over. By late 1951, almost all were gone.

China's intervention in the Korean War bore political relevance to Chinese intellectuals in particular. While exploiting the existing anti-American sentiments among politically assertive young intellectuals for their active support for this action, the CCP leadership also sought to intensify their hostility toward "American imperialism" (often referred to as *Meidiguo zhuyi* or *Meidi*), to root out any lingering "illusions" they might cherish about the United States, and to firm up their loyalty to the new government. To these ends, the Communist-controlled media launched a fierce "Resist America, Aid Korea" (*kangMei yuanChao*) political campaign upon China's entrance into the Korean War. The thought reform of the intellectuals also became an integral part of the anti-American movement.

The previous anti-American student protests paled in magnitude and intensity in comparison with the CCP-organized campaign following China's entry into the Korean War. The Communist-orchestrated political movement against *Meidi* employed most of the techniques (parading and performing on the street, sloganeering, mass rallying, petitioning, among others) and prominent issues (such as the "beastly" behavior of American servicemen in China, the unholy alliance between the imperialist America and the Chiang regime, and the American "rearming" of Japan) that had arisen in the late 1940s.[7]

The sensitive topic concerning the American occupation policy in Japan resumed its significance, and became even more inflammatory in the hostile international environment. In 1949, the United States pronounced its decision to suspend all Japanese reparation payments during the period of the occupation and to allow Japan to proceed with full-scale production in a number of strategic industries. Meanwhile, American plans for building up Japanese police and self-defense forces and for arranging a peace treaty with Japan that excluded the People's Republic of China and the Soviet Union further increased China's suspicion of U.S. intentions. The CCP thus intensified its exaggerated attacks on the United States for resurrecting Japanese militarism and for intending to use Japan as a military base for launching offensives against China and other Asian countries.[8]

Apart from the Japan issue, the incidents involving American GIs and Chinese civilians in the immediate post–World War II China served as the most ready and convenient materials for reuse in the politically charged anti-American atmosphere. Books, wall posters, and cartoons full of unsavory images of American troops in China mushroomed. The Shen Chong Incident in particular assumed new prominence in refreshing urban people's memory of the "brutality" of American troops in China. Of the 27 images collected in *Atrocities of Americans in Pictures*, the cartoon depicting the Shen Chong rape case appeared on the front page (see Figure 6).

The Korean War perpetuated old images and created new ones. Confronting a powerful enemy in a foreign country, Mao's notion of *Meidi* as a "paper tiger" was widely propagated.[9] The official view highlighted the moral degeneracy and lack of fighting spirit on the part of the American soldiers in sharp contrast to the moral superiority and high morale characterizing the Chinese soldiers on the battlefield. The propaganda had a substantial effect on the Chinese of various levels, since they appeared to embrace the official stance of the invincibility of the Chinese soldiers and of the alleged weakness and wickedness of their American counterparts. The effect was particularly felt among many educated urban Chinese as they became actively engaged in the renewed anti-American campaign, whether voluntarily or under political pressure.

From the early 1940s to the early 1950s, Chinese images of American soldiers underwent drastic changes. In the eyes of the Chinese, the GIs switched from courageous, righteous fighters of World War II to arrogant, abusive brutes during their occupation of China in the immediate postwar years to vicious, demoralized cowards of the Korean War. The fluctuating military and political environments as well as effective propaganda dictated the vagaries in the public view.

ESCALATION OF HOSTILITIES BETWEEN BEIJING AND WASHINGTON

The Chinese Communists did not come into official contact with the United States until after the Japanese attack on Pearl Harbor, which made Nationalist China and the United States allies in a war against Japan. The Communists demonstrated shrewdness during the war. In their eagerness to survive and to win the war first against Japan and then against the GMD, they relegated their Marxist ideological claims to a secondary level and endeavored to seek whatever support they could obtain to achieve their objectives against their adversaries.[10] Through contacts with the Americans at various levels, the Communist leaders had attempted to convince the Americans of the GMD's degeneracy and the CCP's promising prospects in order to obtain American military aid. However, the CCP's attempts to open avenues of communication with the United States during World War II and to seek its neutrality during the Chinese Civil War had repeatedly failed. Ever since the failure of Marshall's mediation in January 1947, the Communists had been escalating their verbal attacks on the United States. Even though the American military and economic aid to the Nationalists was of a limited scale and failed to turn the tide in their favor, it further deepened Communist resentfulness and distrust of the United States.

With the unfolding of the Communist victory in China, the CCP leaders, especially Mao Zedong, laid out general principles regarding the new government's foreign policy. The CCP had from its formation in 1921 espoused the ideology of anti-imperialism, which targeted Japan during China's war with Japan and the United States during the Civil War. National Communists at heart, Mao Zedong and his followers were acutely conscious of China's humiliations of the past century. Eager to restore national confidence and to assert China's independence, the Communist leadership intended to make clear its difference from the previous supine Manchu and Nationalist regimes, and to end the privileges enjoyed by the foreign powers in China. The issues of equality and mutual respect for territorial integrity and sovereignty as well as the severing of ties with the GMD served as the fundamental principles in defining the new China's relationship with the rest of the world.[11]

Although CCP leaders demonstrated a willingness to establish diplomatic relations with the United States under these conditions, Washington's refusal to relinquish ties with the GMD, to recognize the official standing of the new Communist leadership, and to accept the new regime's claim of annulling the preexisting treaty obligations left little room for accommodation and reconciliation. Caught in the increasingly polarized atmosphere of the early Cold War years, facing mounting public and congressional anti-Communist sentiments, and confronting rising domestic allegations for having "lost" China, the Truman administration was in no mood to compromise with the CCP.

On the other hand, even though the CCP did not dismiss the prospect of some diplomatic rapprochement with the United States, which would entail such gains as continued economic trade, reduced American support of the GMD, a minimized military threat from the United States, and an enhanced international standing, the CCP leadership had also learned not to anticipate much as a result of repeated frustrations of expectations and hopes in its official dealings with the United States throughout the 1940s. Furthermore, heartened by the sweeping military victories, and emerging as the new ruling party of China, the CCP was now more confident and defiant, eager to correct the wrongs the powers had inflicted upon China and to assert a new order, and had no inclination to budge on the fundamental principles. In mid-1949, the CCP added to the atmosphere of mutual distrust and antagonism by charging American diplomats in Shenyang with espionage, which led to the arrest, trial, and expulsion of U.S. consul general Angus Ward and his staff. Meanwhile, confronting an increasingly hostile United States, the CCP displayed an eagerness to cement ties with the Soviet Union in the early 1950s, following Mao's famous "lean to one side" speech in June 1949. The speech served as the basis for new China's foreign policy.

In the atmosphere of ill will, the U.S. State Department issued *The China White Paper* (officially called *United States Relations With China, With Special References to the Period 1944–1949*) in August 1949, shortly before the establishment of the People's Republic of China. *The White Paper* documented the Sino-American relationship, castigated the CCP as well as the GMD, and contributed further to the CCP's ill feelings toward the United States. Regarded by the Chinese Communist leadership as new evidence of American aggressive intentions toward China and interference in Chinese domestic affairs, *The White Paper* elicited a series of harsh verbal attacks from China. Secretary of State Dean Acheson's "Letter of Transmittal" attached to *The White Paper*, which, among other points, provided a rather unsavory picture of the CCP and emphasized the traditional friendship between China and the United States, drew particular attention. In response to *The White Paper*, the Communist leader Mao Zedong himself wrote five commentaries, which were published in *XinHua ribao*, the official newspaper.[12]

With a view to repudiating Acheson's depiction of U.S. friendship toward China, Mao's "'Friendship' or Aggression?" enumerated the "wrongs" America had inflicted upon China during the past hundred years. Mao ascribed the establishment of higher educational institutions in China by American religious groups and American missionary and philanthropic undertakings to "spiritual aggression." According to him, these activities were meant to fool the Chinese people for the benefit of Western "invaders." As a way of exposing the true color of American "friendship" toward China, Mao also mentioned the case of Shen Chong. "Despite the 'abolition' of extraterritoriality," he asserted, "the culprit in the raping of Shen Chung [Chong] was declared not guilty and released by the U.S. Navy Department on his return to the United States—this counts as another expression of 'friendship.'"[13] Mao's commentaries then set off nationwide public discussion on American imperialistic activities in China in particular and in Asia in general.

The founding of the People's Republic saw manifested coldness between Beijing and Washington. Beijing's animosity toward Washington resulted from many elements. But it was the latter's decision to recognize and continue supporting the Nationalist government in Taiwan, as well as its endeavors to keep

Communist China out of the United Nations and to prevent its allies from recognizing the new government, that especially embittered the Communist leadership.[14] On September 30, 1949, the eve of the inauguration of the People's Republic, Premier of the State Council Zhou Enlai made a lengthy speech in front of the National Committee of the People's Political Consultative Conference, in which he denounced the United States as China's "most dangerous enemy."[15]

The Korean crisis crystallized Sino-American hostility. The employment of the American Seventh Fleet in the Taiwan Strait under President Truman's administrative order two days after the outbreak of the Korean War made Washington China's major obstacle to "liberating Taiwan." The ostensible purpose of stationing the fleet between China and Taiwan was to prevent one side from attacking the other. In reality, the move committed the United States to the protection of the island. The frustration of the Communist plan to recover Taiwan as a result of the American "neutralization" action in the Taiwan Strait incited angry and harsh censure from Beijing, which repeatedly accused the United States of "armed invasion" of Taiwan. Premier Zhou Enlai, in his capacity as foreign minister, issued a public statement condemning the American patrols of the Taiwan Strait as the "armed aggression against the territory of China."[16] General Douglas MacArthur's "March to the Yalu" threatening the Chinese border dispelled any Chinese doubt about U.S. animosity toward the new China. In a speech to the UN Security Council delivered immediately after China entered the Korean War, the Chinese delegate Wu Xiuquan characterized American attitudes toward the People's Republic as an extension of its interventionist policy of the late 1940s.[17] The American involvement in the Korean War and the ensuing Chinese-American military confrontation in Korea ended any hope of reconciliation between the two countries. The Cold War in Asia entered a new stage, and the Chinese image of the United States as the number one enemy of China persisted for two more decades.

"WHEN THE LIPS ARE GONE, THE TEETH FEEL COLD"

On October 25, 1950, the newly established People's Republic of China entered the Korean War against the United States. Fresh from a bloody and protracted war, and faced with the enormous task of national economic rehabilitation and political power consolidation, the CCP leadership sought to generate warm and widespread support for the Central Government's move to send into Korea the Chinese troops, who were called the "Chinese People's Volunteers" (*Zhongguo renmin zhiyuanjun* or CPV).[18] To rally popular support for the war effort, the propagandists worked arduously to expose *Meidi*'s "sinister scheme" to subjugate Korea and invade China. The official version of the Korean War was that South Korea, supported and encouraged by its American master, invaded North Korea. American imperialists, together with their lackeys, then extended the war flames to the Yalu River, and their planes were dropping bombs over China's *dongbei* (northeast, also known as Manchuria). The ill intent of *Meidi* toward China was therefore obvious. The most popular war slogan was thus "Resist America, Aid Korea; Protect Our Homes, Defend Our Homeland" (*kangMei yuanChao, baojia weiguo*). The old Chinese saying "when the lips are gone, the teeth feel cold" (*chunwang chihan*), and such expressions as "we cannot sit idly while our neighbor's house is on fire" and "the flame of *Meidi* will scorch China after Korea; to save Korea is to save China" served as justifications for China's entry into the war.[19] This calculated rhetoric imparted that China needed to have a friendly buffer state between itself and hostile countries. It could not afford to stand idly by while North Korea was falling into enemy hands and the American soldiers were closing in on the Yalu River.

The mass media was then fully utilized by the government and served as its mouthpiece. An article published in *People's China*, an official English-language weekly that was to be later renamed *Beijing Review*, focused on the "menace" posed by the *Meidi* to Asian peoples in general and to Chinese people in particular. Written mainly for the consumption of English-speaking readers, the author emphasized especially the correlation between the Chinese entry into the Korean War and the safeguarding of peace back at home. The Chinese people, he contended, "realized that the American invasion of Korea was merely the prelude to the invasion of China, that the reconstruction of their country could not be completed unless the flames of war started by the American imperialists in neighboring Korea were quenched."[20] Proclaiming the sending of the CPV to Korea as the most "righteous" act, the CCP leadership repudiated the United States in the name of protecting China and defending world peace.

As the war in Korea intensified, the CCP leadership in Beijing declared that local cadres should intensify their propaganda (*xuanchuan*) efforts nationwide to strengthen party leadership.[21] In early February 1951, Mao and the Central Committee of the CCP called on the whole nation to carry out a "propaganda and education campaign for resisting U.S. aggression and aiding Korea." They claimed: "Persistent efforts must be made to push this campaign throughout the country, to deepen it where it is already under way and spread it where it is not, so as to make sure that this education reaches everyone in every part of the country."[22]

Directed by the omnipresent "Resist America, Aid Korea" Associations, government agencies, schools, and universities as well as factories were all actively involved in the anti-American campaign. Millions of Chinese were spurred by mass rallies and took part in the condemnation of the "criminal" behaviors of the Americans in Korea.[23] Colleges and universities became once again hotbeds of the political movement. On many campuses, classes were even suspended for a time so that students and staff could devote themselves completely to examining and denouncing *Meidi*, and to cultivating the correct political attitude toward the Korean issue. Large-scale anti-American student demonstrations and protests filled the streets, a phenomenon familiar to Chinese college campuses. Beijing University (Beida)'s Democracy Wall was once again covered with anti-American big-character posters (*dazibao*) and cartoons assailing *Meidi*.

Meanwhile, many college and high school students went to factories and the countryside to explain to workers and peasants the nature of the Korean conflict and to carry out anti-American propaganda work.[24] Quite a number of students from various universities signed up for military academies.[25] Enthused with

China's entry into the war against the United States, many volunteered to go to the frontline. A small number of those who were eventually inducted to the CPV or who were accepted by military academies were given enthusiastic send-offs.[26] At Qinghua University, an eye-catching slogan poster, proclaiming "Salute Those Who Will Be On Their Way to the Glorious Post," was plastered at the entrance of the school auditorium. At the farewell meeting held inside the auditorium, the chosen military cadets were hailed as heroes, and were carried to the platform by their fellow schoolmates in the midst of firecrackers, applause, and loud music.[27] The glorification of war was intended not only to encourage more young people to volunteer for military service, but also to raise morale on the battleground. The veneration of war on the home front contributed significantly to the display of heroic behavior by many Chinese soldiers on the Korean front line.[28]

"WHO ARE THE MOST BELOVED PEOPLE?" ANTI-AMERICANISM AS REFLECTED IN LITERATURE AND POPULAR ART

To generate anti-American emotions, the government employed all avenues of propaganda. Upon China's entry into the Korean War, newspapers, journals, and books fraught with anti-American themes were issued to urban, educated people to appeal to their patriotic feelings and to play upon their spirit of nationalism. Journals and newspapers were also laden with stories that demonstrated intellectuals' and students' determination to contribute to the "Resist America, Aid Korea" movement. A typical example can be found in an article titled "Motherland, I Answer Your Call," which describes the enthusiasm of the students from Beida who were admitted into military academies.[29]

Articles on young intellectuals' recognition of the true menace of the United States mushroomed. One article published in *Renmin ribao* (People's daily) focused on the process through which this awareness took shape in a young college student. The story begins by asserting that the Communist victory in 1949 had assured a youth named Yuan Baotong of Qinghua University, a civil engineering major, of a peaceful learning environment and a promising future. He therefore devoted himself assiduously to academic studies without thinking much of the "wolf" outside China. The outbreak of the Korean War shocked him, but he reasoned that the United States dared not challenge China; that imperialism would eventually meet its own death and therefore it was unnecessary to clash with it; and that the Korean people would be able to liberate themselves. In a group discussion, however, his thoughts met with severe criticism from his fellow students, who argued that the United States was simply following in the footsteps of the former aggressor Japan and that to aid Korea was to protect China itself. While feeling indignant toward the United States, Yuan was still not fully convinced by the arguments made by his classmates and continued to believe in the saying, "we shall not attack unless we are attacked" (*Renbu fanwo, wobu fanren*). However, the fact that the American soldiers were pressing on the Yalu River and that the American imperialists were bombing China's *dongbei* made him shed his last illusion. Together with other students at Qinghua, he pledged that he would be ready to go wherever the nation needed him most.[30] Articles of this nature also reveal the official wariness of the existing skepticism of taking on a powerful nation for the sake of another country, thus the urgent need to educate people about the flaws in this line of thinking.

In another article titled "Will *Meidi* Allow Us to Construct Our Country?" a student from the College of Agriculture in Beijing claimed that he was initially skeptical about his schoolmates' eager demonstration of patriotism through parading, shouting slogans, singing patriotic songs, plastering written pledges on the wall, and volunteering to go to the front line in Korea. He believed that the most urgent task facing China at the time was economic reconstruction; therefore, students should devote themselves to gaining technical knowledge to help rebuild China. He wondered aloud how empty patriotic slogans could do the job. His more progressive classmates assured him that all patriotic Chinese youths shared his ideals. But, they asked him, would *Meidi* allow the Chinese to realize their dream of building up their country? The Chinese had to deal with the American threat first before they could hope to have a bright future.[31] Articles of this type aimed at instilling in educated youths a correct understanding of the nature of the U.S. government and eradicating any lingering delusions about its intentions.

To make sure that the Chinese people, especially the intellectuals who had returned from the United States, would recognize *Meidi*'s true anti-Chinese nature, the propagandists undertook a drastic revision of the history of Sino-American relations, usually termed the "one-hundred-year history of American aggression against China." The history of Sino-U.S. relations was defined in black and white terms as one of continued American political, economic, and cultural encroachments upon China. It was rewritten with the purpose of letting the Chinese people learn the "truth" about the past. Soon after the Chinese intervention in the Korean War, *Renmin ribao* published "Chronology of American Imperialists' Invasions of China," listing in detail the "aggressions" the United States had committed against China from 1832 when a few American merchants became involved in the illegal opium trade in Qing China to 1950, when the Korean War began.[32] It also carried the piece "One Hundred Year Pictorial History of *Meidi*'s Invasion of China,"[33] and a long series of articles titled "A History of U.S. Invasions of China." To fully achieve the ideological and educational aim of the "Resist America, Aid Korea" campaign, primary and high school textbooks on the subjects of history, geography, and Chinese literature were modified to incorporate themes on American aggression.[34]

One well-known booklet titled *How to Understand America* (*Zenyang renshi Meiguo*) attempted to "fix" the erroneous attitudes that Chinese people of different political persuasions had held toward various aspects of American society. The booklet was widely publicized and printed in all the major newspapers and magazines. Intended also to provide information for the intellectuals to draw on in their speeches to expose American "crimes" in China, it began:

In the past, some Chinese were fooled by American imperialism, and thought that China had to depend on America and should take it as a good friend. Others thought that America was a civilized and democratic nation, so China should learn from America. Some others thought that America was a strong country that could not be challenged. In reality, the pro-America attitude is reactionary, and ideas of worshiping and fearing America are all wrong. Having fully understood the true colors of America, every patriotic Chinese must hate America, despise America, and scorn America!

Then under three subtitles, the booklet urged people to "hate the United States, for it is the sworn enemy of the Chinese people"; "despise the United States, for it is a rotten imperialist nation, the headquarters of reactionary decadence of the whole world"; and "show contempt toward the United States, for it is a paper tiger and can be completely defeated."[35]

To further dispel people's "worship-America" illusions, newspaper articles revealing the flaws of American society multiplied: "The True Colors of the American Educational System" discussed, among other things, racial prejudices in American schools, and poverty and persecution suffered by teachers.[36] "The Militarization of American Education" argued that the American scientific community and universities were tightly controlled by monopoly capital and warmongers.[37] "Look, This Is America," by a scientist who had recently returned from the United States, exposed America as a money-worshiping and politically corrupt society with poor public order, widespread cultural degeneracy, racial prejudice, and the monopoly of capital by a handful of big capitalists.[38]

Anti-American literature in various forms, such as prose, novel, poetry, drama, and literary reportage, proliferated.[39] The editor of the journal *Renmin xiju* (People's drama) reportedly said that he often received over 20 plays on the Korean War in one day.[40] The Chinese Literature Association of Qinghua University published a series of special issues of "Resist America, Aid Korea" literature. In the inaugural issue of the series, literature professor Wang Yao contributed the article "The Anti-American Movement as Reflected in Modern Chinese Literature." It cited primarily anti-American literature related to the 1905 Chinese boycott of American goods and the literary works on the misery of Chinese laborers in the United States.[41]

The official newspaper *Guangming ribao* (Brilliance daily) also published a series of autobiographical articles dictated by Situ Meitang, an ex-immigrant who had spent 70 years in America and had returned to China not long before. The articles were published under one title, "I Thoroughly Despise America" (*Wo tonghen Meiguo*). In the articles, Situ attacked the decadent social environment in America, and castigated its harsh immigration laws and racial discrimination. [42]

The Korean War also led to the glorification of Chinese soldiers and set the precedent for identifying and glorifying heroic fighters for nationwide public consumption. Traditional China had usually assigned low social status for soldiers; as the old saying goes, "good iron is not used for making nails, and good men do not become soldiers." In the old social hierarchy, the scholarly class stood at the top while the military class was placed at the very bottom. China's entry into the Korean War, however, saw an official effort to elevate the military class into a privileged one. People were told to love and respect soldiers, and to offer physical and material assistance to families with sons or husbands fighting in Korea. Meanwhile, families with servicemen had priority in receiving officially rendered services. It also became a common practice for the local government to plaster a large piece of red paper with big characters, "Glorious Family," on or near the door of a house with a "martyr" or a combat hero.[43]

Fighting the most powerful nation in the world, Mao and the Communist leadership were well aware of the military disadvantages China faced and of the possible misgivings in many people's minds. The propagandists therefore spared no effort in perpetuating the image of the CPV's noble heroism and invincibility, which reinforced the value of sacrifice and revolution. Korean War heroes, such as Huang Jiguang and Qiu Shaoyun, became famous nationwide and remained so for decades afterwards. Almost every school child could relate their heroic deeds, told and retold in school textbooks and picture books.[44] The near deification of the Chinese war efforts on the home front also aimed to raise morale and encourage the spirit of endurance and self-sacrifice on the battlefront.

Perhaps the most famous literary piece in glorifying the CPV was "Who Are the Most Beloved People?" by the war journalist Wei Wei. Written in the form of literary reportage in April 1951, Wei asked his "dear readers" to remember that the peace and happiness they were enjoying back in China were made possible by the numerous sacrifices of the Chinese soldiers in Korea. These soldiers were therefore "the most beloved people." The story won praise from top Chinese leaders and was widely read. It has since been used repeatedly in school textbooks.[45] Written as propaganda, Wei's story nonetheless was smooth reading and moving, provoking even more resentment toward the U.S. government among readers in the early fifties.

On the other hand, to rid people of the "fear-America" mentality, the Party agencies and members associated with the "Resist America, Aid Korea" movement worked assiduously to expose fully the "weakness" of the American "paper tiger." A characteristic depiction of American soldiers on the battlefield was their abject cowardice. While a Chinese soldier would sacrifice his own life to save his comrades, an American soldier's first instinct upon encountering danger was to either flee or surrender. In another literary reportage, Wei Wei described a pep talk delivered by a division commander to his soldiers: "Don't forget the enemy's fundamental weakness is cowardice. He can't overcome it! Now we're better equipped with artillery, the folks at home have given us all these big guns! If we can send the enemy infantry slinking off like dogs with their tails between their legs, can't we do the same to their artillery?"[46]

To further boost morale, the "Resist America, Aid Korea" Associations sent groups of performers, including some prominent figures in the cultural circles, to entertain the Chinese troops in Korea and to deliver emotional patriotic talks. Upon their return to China, members of these groups went to various regions to report on the valiant behavior of the Chinese soldiers and the alleged cowardice of the Americans.

The "Resist America, Aid Korea" Association at Central Academy of Fine Arts in Beijing concentrated on producing posters and cartoons, and issued a series titled *Reference Materials for Propaganda Posters*. These were reproduced by local "Resist America, Aid Korea" clubs, schools, and universities as street and wall posters. In general, the posters endeavored to demonstrate *Meidi*'s wickedness and weakness and the strength and righteousness of the Chinese people. The table of contents of one such issue, for example, includes the following subjects: "We will win victory to protect peace"; "Launch a patriotic competition for industrial production"; "People of the world oppose the war of aggression"; "Do not allow *Meidi* to violate the Potsdam Agreement"; "American and Japanese reactionaries reduce the life of Japanese people to that of slaves"; "*Meidi*'s re-arming of Japan is unlawful"; "Take on the task of maintaining world peace and stop new wars"; "American imperialists and their lackeys, Chiang Kai-shek and Syngman Rhee, are clamoring for wars"; and "The bandit gangs of Americans and Syngman Rhee commit bloody crimes."[47]

Many cartoons provide poignant images that were intended to expose the United States as a great threat to Asia, especially China. One cartoon, for example, in the top half depicts an armed Japanese soldier who had crossed the Yalu River and landed in China's *dongbei*, and in the bottom half shows an armed U.S. soldier fighting a Korean on the banks of the Yalu River. Moreover, to stir up feelings of deep contempt among the Chinese for things American, many posters portrayed in a most unfavorable light the American way of life, as full of vice, violence, and degeneracy (see Figures 7 and 8).

Meanwhile, to emphasize the righteousness of China's move to send the "People's Volunteers" to Korea and the importance of domestic contributions to the war effort, the government encouraged urban "cultural workers," including professional players and particularly amateur student performers, to perform patriotic plays related to anti-American themes. "Living newspapers" (*huobaoju*) became a popular form of performance. It was a kind of vaudeville with a focus on current political issues or movements, performed on street corners or on the stage. Better-known titles of "living newspapers" include: "Paper Tiger," "People's Will," "Protecting Our Peace at Home," "Victory Belongs to the People," "Atrocities of American Soldiers," and "American Espionage."[48]

An article published in *People's China* reported the great number of people involved in this propaganda work and the effectiveness of their performances:

Every day during the last few days in Peking alone, more than 5,000 players from schools, institutions, and dramatic clubs have given various street corner shows. Among the most effective "living newspapers" plays are "Truman Dreams of Hitler," and the "Dance of the Devils," the devils being Truman, MacArthur, Chiang Kai-shek and many others. All these troupes are amateur groups organized by the people with the help of the drama workers.

Through the countryside of Hopei [Hebei] province, 2,000 locally organized amateur troupes are traveling from village to village to give performances for the peasants in the long winter evenings. Around the theme of "protect the homeland," their plays are woven out of the stuff of their own experiences. Their true life stories impress the audiences profoundly and often at the end of the shows, the onlookers themselves join the players in shouting slogans. Many enroll immediately as volunteers for Korea on the spot.[49]

Party propagandists tried various tactics to intensify hostility toward the United States, and sometimes did so with some imagination. For example, a story of this nature was told in a booklet titled *How to Be a Propagandist*. When a group of workers were on their way to the factory early in the morning, one worker stepped into a puddle of muddy water. The propagandist among them then commented that once he had had a similar accident, and he had surely cursed hard. When asked what he had cursed, the propagandist replied: "American devils." He then explained that "if the American devils had not invaded us and bombed our Northeast, would we have to protect ourselves from air raids and always be in a black-out?" He thus continued, "We would have our street lights lit until morning and then we wouldn't fall or step into puddles. Whom do you think I would curse but those American devils?"[50]

Popular writings, movies, cartoons, or songs related to the anti-U.S. campaign, even though they served a political purpose, had a strong appeal, and often achieved their intended effect.[51] Slogans and songs constitute an essential part of war propaganda for any modern nation. These sources can be difficult to handle, but are useful in "re-creating the ethos which underlay the attitudes and actions of men and women" at the time.[52] As with past Chinese patriotic movements, songs were created as a great morale builder during the "Resist America, Aid Korea" campaign. One song, "March of the Chinese People's Volunteers," even survived the Korean War to become a favorite with students at all levels until the late 1970s. It goes as follows:

With vigor and high spirits,
[We] cross the Yalu River.
To safeguard peace and defend motherland is to protect our hometown.
China's good sons and daughters, unite!
Resist America and Aid Korea,
Defeat the vicious wolves of American Imperialism.

Two Korean War movies, *Yingxiong ernu* (*Heroic Sons and Daughters*) and *Shangganling*, served to immortalize the heroic deeds of the CPV soldiers. During China's Cultural Revolution of the 1960s and 1970s when the goal of entertainment was solely to serve political purposes and the limited number of available movies were invariably dominated by the drab messages of class struggle and impersonal devotions to Mao Zedong and the CCP, the two war movies, with more humane characters and slightly smacking of romance, drew youngsters back to the movie theaters repeatedly. The scene from *Yingxiong ernu* that was engraved on the minds of the young audience, however, was the courageous death of the soldier, Wang Cheng. After resisting repeated enemy attacks, Wang Cheng was the only one left of his squad guarding a hill. As the American soldiers approached the hill, Wang Cheng shouted into the radio asking the headquarters to bombard the hill. As such a move would surely kill Wang Cheng as well, the headquarters refused to issue the order. Wang thus waited calmly for the enemies to come nearer, and then pulled the fuse of a bomb, killing himself and the enemy soldiers. This scene often drew tears from the young audience, whose admiration for the heroic Wang Cheng was then translated into aversion to American soldiers, whose evil action caused the deaths of such noble Chinese young men as Wang Cheng. The other popular war movie, *Shangganling*, is about a long and bloody battle fought in a place called Shangganling, a small town in Korea. It also focused on the notions of endurance and revolutionary heroism. The popularity of the movie made the battle of Shanganling the best known one for the Chinese.

The catchy songs of the two movies explain to a large extent the fact that the movies are still remembered today. Such harsh lines as "people's soldiers fight against wolves and sacrifice themselves to fight for peace" or "we entertain friends with wine and meet wolves with hunting guns" were fused into haunting music, which immediately popularized the songs. Today, almost five decades after the end of the Korean War, people still occasionally sing the old songs from the two movies at national galas, alumni reunions, or even karaoke bars. The songs that used to inspire hatred of American "wolves" and patriotic nationalism no longer carry any political or historical significance, but their beautiful lyrics serve to bring back a degree of nostalgia for the old days.[53]

ERADICATE *MEIDI'S* INFLUENCE: THOUGHT REFORM

With the establishment of the People's Republic of China in October 1949 and Mao's declaration that the Chinese people had finally stood up, Chinese intellectuals, together with the larger population, experienced a sense of patriotic joy and pride over China's unification and the prospect of modernization. Although a large number of wealthy urban Chinese left for places such as Hong Kong, Taiwan, and the United States in 1949 and 1950, many others chose to stay and some returned from abroad to help build a new society. Having borne the psychological burdens of China's past humiliations, and inspired by the final unification of the country and by the high-sounding, heart-stirring words and songs of a glorious future, many were jubilant at the prospect of realizing their long-frustrated desires to see a rejuvenated China. They therefore embraced the new order and chose to follow their social conscience at the expense of individual freedom, and were keen on making contributions to the new "socialist construction" (*shehuizhuyi jianshe*).[54] In his book on the prominent Chinese sociologist Fei Xiaotong, R. David Arkush depicts Fei's initial enthusiasm over the possibilities a new system could promise:

Reading Fei's 1949–1950 articles on thought reform and the reform of the universities, one is struck by the theme of social unity that runs through them: the enormous power of nation and people united in common purpose; the importance of intellectuals overcoming individualism, factionalism, and divisiveness so that they could unite with the laboring masses; the benefits of cooperation and of pooling risks and resources; and so on. In those first two years, Fei must have thought the social cohesion he had looked for for so long was increasing, and he and the other intellectuals, instead of being cut off from most of society, were at last going to be able to contribute their skills to constructing a new China.[55]

Upon taking over the leadership of China, the CCP faced the massive task of national economic and political reconstruction. Having driven the Nationalists to the island of Taiwan, the Communist leaders needed time to consolidate their newly gained national power. Initially they had allowed some latitude in terms of intellectual freedom. But this policy of leniency did not last long. With China's entrance into the Korean War, the intellectuals, characterized as being "petty bourgeois" in their outlooks by the new order, received the first round of Communist reeducation.

Many intellectuals, especially the younger ones, had in the recent past been embittered by the U.S. government's actions in China and Japan and had actively participated in anti-American demonstrations. However, the fact that many well-established intellectuals were educated in the United States or in American-sponsored schools in China ensured the influence of American ideas on their thinking to varying degrees. Well aware of the patriotic anti-American fervor that had swept the nation's major cities since the late 1940s, Communist leaders nevertheless suspected that many intellectuals still admired some aspects of American life and could inadvertently become its major spokesmen in China, however much they condemned certain actions of the U.S. government. The newly established government harbored suspicions regarding intellectuals' liberal views and was by no means certain of the educated elite's steadfast support.

Certain references made by American spokesmen did not help to alleviate the CCP leadership's reservation about Chinese intellectuals' anti-American stand. The publication of *The White Paper,* for example, served to intensify the fear. Secretary of State Dean Acheson's "Letter of Transmittal" had suggested an American policy of cultivating the support of "liberal, independent" groups in China to resist Communist control. Mao was especially sensitive to Acheson's suggestion of the existence of pro-American intellectual elements in China. He acknowledged that Acheson's comment had some truth in it and asked Chinese intellectuals to cast away whatever illusions they might still cherish about the United States. Mao himself had never truly trusted the intellectuals. In his series of articles attacking *The White Paper*, he devoted much space to warning those "muddle-headed Chinese intellectuals" to discard their illusions about the U.S. imperialists. He wrote:

Part of the intellectuals still want to wait and see. They think: the Kuomintang [Guomindang] is no good and the Communist Party is not necessarily good either, so we had better wait and see. Some support the Communist Party in words, but in their hearts they are waiting to see. They are the very people who have illusions about the United States. They are unwilling to draw a distinction between the U.S. imperialists, who are in power, and the American people, who are not. . . . They are the supporters of what Acheson calls "democratic individualism."

Mao concluded that the American imperialists had "a flimsy social base in China."[56] According to him, the Communist policy toward these liberal middle-of-the-roaders or the supporters of "democratic individualism" should aim to "win them over, educate them and unite with them" so that they would not be fooled further by imperialism.[57]

In response to Mao's commentaries on *The White Paper*, intellectuals, especially those in the Beijing-Tianjin area, were called upon to join the Party in denouncing it. Over four hundred professors and staff members of Beida signed a protest against American imperialistic behavior in China as evinced in *The White Paper*.[58] In an article titled, "A Sad Confession," published in *Guangming ribao*, a professor at Beida claimed that the publication of *The White Paper* provided documentary evidence that the American leaders had consistently plotted to intervene in Chinese domestic affairs to promote their own selfish ends. Consequently, the author argued, *The White Paper* was a confession by American imperialists of their crimes of aggression against China.[59] The distinguished sociologist Fei Xiaotong, in an article written in late 1949, went even further by asserting that *The White Paper* demonstrated that the United States' true intention all along had been "to make China into an American colony."[60]

The speech by Warren Austin, U.S. representative to the United Nations, to the Security Council on November 28, 1950, also served to deepen the Communist apprehension over continued mental linkage on the part of Chinese intellectuals with the United States. In his speech, Austin enumerated the actions of friendship between China and the United States, and the various aids the United States had extended to China in the past. He emphasized that American generosity had made possible the education of a great number of Chinese either in the United States or in American-sponsored schools in China, and that they therefore retained a sense of gratitude for American assistance. He thus suggested that "thousands upon thousands of Chinese and Americans share a community of experience and a compatibility that cannot be erased by evil propaganda."[61]

Austin's speech elicited fierce responses inside China, mostly from educational institutions and also from religious organizations. Intellectuals vied with one another to condemn Austin's speech and to dissociate themselves from the category Austin referred to. Just as previously Consul Cabot's and Ambassador Stuart's references to the Chinese lack of gratefulness grated on the nerves of many sensitive Chinese, Austin's allusions to Chinese indebtedness to America aroused some heated patriotic sentiments. Many people wrote with a view to challenging the notion of American benevolence.

Austin's speech also incurred a bitter diatribe against American cultural aggressions in China. Much of the denunciation in this aspect appeared, however, to be dictated by the Party line and was highly exaggerated. A typical example is an article written by a scholar named Liu Butong, who interpreted the cultural exchanges between China and the United States in unflattering terms. The central targets of Liu's attack were American missionaries. "Holding bibles in their bloody hands," Liu asserted, "missionaries paved the way for the capitalistic predators" who colonized other countries. "Wherever they went, missionaries turned the place into a capitalist's paradise and a laborer's hell."[62]

With the Korean War and "Resist America, Aid Korea" campaign in full swing, all foreign missionary endeavors in China, condemned as tools of cultural imperialism, found themselves under attack. Private Christian colleges and universities, sponsored in most cases by funds from abroad—a tangible reflection of American "cultural aggression"—became some of the most unattractive places in China. In early 1951, Vice Minister of Education Zeng Zhaolun, a prominent American-trained physicist, issued a statement titled "The Disposal of American-Subsidized Schools Is the Foremost Task on the Current Cultural Front." In sensational language Zeng condemned the "criminal" acts of American imperialist cultural aggression. According to Zeng, the exposure of American cultural crimes would "raise the students' understanding of the aggressive nature of American imperialism, and increase their hatred toward the American imperialists." He claimed that during the past one hundred years, the American imperialists had tried every means to achieve the spiritual enslavement of Chinese children and youths through the dissemination of poisonous pro-America, revere-America, and fear-America sentiments; to ally themselves with the Chiang bandits to harm and persecute progressive teachers and students; and to use schools as a camouflage to engage in espionage activities against the interests of the Chinese people.[63] Writings denouncing American cultural imperialism proliferated between 1950 and 1951. By 1952, religious and foreign-run colleges were nationalized.[64]

Along with the intensification of the Korean War, the Central Committee of the CCP in Beijing decided that it was time to inculcate in the intellectuals a correct understanding of the malevolence of the leading capitalist power, and ideologically reform them into individuals politically loyal to the Party and technically useful for the physical reconstruction of the nation. The Korean War, therefore, stimulated the first concerted Communist move to integrate intellectuals into the new political order. Thought reform and the revamping of the universities soon became a top priority on the political agenda of the new government. The thought reform movement started in earnest following a speech on the topic given by Premier Zhou Enlai to over three thousand college teachers of the Beijing and Tianjin areas in September 1951. Toward the end of 1951, over six thousand college teachers in Beijing and Tianjin alone were reported to have been involved.[65] An important aspect of thought reform was the denunciation of American imperialistic practices so that the intellectuals could develop a uniform socialist outlook. Those who had studied in the United States were called upon to report their unpleasant experiences there and to expose the weaknesses of American society.

Well-established intellectuals articulated views in a dramatic fashion that had been more characteristic of radical youths and known leftists of the previous years. One example of anti-American writing is provided by Nie Rongzhi, a professor of Yanjing University (Yanda) who spent four months in the United States in late 1948. In a short commentary on his impressions about the country, Nie dealt with two issues: American public order and American movies. He claimed that many Chinese held the wrong notion that America was a rich country where robbery must be very rare. As a matter of fact, Nie wrote, petty thefts happened all the time, because only a small number of capitalists could boast of wealth; the majority of American people did not live so well. Therefore, many turned into petty thieves. As for the American movies, the three he saw while he was in the country involved robbery, violence, and women. As movies served an educational purpose, Nie reasoned, the American public's love for movies of such low taste showed their poor state of mind.[66]

The encompassing attacks made by the intellectuals were directed at a wide range of "depraved" social and political phenomena in the United States: low moral standards; the obsession with money, sex, and meaningless but violent detective stories; the exploitation of workers; lack of true democracy; and racial prejudice. The image of a decaying, crime-ridden, decadent, avaricious, and exploiting American society created in the early years of the 1950s was officially perpetuated during most of the Cold War era. The negative image served as a justification for the new government's policy of isolating China from the United States in order to prevent unhealthy elements from a highly undesirable society from contaminating China.

Meanwhile, thought reform was accompanied by numerous small group discussions, self-criticisms, and "thought summaries" by college teachers and professors all over China. Even intellectuals who had previously enthusiastically supported the CCP and denounced the U.S. government had to make confessions and go through indoctrination. Meanwhile, college students participated in endless anti-American study sessions and demonstrated great zeal for China's war efforts against the United States.

Intellectuals who had received their education in the West, especially in the United States, were the primary targets of the thought reform movement. They had to undergo serious thought reform since the Party officials were convinced that they must have been poisoned by the decadent Western culture and were therefore politically backward. Many had to publicly confess their "fraudulent" pro-America, worship-America mentality and renounce the United States. While it is sometimes hard to distinguish between personal views and political lines, many intellectuals must have had to work hard to meet the official standard.

A number of intellectuals confessed that their pro-America mentality had led them to abandon national patriotism and side with American imperialism. Others claimed that, even though they were exasperated by the U.S. China policy, they had blindly admired *Meidi*'s science, technology, and culture; the "Resist America, Aid Korea" campaign, however, had made them fully realize the degeneracy of American society and the true nature of American cultural aggression.

A typical example of self-criticism is found in the "thought summary" in early 1952 by the prominent professor of philosophy Jin Yuelin, chairman of the Department of Philosophy at Qinghua University, who had been known for his independent mind.[67] The part he wrote on *Meidi* described how he had fallen under the "evil" American influence and was subsequently led astray. He claimed that his prolonged exposure to the bourgeois education in the United States and his constant contact with Americans had instilled in him pro-American thoughts and prevented him from realizing *Meidi*'s plots of aggression against China during the past hundred years. He was therefore turned into an unconscious instrument of "American imperialistic cultural aggression." He had cried bitterly over the humiliating "21 Demands" that Japan had tried to enforce on China, but had taken no notice of the Sino-American Treaty of Friendship, Commerce, and Navigation. Having examined the thorough "corruptness" of his political attitude, Professor Jin then claimed that over the years, he had changed from a hot-blooded and patriotic young man to a "fool."[68] Many self-criticisms made by intellectuals adhered to a similar pattern: an examination of their false notions about the United States in the past, followed by a harsh repudiation of *Meidi*.

Those intellectuals whose confessions indicated their reservations about indiscriminate attacks on the American society often suffered condemnation themselves as in the case of Lu Zhiwei of Yanda, who had received his doctoral degree from the University of Chicago and was a leading psychologist in China at the time. Lu assumed the presidency of Yanda in April 1949, shortly after the Communists had taken over the city of Beiping.[69] Even though he had enjoyed a good relationship with the CCP, Lu soon found himself under attack from his friends and students who began to accuse him in front of the whole university of "serving as the running dog of American imperialists." In February 1951, Lu made a public confession titled "U.S. Imperialist Cultural Aggression as Seen in Yenching [Yanjing] University." He then retreated to a small isolated room to work on his self-criticism.[70] Lu seemed to have failed to satisfy his accusers because he maintained that, although he despised Americans, he did not hate them because a "scholar's training" taught him "not to rave at people." Shortly afterwards, his daughter, Lu Yaohua, a graduate student at Yanda, repudiated him in a public meeting, exposing him as "a total claw of imperialism and a tool faithful to U.S. imperialism for its cultural aggression."[71] Declaring publicly her desire to be progressive, Lu Yaohua had effectively contributed to her father's downfall. Lu Zhiwei was soon removed from his office and his daughter was rewarded by being selected as a representative to the Municipal People's Congress of Beijing.

It is difficult to evaluate the effectiveness of the anti-American thought reform on the true thinking of Chinese intellectuals. However, their apparent compliance with the Party line did not result entirely from political pressure. Suspicion of the U.S. government had been accumulating in the late 1940s, and the outbreak of the Korean War had certainly deepened the hostility among Chinese intellectuals in the same way public opinion in America had turned sour toward China when the two countries went to war.

Furthermore, initial favorable intellectual reactions to the Communist endeavors and commitment to reconstruct the society might have prompted their support of the Communist call to condemn *Meidi* with some genuine enthusiasm. On the other hand, indiscriminate attacks on various aspects of American culture by many established scholars who had had long personal experiences in the United States and friendship with individual Americans sound flimsy. A student, who had maintained a strong pro-Communist stand during the Civil War period, is recorded to have said after the Communist takeover that while the Americans were in China, people hated them and wanted them to leave. Now that they were gone, with their movies, music, and money, people rather missed them.[72] Wu Ningkun, a professor at Yanda, after returning to China in the middle of 1951 from years of education in the United States, recalls his strong misgivings at the time about "the self-righteous demands for conformity and the unconditional submissiveness of the individual to the party [Party] or the state."[73]

Leaving aside the issue of sincerity regarding the manifested resentment among the intellectuals toward the United States, the fact remains that many went along with the movement and were submissive in their self-criticism during and after the thought reform, and appeared to be enthusiastically supporting the Party line. As one historian points out, Chinese intellectuals received a clear message from the thought reform, that is, the only way for them to meet the demands of the new society was to stop being themselves and give up independent and critical thinking.[74]

The overhauling of the educational field also quickened with the intensification of the Korean War. Issues such as loyalty to the Communist Party, dissociation from the American model of development, and learning from the Soviet Union gained prominence. The essential guidelines of the new educational system therefore were to aim to be anti-imperialistic in orientation and to eliminate remaining American influence.[75]

Proclaiming themselves as the champions of anti-imperialism, the Communist leaders had endeavored to channel Chinese nationalistic feelings exclusively against *Meidi* during the Korean War. Their task was made relatively easier by the preexisting anti-American mentality among many young politically active intellectuals and by China's military confrontation with the United States in Korea. On the other hand, the early years of the 1950s saw pervasive Soviet influence in China. Since the Sino-Soviet alliance served as the basis of the Chinese foreign policy in the early years of the 1950s, the Chinese leadership intended to prevent any development of suspicious and hostile attitudes among the intellectuals toward China's close relationship with the Soviet Union, and to transform their enmity toward America into admiration for Russia. The Soviets were now acclaimed as the "elder brothers" of the Chinese.[76] Sociologist Fei Xiaotong was one of the scholars who sang praises of China's "friendship" with the Soviet Union. With regard to the Sino-Soviet Treaty, Fei wrote that it safeguarded world peace and deterred U.S. imperialism, and that the U.S. charge of the Soviet territorial ambition on China was a vicious lie.[77]

In the drive to forge unity with the Soviet Union, the Soviet-style pedagogical programs and materials were adopted.[78] Even Soviet textbooks for teaching the English language were claimed to be superior to those of the imperialistic English-speaking countries. In an article titled "Superiority of Soviet Russian Teaching Materials of the English Language," a professor of Shandong University exposed the "evil" effects of the "capitalistic teaching materials of English language," and favored the Soviet textbook *Advanced Readings of the English Language*, which his university adopted in early 1953.[79] A craze for the Russian language followed in higher education.

China paid dearly for the Korean conflict. Based on the estimated figures, China sustained staggering war casualties of 900,000. Despite the tremendous human toll, the immense drain on its scarce economic resources, and the end of hopes for a quick recovery of Taiwan, the Beijing government did reap significant political benefits. While Chinese troops were mounting costly charges against well-entrenched American soldiers in battlefronts in Korea, the Chinese government carried out a fierce propaganda war back home. The campaign began in earnest in late 1950 and lasted until Mao Zedong declared "a great victory in the war to resist U.S. aggression and aid Korea" in September 1953.[80] The "Resist America, Aid Korea" campaign appealed strongly to the Chinese patriotic sentiments, and intensified popular nationalist support for the Communist leadership. The fact that the "People's Volunteers" fought the world's most powerful army to a stalemate rekindled an enormous sense of national pride and confidence. The Korean War also reinforced the Chinese outlook of a hostile *Meidi* working tenaciously against the interests of China and Chinese people.

In the early 1950s, while both the Cold War and McCarthyism were in full swing, America was hunting out the "Reds," purging universities and government agencies of Communist sympathizers in a way that was reminiscent of the thought reform in China. The Korean War seemed to have provided justification for the official American verdict on Communist China as a menace to its neighbors and to the world. The U.S. government subsequently hardened its policy toward the People's Republic, and the attitudes of the American public toward China turned hostile. Concurrently, in China many intellectuals, especially those who had returned from America, were under severe pressure to eradicate any possible lingering affinity they still had with the American "imperialists." As a result of direct confrontation in the battlefield, the Communist leadership attempted to completely oust American influence from China.

Against the backdrop of widespread anti-Americanism among "progressive intellectuals," which was a political legacy of the pre-1949 era, the "Resist America, Aid Korea" campaign became one of the most pressing political issues in China during the first years of the 1950s. Anti-American demonstrations, once propelled by the student leaders, were now organized by the government. To galvanize patriotic support for the war in Korea, Party propagandists borrowed directly from the student anti-American protests of the 1940s for vocabulary and techniques to garner support for the fledgling regime and to shape public opinion. Artists and cartoonists incorporated recent anti-American issues into their works, and produced a flood of picture books, cartoons, and posters that portrayed American soldiers who were stationed in immediate post–World War II China as outright robbers, thieves, rapists, and murderers, brutal and bestial men with little regard for Chinese life, property, and dignity. The American soldiers in Korea, however, were depicted as moral weaklings whose cowardly behavior contrasted sharply with noble heroism as demonstrated by the Chinese CPV. The officially sanctioned mass media of the "Resist America, Aid Korea" movement, therefore, reinforced in a sensational manner old negative images as well as created new poignant images of American soldiers and American society that persisted throughout most of the Cold War period.

The intellectuals, including university students, who had voiced opposition essentially against the U.S. government's policies in the late 1940s, were now called upon to condemn anything American. Given the unfavorable attitudes many educated Chinese had held toward the American government in the recent past, their initial enthusiasm over the establishment of the People's Republic, and especially the fact that China and the United States were at war with each other, their denunciation of *Meidi* cannot be dismissed simply as a result of their involuntary cooperation with the Communist government. In the early 1950s, the Chinese government was able to count on national loyalty. Its efforts to build a strong country and its military confrontation abroad gained it the support of Chinese intellectuals even though the latter lost an unprecedented degree of political freedom. On the other hand, the intellectuals also seemed to have recoiled before the massive indoctrination machine and under duress rephrased their rhetoric in revolutionary terminology. In the final analysis, the intellectuals' censure of *Meidi* can probably be attributed to a mixture of spontaneity and government coercion.

NOTES

1. The origins of the Korean conflict have been much debated. Newly available sources indicate that Soviet leader Joseph Stalin as well as Chinese Communist leader Mao Zedong were aware of and gave approval to the North Korean leader Kim Il Sung's plan to attack South Korea. An earlier statement by Secretary of State Dean Acheson that the United States did not consider South Korea and Taiwan part of the U.S. "defensive perimeter" in the Pacific might have precipitated such a move. However, Mao did not seem to contemplate the prospect of major Chinese involvement, as the new government was preoccupied with rebuilding an economy that was in a shambles, and with making preparations for taking Tibet and GMD-controlled Taiwan. (See, for example, Chen Jian, *China's Road to the Korean War: The Making of the Sino-American Confrontation* [New York: Columbia University Press, 1994], 85–90; Michael H. Hunt, *The Genesis of Chinese Communist Foreign Policy* [New York: Columbia University Press, 1996], 183–89.)

2. Allen S. Whiting, *China Crosses the Yalu: The Decision to Enter the Korean War* (Stanford: Stanford University Press, 1968); Chen, *China's Road to the Korean War*; Zhang Shu Guang, *Mao's Military Romanticism: China and the Korean War, 1950*–1953 (Lawrence: University Press of Kansas, 1995). Other accounts of the Korean War based on newly available sources from China and Russia include William Whitney Stueck, *The Korean War: An International History* (Princeton: Princeton University Press, 1995); Sergei N. Goncharov, John W. Lewis, and Xue Litai, *Uncertain Partners: Stalin, Mao and the Korean War* (Stanford: Stanford University Press, 1993); and some articles in Odd Arne Westad, ed., *Brothers in Arms: The Rise and Fall of the Sino-Soviet Alliance, 1945–1963* (Washington, D.C.: Woodrow Wilson Center Press, 1998).

3. See Chen Wen-hui, *Wartime "Mass" Campaigns in Communist China: Official Country-wide "Mass Movements" in Professed Support of the Korean War* (Lackland Air Force Base, Tex.: Air Force Personnel and Training Research Center, 1955).

4. See, for example, David Kidd, *Peking Story* (New York: Clarkson N. Potter, 1988), 142.

5. Suzanne Pepper, *Radicalism and Education Reform in 20th-Century China: The Search for an Ideal Development Model* (New York: Cambridge University Press, 1996), 171–72. For an analysis of Chinese reactions to American missionary efforts in China, see Michael H. Hunt, *The Making of a Special Relationship: The United States and China to 1914* (New York: Columbia University Press, 1983), 154–77.

6. Bai Ren, "Tangyi paodan" (Sugar-coated bullets), in *Sufan juzuo xuan* (Selected works on elimination of counterrevolutionaries), ed. Wang Su (Beijing: Qunzhong chubanshe, 1979), 92.

7. See, for example, Xinhua shishi congkanshe, eds., *Meijun zhuHua shiqi de xuezhai* (The bloody debts American troops stationed in China incurred) (Beijing: Renmin chubanshe, 1950); Li Cunsong et al., *Meijun baoxingtu* (Atrocities of American troops in pictures) (Beijing: Renshijian chubanshe, 1951); Zhongyang meishu xueyuan kangMei yuanChao weiyuanhui, eds., *Xuanchuanhua cankao ziliao* (Reference materials for propaganda posters) (Beijing: Zhongyang meishu xueyuan, 1951); "Meidi qinHua nianbiao" (A chronology of American imperialists' invasion of China), *Renmin ribao*, November 16, 1950.

8. The Chinese delegate Wu Xiuquan proclaimed in the United Nations that "since the Chinese people won their victory on the Chinese mainland, the United States Government has still more frantically carried out a policy of rearming Japan to oppose the Chinese people and the other Asian peoples. At present, the United States Government has not only turned Japan into its main base in the Far East in preparation for aggressive war, but it has already begun to use this base as a means to launch aggressive wars against a series of

Asian countries." United Nations, *Security Council Official Records*, No. 69, 527th Meeting, November 28, 1950, 2–25.

9. In an interview with the American leftist correspondent Anna Louise Strong in Yanan in 1946, Mao first illustrated his theory of the "paper tiger." According to him, the U.S. reactionaries were all paper tigers. He claimed that "speaking of U.S. imperialism, people seem to feel that it is terribly strong. . . . But it will be proved that the U.S. reactionaries, like all reactionaries in history, do not have much strength." (See Mao Tse-tung, *Selected Works of Mao Tse-tung* [Peking: Foreign Languages Press, 1961], 4:97–101.)

10. For an analysis of the pragmatic approach of the CCP at the time, see James Readon-Anderson, *Yenan and the Great Powers: The Origins of Chinese Communist Foreign Policy, 1944–1946* (New York: Columbia University Press, 1980), 51–67.

11. For a detailed discussion, see Chen Jian's *China's Road to the Korean War*, 33–63.

12. The five articles include: "Cast Away Illusions, Prepare for Struggle," "Farewell, Leighton Stuart!" "Why It Is Necessary to Discuss *The White Paper*," "'Friendship' or Aggression?" and "The Bankruptcy of the Idealist Conception of History." See Mao Tse-tung, *Selected Works of Mao Tse-tung*, 4:425–559.

13. Mao, *Selected Works of Mao Tse-tung*, 4:447–50.

14. The Nationalist government in Taiwan occupied China's seat in the United Nations until the early 1970s, when Beijing was admitted into the United Nations.

15. *New York Times*, October 1, 1949.

16. Whiting, *China Crosses the Yalu*, 58.

17. See United Nations, *Security Council Official Records*, 2–25.

18. This particular title suggested that China's involvement was an extension of brotherly assistance to a neighbor in need.

19. *Renmin ribao* and *Guangming ribao* were two of the most important newspapers that closely represented the views of the CCP. The two newspapers were full of such expressions after China entered the war.

20. See C.C. Fang, "The Way of the US Aggressor: Korea," in *People's China* 2 (December 1950): 5–7.

21. *Renmin ribao*, January 1, 1951.

22. Mao Tse-tung, *Selected Works of Mao Tse-tung* (Peking: Foreign Languages Press, 1977), 5:45.

23. See *Renmin ribao* and *Guangming ribao* in the months of October, November, and December.

24. See *Renmin ribao*, November 1, 15, 1950.

25. See, for example, "Xiangying zuguo haozhao relie canjia junxiao" (Respond to the call of the motherland and join the military schools enthusiastically), *Guangming ribao*, December 19, 1950.

26. See *Guangming ribao*, December 17, 26, 27, 1950.

27. Chen, *Wartime "Mass" Campaigns*, 35.

28. The warm welcome home accorded the Korean War heroes contrasted sharply with the ignominious fate that awaited the Chinese POWs, who were often condemned as traitors and ostracized by the society. For a study of the experiences of the Chinese POWs, see Philip West with Li Zhihua, "Interior Stories of the Chinese POWs in the Korean War," in *Remembering the "Forgotten War": The Korean War Through Literature and Art*, ed. Philip West and Suh Ji-moon (Armonk, N.Y.: M.E. Sharpe, 2001), 152–86.

29. Shao Feng, "Zuguo, wo xiangying nide haozhao!" (Motherland, I answer your call) *Guangming ribao*, December 17, 1950.

30. Jin Feng, "Yige daxuesheng de juexin" (A university student's resolution), *Renmin*

ribao, November 6, 1950.

31. See *Renmin ribao*, January 5, 1951.

32. Ibid., November 16, 1950.

33. Ibid., November 20, 1950.

34. "Shi kangmei yuanchao sixiang jiaoyu pubian shenru" (Deepen the resist America, aid Korea ideological education to every level), *Guangming ribao*, December 26, 1950.

35. *Renmin ribao*, November 5, 1950.

36. Liu Eyie, "Meiguo xuexiao jiaoyu zhenmianmu" (The true colors of the American educational system), *Guangming ribao*, December 17, 1950.

37. Cheng Zhi, "Meiguo jiaoyude junguozhuyihua" (The militarization of American education), *Guangming ribao*, December 18, 1950.

38. Ding Jing, "Kan, zhe jiushi Meiguo!" (Look, this is America) *Renmin ribao*, November 16, 1950.

39. See, for example, Zhang Wenyuan, ed., *KangMei yuanChao sanwen xuancui* (Selected prose on resist America, aid Korea) (Beijing: Jiefangjun wenyi chubanshe, 1990); Tianjinshi wenyijie baowei shijie heping fandui Meidi qinlue weiyuanhui (Committee of the Tianjin cultural circles on safeguarding world peace and opposing American imperialist invasion), eds., *KangMei yuanChao dumuju xuan* (Selected one-act dramas on resist America, aid Korea) (Beijing: Dazhong shudian, 1950); Huang Di et al., *Ba paodan da shangqu!* (Shoot the artillery skyward) (Beijing: Sanlian shudian, 1951).

40. See "Art Fight in Korea" *People's China* 3 (January 1951):26.

41. See Wang Yao, "Fanmei yundong zai zhongguo wenxue shang de fanying," *Guangming ribao*, December 16, 1950.

42. Situ Meitang was one of the well known "democratic personages" (*minzhu renshi*) in China in the fifties.

43. See Chen, *Wartime "Mass" Campaigns*, 32–35.

44. Huang Jiguang died as a result of blocking the gunport of an enemy pillbox with his body to shield his company's advance. In the case of Qiu Shaoyun, he and his fellow soldiers hid themselves in the grass right in front of an American fortification. Then a stray American incendiary bomb hit near where Qiu was hiding. His clothes were soon on fire. However, in order not to endanger the life of other soldiers, Qiu kept still and was in the end burned to death.

45. For more details on the appeal of Wei's "Most Beloved People," see Philip West, "The Korean War and the Criteria of Significance in Chinese Popular Culture," *The Journal of American-East Asian Relations* 1 (winter 1992): 383–408. For a full text of this article in Chinese, see Wei Wei, "Shui shi zui keaide ren?" (Who are the most beloved people?), in *Kangmei yuanChao sanwen xuancui*, 3–7.

46. Wei, "Get Them Down," in *Chinese Literature* 2 (1953): 120.

47. Zhongyang meishu xueyuan, *Xuanchuanhua cankao ziliao* (Reference materials for propaganda posters), no. 6.

48. See "Shoudu kangMei yuanChao zhongde xiju huodong" (Resist America, aid Korea drama activities in the capital), *Guangming ribao*, December 27, 1950.

49. "Art Fight for Korea," *People's China* 3 (January 1, 1951): 26.

50. Renmin chubanshe bianjibu, eds., *Zenyangzuo xuanchuanyuan* (How to be a propagandist) (Beijing: Renmin chubanshe, 1951), 11–12; see also Frederick T.C. Yu, *The Propaganda Machine in Communist China—With Special Reference to Ideology, Policy, and Regulations, as of 1952* (Lackland Air Force Base, Tex.: Air Force Personnel and Training Research Center, 1955), 24.

51. See West, "The Korean War and the Criteria of Significance in Chinese Popular Culture," for a discussion on the effect of the appeal-centered literature on the general public.

52. John D. Dower, *War without Mercy: Race and Power in the Pacific War* (New York: Pantheon Books, 1986), x.

53. See also Pingchao Zhu, "The Korean War at the Dinner Table"; and James Gao, "Myth of the Heroic Soldier and Images of the Enemy," in *America's Wars in Asia: A Cultural Approach to History and Memory*, ed. Philip West, Steven I. Levine, and Jackie Hiltz (Armonk, N.Y.: M.E. Sharpe, 1998), 183–91; 192–202.

54. In *China's Intellectuals and the State: In Search of a New Relationship*, ed. Merle Goldman and Timothy Cheek (Cambridge: The Council on East Asian Studies, Harvard University, 1987), Goldman and Cheek point out that "although intellectuals in modern times have switched from serving their culture to serving their nation, their service to the nation has severely limited their intellectual and moral autonomy," 1.

55. R. David Arkush, *Fei Xiaotong and Sociology in Revolutionary China* (Cambridge: Harvard University Press, 1981), 225. During the anti-rightist campaign of 1957, which branded 300,000 intellectuals "rightists" and effectively ended their careers, Fei, however, was labeled as an agent of American cultural aggression and was denounced as a "rightist."

56. Mao Tse-tung, "Cast Away Illusions, Prepare for Struggle," 4:427.

57. Mao Tse-tung, "Farewell, Leighton Stuart!" 4:438.

58. *Renmin ribao*, September 1, 1949.

59. *Guangming ribao*, August 23, 1949.

60. Arkush, *Fei Xiaotong,* 218.

61. United Nations, *Security Council Official Records*, No. 68, 526th Meeting, November 28, 1950, 12–26.

62. Liu Butong, "Zhaoyaojingxia kan Meiguo duihuade wenhua 'yuanzhu,'" (Examine the American cultural "assistance" to China under the monster-revealing mirror) *Renmin ribao*, January 10, 1951.

63. Tseng Chao-lun (Zeng Zhaolun), "The Disposal of American-Subsidized Schools Is the Foremost Task on the Current Cultural Front Now," in *Chinese Communist Education: Records of the First Decade*, ed. Stewart Fraser (Nashville: Vanderbilt University Press, 1965), 99.

64. For a study of the accommodation of the prestigious Yanjing University, an American-founded Christian university, to the new order and its demise in 1952, as a result of Chinese nationalism, the Communist revolution, and especially the Korean War, see Philip West, *Yenching University and Sino-American Relations, 1916–1952* (Cambridge: Harvard University Press, 1976), 195-243.

65. See *Renmin ribao*, November 13, 1951.

66. Nie Rongzhi, "Liumei ganxiang" (Impressions from a visit to America), *Guangming ribao*, December 28, 1950.

67. For more information on Jin Yuelin, see John Israel, *Lianda: A Chinese University in War and Revolution* (Stanford: Stanford University Press, 1998), 127, 157–58, 193–94.

68. Chin Yueh-lin (Jin Yuelin), "Criticizing My Decadent Bourgeois Ideology," in *Chinese Communist Education*, 150–51.

69. For more discussions on Lu Zhiwei and the issues involving his presidency at Yanjing, see West, *Yenching University and Sino-American Relations,* 133–35.

70. Maria Yen, *The Umbrella Garden: A Picture of Student Life in China* (New York: Macmillan, 1954), 260–61.

71. See Lu Chih-wei, "U.S. Imperialist Cultural Aggression as Seen in Yenching University," in *Chinese Communist Education*, 105; Lu Yao-hua, "I Denounce My Father, Lu Chih-wei," in *Chinese Communist Education*, 139.

72. Kidd, *Peking Story*, 161.

73. Wu Ningkun, *A Single Tear: A Family's Persecution, Love, and Endurance in Communist China* (Boston: Little, Brown and Company, 1993).

74. Israel, *Lianda,* 386.

75. The new guideline also highlighted "revolutionary patriotism, passion for the Party, the army, and the leaders" and opposed "narrow-minded nationalism," which entailed skepticism about unity with the Soviet Union. See Chung Shih, *Higher Education in Communist China* (Hong Kong: The Union Research Institute, 1958), 9.

76. For a study based on new Russian and Chinese documentary sources on the history of the Sino-Soviet alliance, with its rise in the late 1940s, peak in the 1950s, and collapse by the early 1960s, see Westad, ed., *Brothers in Arms*.

77. Arkush, *Fei Xiaotong*, 218.

78. In *Radicalism and Education Reform in 20th-Century China*, Pepper details the overhauling of the higher educational system to conform to the Soviet pattern, 164–91.

79. See *Guangming ribao*, March 28, 1953.

80. Mao Tse-tung, *Selected Works of Mao Tse-tung*, 5:115.

CONCLUSION

In modern China, the themes of national unity and independence have been critical components of its political discourse. Patriotic nationalistic tides, the driving force of Chinese revolution of the twentieth century, "engulf all that stands in their path—imperial, Republican, and Communist institutions."[1] The CCP was propelled to power partly by championing China's freedom from foreign influence. The Communist leadership today still voices loudly and clearly such political rhetoric as "no interference in China's internal affairs" and "no violation of China's sovereignty," which characterized the student anti-American movement in late forties. An examination of such political expressions asserted vehemently in the middle of the twentieth century can provide a historical perspective to contemporary Chinese political values and offer insights into the dynamics of Chinese-American relations.

With Japan's unconditional surrender in the fall of 1945, China seemed to be emerging as an independent nation at long last. Foreign powers' unequal treaties with the country had been relinquished, which erased the vestiges of its semicolonial status. However, Japan's surrender ended the war, but did not usher in peace. The political reality in China served as a blow to the high expectations cherished by educated Chinese. Far from fulfilling a vigorous function in the postwar world, China was on the brink of another war. The political and military crises provided fertile soil for student activism. Domestic instability pushed many young intellectuals to take direct action in the hope of shaping their country's political landscape. While the power struggle between the GMD and the CCP entered its crucial stage, Chinese intellectuals, especially the students, became a potent force. As one historian asserts: "During the unrelenting crises of the 1940s, people had heightened political concerns, and many became politically active. Even those formerly aloof from politics became involved for the first time."[2]

The United States figured importantly in China's revolutionary transformation in the mid-twentieth century. From the end of World War II until 1949, the

United States, as the strongest Western power, had a conspicuous presence in China. The period, however, saw the expression of growing ill feelings toward the American presence in urban China, manifested largely and explicitly in the media, in scholarly opinions, and especially in student movements. During this period, warm Chinese memories of America as a crucial ally during World War II gave way to suspicion and even resentment.

What led to the shift in young, urban Chinese intellectual opinion of the United States from warm friendship fostered during World War II to bitterness in the postwar period? Vehement youth protests had to be understood in the broader political context of modern China's passion for national salvation. In their search for ways to achieve national autonomy, politically conscious Chinese displayed a strong antiforeign tendency. In the aftermath of World War II, the U.S. government involved itself in China's internal conflicts in the hope of promoting a pro-American political regime and minimizing the Soviet influence in the country. Its involvement, however, embittered many educated urbanites. Sensitive to any foreign action that appeared to jeopardize China's national integrity and autonomy, the increasingly hostile educated Chinese, especially the younger ones, became highly suspicious of the visible American presence in their country. Meanwhile, the absence of national unity in the late forties rendered them suspicious of American "interference" in Chinese affairs. Perceptions and nationalism, therefore, reinforced each other and produced anti-American thunder.

The presence of GIs in the immediate post–World War II China constituted an important chapter in Sino-American relations. It further politicized and radicalized a large number of young Chinese elite; the negative images of the GIs developed among the urban populace were deliberately cultivated and propagated by the Communists during not only China's Civil War, but also its confrontation with the United States in the Cold War era. A great number of incidents involving American servicemen and local Chinese were reported in Chinese newspapers between 1946 and the early part of 1947. In the eyes of the Chinese, the accidents did not stem simply from reckless behavior on the part of American troops, but also reflected American insensitivity and racial arrogance. They became issues of national pride, thus provoking particular exasperation from the Chinese who were keenly conscious of the lowly position that their country had occupied in the past hundred years. Consequently, the presence of American servicemen, compounded with their rowdy behavior in the immediate postwar China, took on a larger political and cultural significance. It greatly impacted Sino-American relations, since many embittered urban Chinese looked upon the United States as simply continuing the legacy of imperialism. In this sense, the direct contact between U.S. servicemen and Chinese civilians had results that were far greater in importance than might have been expected from the limited American military involvement. This contact served as a prism through which politically sensitive Chinese perceived the postwar Chinese-American relationship. A few years later, when Communist China and the United States confronted each other in Korea, the incidents involving American soldiers served as effective ammunition for attacks against

U.S. "imperialism." They were rewritten in exaggerated and black-and-white terms to rekindle people's indignation toward a country at war with China.

Gender and class assumed new importance when compounded with ethnicity and nationalist discourse. The interplay of nationalism and gender, class, and race was revealed visibly in the outburst of nationwide student outrage over the sensational Shen Chong *shijian* (incident), which inaugurated large-scale student demonstrations of the Civil War period. The rape of "a weak, helpless, and virtuous young woman from a distinguished family by an American bully,"[3] which caused the loss of her chastity, a young woman's most intrinsic value as commonly perceived by the society, assumed great symbolic significance. In the eyes of many, it epitomized the rape of a weak China by the United States, and was therefore tantamount to the loss of national honor and integrity.

The celebrated rape case served as a powerful political tool. Immediately after the Shen Chong *shijian*, the GMD officials demonstrated deep concerns over the possible Communist exploitation of the issue, while the CCP members were elated over its bigger significance for their cause. Both parties recognized the sensitive, inflammable, and exploitable nature of the incident. While one saw in it potential political harm, the other perceived potential political gains.

The Shen Chong *shijian* crystallized the poignant urban Chinese images of American soldiers and provides a unique lens for studying the deterioration of Chinese-American relations. Many Chinese today who were students in the late 1940s still remember the rape of Shen Chong because of the nationwide sensation it aroused.[4] Upon the Communist triumph in 1949 and especially during China's open hostilities with the United States in the Korean War, the rape case received renewed and invigorated publicity and served as the most vivid and glaring example of the American imperialistic insult to the Chinese.

During the Maoist years of the 1960s and 1970s when politics was often combined with the teaching and learning of the Chinese language and literature, the Shen Chong rape case was incorporated into textbooks in elementary schools and became mandatory reading. Since dreary political stories on "class struggle" and Mao's writings dominated the teaching materials, the story of Shen Chong involving the "American devils" (*Meiguo guizi*) and the rare and sensational topic of rape made a relatively more interesting reading and a deeper impression on young students. The younger generation of Chinese thus learned from the text that the drunken American soldiers did something "inhuman" to an innocent college student named Shen Chong.

In the post-Mao period, the Shen Chong *shijian* continued to be molded to serve political ends. In 1984, almost 40 years after the incident, the Beijing Institute of Research on the History of the Chinese Communist Party compiled a detailed collection of primary materials related to the incident, as part of its project to publish source information on "significant historical events that had originated in Beijing, but had great impact on the course of the Chinese Revo-lution."[5] The publication of materials on the Shen Chong *shijian* by the Beijing University Press in the immediate aftermath of the Chinese government's military crackdown on student protesters in Tiananmen Square on June 4, 1989, was hardly coincidental. The Shen Chong rape case was again used as a symbol of American violation of Chinese "human rights" and served as an official Chinese counterattack to the American charge of the Chinese government's disregard of human rights.

The vigorous expression of educated youths' enmity toward the United States provided a strong stimulus to the Communist urban revolution, and constituted an important political issue in the course of the Chinese Civil War. The CCP found in it an excellent opportunity to openly attack the GMD and the U.S. government. Student demands for the departure of American troops from China, and for a stop to American interference in Chinese affairs, and nationwide demonstrations against the shift in American occupation policy in Japan, dovetailed nicely with the Communist propaganda line. Furthermore, the GMD inadvertently assisted the Communist cause by identifying the CCP with the popular nationalistic, anti-American movements and by resorting to repressive measures against intellectual dissent under the pretext of fighting Communist penetration. Accordingly, the CCP appeared to be the better defender of Chinese national interests, garnered more credibility, and was perceived by many urban Chinese as an alternative solution to China's political crisis. The Communist leader Mao Zedong affirmed with great joy in the aftermath of the Shen Chong *shijian* that the student movement in the GMD-controlled cities constituted a "second front" in the ongoing power struggle between the CCP and the GMD.

The Chinese anti-American sentiment proved to be a disturbing phenomenon of grave concern to American diplomats and other observers. It often baffled and offended American officials, who failed to comprehend the profound nationalist sentiment behind the forceful expression of young intellectual resentment and, consequently, underestimated its implications for the course of Sino-American relations. U.S. officials in the late 1940s had hoped to win the support of educated Chinese. American postwar activities, however, gravely undermined the image of the United States among the group of people whose support the Americans had solicited. Even before the Communists assumed national power, the U.S. government as well as the GMD had already alienated many urban elite.

The animosity that many young Chinese intellectuals displayed toward the United States manifested itself mainly in the political realm. In the midst of expressions of anti-American sentiment, admiration for American scientific and technological progress and material wealth persisted, and private friendships continued. What the educated youths attacked were essentially U.S. policies toward China and Japan. Nevertheless, as the decade of the 1940s drew to a close, a general disillusionment among politically engaged Chinese threatened to warp the future of the Sino-American relationship. In 1948, a Chinese student who had graduated from the Missouri School of Journalism wrote down "c/o Monkey King" when asked to supply his home address to the school alumni network, since he saw no prospect for the establishment of a lasting friendly relationship between the two countries.[6]

While many students in urban China in the late forties became increasingly critical of the role the United States played in a country undergoing revolution, many Americans in the fifties began to question their government on how it could have allowed China to turn Communist. In other words, while many educated youths in China in the late forties were calling for no more American interference, the American public of the fifties looked with dismay at a "friendly" China transforming itself into a "Red menace," and concluded that their government had failed to intervene more to forestall the Communist triumph there. The pained surprise also pointed to a persistent, yet erroneous American thinking that "China was made up of people who in their hearts wanted to become just like them."[7]

The search for the reasons why the United States had "lost China" dominated the McCarthy era of anticommunism, mainly because the Chinese revolution and the Korean War had created in the country "the atmosphere hospitable to the spasms of fear and frustration."[8] American literature of the 1950s and early 1960s on U.S. policy toward China in the late forties centered largely on what the United States could have done in China. The main argument suggested that if the United States had fully equipped and supplied the Chinese Nationalist forces, and pressured the Nationalist government to reform, the GMD would not have lost to the CCP in 1949 and fled to Taiwan.[9] What the writers failed to realize was that American involvement in China's political disputes as well as American efforts to bolster the GMD served only to further provoke intellectual opposition and to advance the Communist cause. Their arguments were severely challenged in the following decades, when, disillusioned with the Vietnam War and enthused by the reestablishment of relationships between China and the United States following President Richard Nixon's visit to China, the new generation of American diplomatic historians argued that China was not America's to lose or to have in the first place and that the United States could not have changed the course of the Chinese revolution. According to one historian, the answer to the question of "what, if anything, was lost?" in China was simple: "nothing."[10] On the other hand, one may argue that the U.S. government had indeed "lost China" prior to the Communist takeover, for it had lost the goodwill of an important segment of the Chinese population: politically articulate Chinese youths.

The prevailing anti-American sentiment among educated Chinese worked to the advantage of the CCP not only in its contest for power with the GMD, but also in its later confrontation with the United States during the Cold War era. The CCP was swept into power in 1949 with a record of avowed commitment to ending foreign impingement on China. Upon seizing power, the new CCP leadership, in order to maintain and enhance the momentum of the Chinese revolution, continued its committed role as the anti-imperialist champion and exploited fully the accumulated public hostility toward the United States.

China's military confrontation with the United States during the Korean War had profound domestic significance. The nationwide "Resist America, Aid Korea" campaign became one of the most inflammatory political causes in China in the early 1950s. The Communist-sponsored anti-American movement bore significant political relevance to the Chinese intellectual community. On the one hand, the Communist authorities counted on the existing anti-American sentiment among politically assertive young intellectuals for their active support for China's involvement in the Korean War and appealed strongly to their patriotism. On the other hand, they used this opportunity to eradicate whatever lingering "illusions" the intellectuals, especially those who had received education in the United States or who had been educated in American-sponsored schools in China, might cherish toward the United States, to heighten their hostility toward the Americans, and to further secure their loyalty to the CCP. In this sense, the Communist leaders saw in the Korean War both a challenge and an opportunity.[11]

In staging the anti-American campaign, Communist organizers co-opted and employed most of the techniques and political rhetoric of the student anti-American movements of the late forties, and molded and remolded them to serve political ends and reshape public opinion. Stories about the "atrocities" committed by American soldiers, the Marshall Mission, the American military assistance to the Nationalist government, the Sino-American Commercial Treaty, the Shen Chong rape case, and the American occupation policy toward Japan assumed new importance and served as examples of "American imperialistic aggression against the Chinese people." The government-sanctioned propaganda had a substantial effect on the Chinese of various levels, since they appeared to embrace the official view of the celebrated heroism and invincibility of the Chinese soldiers and the alleged cowardliness and wickedness of their American counterparts. The effect was particularly felt among many young, educated urban Chinese as they became actively engaged in the renewed anti-American campaign.

The task of the CCP propagandists was made easier because the seed of enmity had been planted prior to the Korean War. Distrust of the political intentions of the U.S. government was nothing new to the Chinese intellectual circle. Anti-American sentiment in China had been building up its momentum in the late 1940s. Now faced with what they perceived to be U.S. hostility toward the People's Republic, many Chinese became genuinely resentful of the United States. With the proliferation of war literature, Chinese college students and established intellectuals as well as ideologues turned the home front into a front of demonizing the American government, vilifying American soldiers, vulgarizing American society, and glorifying "New China" (xin Zhongguo) and its heroic fighters. The vitriolic images became an important part of the Cold War repertoire of expressions directed at the United States.

Chinese obsession with national self-determination is by no means a thing of the past. In the aftermath of the 1989 Tiananmen massacre and the collapse of Soviet and East European communism, the Chinese Communist leadership suffered a severe erosion of credibility internationally and has repeatedly resorted to the use of patriotism to counteract political pressure and censure from the West. Confronted with the rapid decline of Marxist and Maoist beliefs, it has relied increasingly upon nationalism as a unifying ideology to maintain stability within the Party, to buttress its political legitimacy, and to elicit public support. The eclipse of communism in China has left a political vacuum that nationalism has been filling.

Patriotic nationalistic sentiment has also reemerged as an intellectual force in China. The upsurge of nationalism corresponds with the country's rapid economic development and modernization and its growing prominence in the global political economy. In 1978, two years after the death of China's revolutionary leader Mao Zedong, Deng Xiaoping emerged as the new paramount leader and launched drastic economic reforms. The impact of the reforms has become more pronounced since early 1992, when Deng reaffirmed the government's determination to quicken the pace of modernization, which had suffered a setback since the Tiananmen Incident. Since the 1990s, record economic growth has instilled in many Chinese a strong sense of national pride and self-confidence. On the other hand, China's growing economic power and seemingly assertive irredentism over "lost territories" have aroused concerns in the United States about the "China threat." Although the proclaimed official U.S. policy toward China has centered for the most part on engagement, many in the country also call for a policy of "containing" China,[12] and the mainstream media has swung largely to the negative side of the pendulum.[13]

It took China and the United States over two decades to reestablish official relations after the Communist triumph in 1949. Today, more than 20 years later, the relationship between the two countries is again characterized by high-sounding rhetoric, irritants, and crises. The U.S.-China relationship has been fraught with contentious issues ever since the Tiananmen Incident, which shattered the American illusion that China was on its way to becoming just like the United States.[14] Debates over such issues as Taiwan, Hong Kong, Tibet, nuclear arms proliferation, arms sale, most-favored-nation trading status, human rights, and China's entry into the World Trade Organization (WTO) have bred suspicion, frustration, and resentment in both countries. More recently, NATO's bombing of the Chinese embassy in Belgrade, which killed three Chinese journalists (May 1999), was perceived by many Chinese as master-minded by the United States and led to student demonstrations and stoning of the U.S. embassy in Beijing;[15] the U.S. Spy Plane Incident (April 2001) again pushed Chinese nationalism to the forefront, although this time the expressions of anti-American sentiment were confined mainly to Internet chatrooms.

Today, overwhelming evidence of American commercial and cultural influence in China and Chinese admiration for American material wealth and things made in the U.S.A. have not deterred the intellectuals from being critical of U.S. policy toward their country. As a result of its historical connection to independence from Western dominance, nationalism still exerts a strong appeal in China. Sensitive to the issue of national self-determination, the Chinese intelligentsia is quick to discern American initiatives in thwarting Chinese national aspirations and to charge the United States of acting as a "global hegemon."[16] The century-old Chinese national aspiration and growing anti-American sentiment have been reflected in a number of recent publications. In 1996, the book *China Can Say No*,[17] written by five young intellectuals, became an instant best-seller in Beijing with the first edition selling about fifty thousand copies.[18] The book demonstrates passionate anti-Americanism as well as a strong faith in China. Resplendent with nationalistic rhetoric, *China Can Say No* was immediately followed by a series of books by the Chinese writers in and outside of the country all pointing essentially to American endeavors to "contain" China. Such books as *Why Does China Say No, China Does Not Just Say No, Containing China, Surpass U.S.A., The True Story of Sino-American*

Contests, and *Behind a Demonized China*[19] have received warm responses from intellectual circles.[20] As happened in the past, such sentiment has been exploited by the Communist leadership, which has allowed the intellectuals some degree of freedom to assert their nationalistic outrage. Following the publication of a spate of literature critical of the United States, an article from *Beijing Review*, an official English-language weekly, highlighted the disillusionment of young Chinese with U.S.-China relations:

The fact that these books have emerged from fresh pens suggests that younger intellectuals are disappointed and even disgusted with American values, politics and especially, the country's China policy. It also implies that Washington's non-secret scheme to nurture a "pro-US" generation among younger Chinese has come to little avail. Needless to say, what Uncle Sam is going to deal with in the next century is still an "oriental dragon" both peace-loving and tough.[21]

At the turn of the twenty-first century, many Chinese intellectuals have again viewed the United States as an obstacle to China's self-determination and political aspirations. On the issue of nationalism, the Chinese Communist leaders and politely sensitive intellectuals have again reached a broad consensus. On the other hand, behind the surging nationalistic sentiment is a country that has extricated itself from the isolation of the Maoist decades and is immersing itself deeply in global connection.[22] Despite the political rhetoric and the existence of anti-American sentiment, very few Chinese today contemplate a severance of the relationship between the two countries. Instead, many have been calling for better mutual understanding and an improved relationship.[23] Simplistic and black-and-white Chinese images of the United States of the Cold War era have largely been replaced by a more thoughtful view that, amid conflicts and disagreements, a constructive relationship between the two countries is more desirable and still possible.[24] In the final analysis, as the editors of *China Beyond the Headlines* point out, although demonizing each other may serve immediate political interests, mutual understanding and respect will serve the interest of both countries in the long run.

NOTES

1. James Townsend, "Chinese Nationalism," *The Australian Journal of Chinese Affairs* 27 (January 1992): 97.

2. Mary G. Mazur, "Intellectual Activism in China during the 1940s: Wu Han in the United Front and the Democratic League," *The China Quarterly* 133 (March 1993), 26.

3. Zhonggong Beijing shiwei dangshi yanjiushi, eds., *Kangyi Meijun zhuhua baoxing yundong ziliao huibian* (Collected materials on the movement protesting the brutalities of U.S. troops in China) (Beijing: Beijing daxue chubanshe, 1989), 147.

4. In the summers of 1997 and 1998, I interviewed 16 retired professors who were college students in cities such as Beijing, Shanghai, Xian, Qingdao, and Harbin in 1947. All remembered the so-called Shen Chong *shijian*, although only 6 of them directly participated in the demonstrations.

5. Zhonggong Beijing shiwei, *Kangyi Meijun zhuHua baoxin*, vii.

6. Yuan Ming, "Chinese Intellectuals and the United States: The Dilemma of Individualism vs. Patriotism," *Asian Survey* 29 (July 1989), 648.

7. T. Christopher Jespersen, *American Images of China: 1931–1949* (Stanford: Stanford University Press, 1996), 82.

8. Harold R. Isaacs, *Scratches on Our Minds: American Images of China and India* (New York: The John Day Company, 1958), 216.

9. For a full argument on this theme, see Tang Tsou, *America's Failure in China, 1941-50* (Chicago: University of Chicago Press, 1963).

10. See Jespersen, *American Images of China*, 172. For a recent discussion of the American sentiment regarding the issue of "Who Lost China," see also Richard Madsen, *China and the American Dream: A Moral Inquiry* (Berkeley and Los Angeles: University of California Press, 1995), 30–33.

11. Chen Jian, *China's Road to the Korean War: The Making of the Sino-American Confrontation* (New York: Columbia University Press, 1994), 219.

12. For an analysis of this argument, see Yong Deng and Fei-ling Wang, eds., *In the Eyes of the Dragon: China Views the World* (Lanham, Md.: Rowman & Littlefield Publishers, 1999), 2. Typical of the view of the "China Threat" is a book by two American journalists titled *The Coming Conflict with China*. The book argues that military confrontations between China and the United States will be inevitable. See Richard Bernstein and Ross H. Munro, *The Coming Conflict with China* (New York: Alfred A. Knopf, 1997).

13. In his perceptive article, "Big Bad China and the Good Chinese: An American Fairy Tale," Jeffrey N. Wasserstrom discusses the American "sunshine and noir" images of the Chinese. The sunshine version romanticizes the Chinese as a people determined to "Americanize" their country and to become just like the Americans, while the "noir" view demonizes the Chinese and portrays China as a growing military menace out to undermine the American way of life. See the article in *China Beyond the Headlines*, ed. Timothy B. Weston and Lionel M. Jensen (Lanham, Md.: Rowman & Little Field Publishers, 2000), 13–35. In fact, the edited book, *China Beyond the Headlines*, was published with the view of moving beyond the headlines and looking upon China and its interests "in more complex terms than the vast majority of U.S. media presentations permit," 8.

14. For a thoughtful discussion of the American obsession with the Tiananmen crisis, and the ways in which the crisis challenged the established American notions, see Madsen, *China and the American Dream*, 1–27.

15. For an interesting study of the connections between recent student demonstrations and those of the early twentieth century, see Jeffrey N. Wasserstrom, "Student Protests in Fin-de-Siècle China," *New Left Review* 237 (September/October 1999): 52–76.

16. For discussions along this line, see Yang Yusheng, *Zhongguoren de Meiguoguan* (Chinese views of America) (Shanghai: Fudan daxue chubanshe, 1996), 279–87.

17. Song Qiang, Zhang Zangzang et al., *Zhongguo keyi shuobu* (China can say no) (Beijing: Zhonghua gongshang lianhe chubanshe, 1996).

18. Maria Hsia Chang, "Chinese Irredentist Nationalism: The Magician's Last Trick," *Comparative Strategy* 17 (1998), 86.

19. Peng Qian, Yang Mingjie, and Xu Deren, *Zhongguo weishenme shuobu? Lengzhanghow Meiguo duihua zhengce de wuqu* (Why does China say no? Mistakes in post–cold war U.S. China policy) (Beijing: Xinshijie chubanshe, 1996); Jia Qingguo, *Zhongguo bujinjin shuobu* (China does not just say no) (Beijing: Zhonghua gongshang lianhe chubanshe, 1996); Sun Geqin and Cui Hongjian, *Ezhi Zhongguo: Shenhua yu*

xianshi (Containing China: myths and realities) (Beijing: Zhongguo yanshi chubanshe, 1996); Xi Yongjun and Ma Zaihuai, *Chaoyue Meiguo: Meiguo shenhua de zhongjie* (Surpass U.S.A.: The end of the American myth) (Huhehaote: Neimengu daxue chubanshe, 1996); Chen Feng et al., *ZhongMei jiaoliang daxiezhen* (The true story of Sino-American contests) (Beijing: Zhongguo renshi chubanshe, 1996); Liu Kang, Li Xiguang et al., *Yaomohua Zhongguo de beihou* (Behind a demonized China) (Beijing: Zhong shehui kexue chubanshe, 1996).

20. Peter Hays Gries's dissertation, "Face Nationalism: Power and Passion in Chinese Anti-Foreignism" (Ph.D. diss., University of California, Berkeley, 1999), deals mainly with the development of Chinese antiforeign sentiments at the popular level in the 1990s.

21. Li Haibo, "Books on Sino-US Relations," *Beijing Review* 40 (May 1997), 4.

22. For a study of the ambiguity of contemporary Chinese nationalism, see Tong Lam, "Identity and Diversity: The Complexities and Contradictions of Chinese Nationalism," in *China Beyond the Headlines*, 147–70.

23. For more discussions on the various Chinese views of the post–Cold War world and China's position in it, see Deng, *In the Eyes of the Dragon*.

24. See Ming Wang, "Public Images of the United States," in *In the Eyes of the Dragon*, 156.

SELECTED BIBLIOGRAPHY

CHINESE LANGUAGE SOURCES

Archival Collections Consulted

Beijing dangan guan (Beijing archives), Beijing, China

"Wei Shen Chong shijian kangyi Meijun baoxing shiliao xuan" (Collected historical materials on anti-American brutality movement in response to the Shen Chong incident). *Beijing danan shiliao* (Archival materials on the history of Beijing) 5, no. 1 (1987): 37–44.

"Hu Shi danan zhong youguan Shen Chong shijian laiwang handian xuan" (Collected telegrams related to the Shen Chong incident in the Hu Shi file). *Beijing danan shiliao* (Archival materials on the history of Beijing) 34, no. 2 (1994): 34–37.

"Beiping shizhengfu youguan Shen Chong shijian laiwang handian xuanbian" (Selected documents and telegrams of the Beiping municipal government on the Shen Chong incident). *Beijing dangan shiliao* (Archival materials on the history of Beijing) 33, no. 1 (1994): 13–20.

Periodicals and Newspapers Quoted

Beijing wenshi ziliao (Cultural and historical materials of Beijing)
Beiping ribao (Beiping daily)
Dagong bao (L'impartiale)
Guangming ribao (Brilliance daily)
Guomin gongbao (National news)
Jiefang ribao (Liberation daily)
Jindaishi yanjiu (Modern history studies)
Lianhe ribao (United daily)
Lianhe wanbao (United evening news)
Meiguo yanjiu (American studies)

Mingguo chunqiu (The republican years)
Minzhu bao (Democracy news)
Qinghua yuekan (Qinghua monthly)
Renmin ribao (People's daily)
Shangwu ribao (Business daily)
Shen bao (Shanghai news)
Shijie lishi (World history)
Shijie ribao (World daily)
Wen hui bao (Collected news)
Wenshi ziliao xuanbian (A selected collection of cultural and historical materials)
Xin wan bao (New evening news)
Xinhua ribao (New China daily)
Xinmin bao (New people's news)
Xinwen bao (The news)
Xinwen wanbao (The evening news)
Yanda sannian (Three years in Yanda)
Yi shi bao (Benevolence news)
Zhongguo jindaishi (Modern Chinese history)
Zhongguo xiandaishi (History of modern China)
Zhongyang ribao (Central news)
Zongheng (Crisscross)

Books and Articles

A Ying, ed. *Fanmei Huagong jinyue wenxueji* (Collected literature on opposition to the American treaty excluding Chinese laborers). Beijing: Zhonghua shuju chuban, 1960.
A Zhe. *Zhongguo xiandai xuesheng yundong jianshi* (A short history of modern Chinese student movement). Hong Kong: Dasheng chubanshe, no date.
Aiguo yundong chubanshe, eds. *Meiguobing gun chu qu* (Roll out, American soldiers). Beiping: Aiguo yundong chubanshe, 1947.
Bai Ren. "Tangyi paodan" (Sugar-coated bullets). In *Sufan juzuo xuan* (Selected works on elimination of counterrevolutionaries), ed. Wang Su. Beijing: Qunzhong chubanshe, 1979.
Beijing daxue lishixi, *Beijing daxue xuesheng yundongshi, 1919–1949* (A history of the student movement of Beijing university, 1919–1949). Beijing: Beijing chubanshe, 1979.
Beijing daxue xuesheng zizhihui, eds. *Beida in 1946–1948*. Beiping, 1948.
Beijing daxue yuanxi lianhehui, eds. *Beida yinian* (One year in Beida). Beiping, 1947.
Chen Feng et al. *ZhongMei jiaoliang daxiezhen* (The true story of Sino-American contests). Beijing: Zhongguo renshi chubanshe, 1996.
Chen Xiqing. "Shilun kangbao yundong jiqi yiyi" (A preliminary analysis of the anti-brutality movement and its significance). In *Jiefang zhanzheng shiqi xuesheng yundong lunwenji* (Essays on the student movement during the war of liberation), ed. Zheng Guang et al., 134–40. Shanghai: Tongji daxue chubanshe, 1988.
Chen Xulu et al. *Jindai Zhongguo bashinian* (The Chinese history of the last eighty years). Shanghai: Shanghai renmin chubanshe, 1983.
Chu E. "Zhengyue geyao" (A rhyme on fighting the exclusion law). In *FanMei Huagong jinyue wenxueji* (Collected literature on opposition to the American treaty excluding Chinese laborers), ed. A Ying. Beijing: Zhonghua shuju chuban, 1960.
Deng Hong. "Zhanghou ZhongMei duanxi de yiyi: 1948nian Zhongguo renmin fandui Meiguo fuzhi Riben yundong " (A chapter in postwar Chinese-American relations: The Chinese people's movement opposing the U.S. support of Japan in 1948). *Zhongguo jindaishi yanjiu*, no. 4 (2000): 13–16.

Gongqingtuan Shanghai shiwei. *1945–1949: Shanghai xuesheng yundongshi* (1945–1949: A history of the Shanghai student movement). Shanghai: Shanghai renmin chubanshe, 1983.

He Jiliang, and Lu Jing. "Jiefang zhanzheng shiqi Shanghai gaoxiaode jiaoyun he xueyun" (Educational and student movements of Shanghai colleges and universities during the war of liberation). In *Jiefang zhanzheng shiqi xuesheng yundong lunwenji* (Essays on the student movement during the war of liberation), ed. Zheng Guang et al., 196–213. Shanghai: Tongji daxue chubanshe, 1988.

Huang Di et al. *Ba paodan da shangqu!* (Shoot the artillery skyward). Beijing: Sanlian shudian, 1951.

Jia Qingguo. *Zhongguo bujinjin shuobu* (China does not just say no). Beijing: Zhonghua gongshang lianhe chubanshe, 1996.

Li Cunsong et al. *Meijun baoxingtu* (Atrocities of American troops in pictures). Beijing: Renshijian chubanshe, 1951.

Li Haibo. "Books on Sino-US Relations." *Beijing Review* 40 (May 1997): 4.

Li Xiguang, and Liu Kang et al. *Yaomohua Zhongguo de beihou* (Behind a demonized China). Beijing: Zhongguo shehui kexue chubanshe, 1996.

Li Zhancai. "Shi xi Wusi shiqi Meiguo duihua yingxiang" (An analysis of American influence on China during the May fourth era). *Zhongguo xiandaishi* (History of modern China), no. 1 (1994): 67–71.

Liao Fengde. *Xuechao yu zhanghou Zhongguo zhengzhi* (Student movements and postwar Chinese politics). Taibei: Dongda Tushu gongsi, 1994.

Lin Guanhong. "Jinggao er wan wan tongbao jiemei" (A plea to the two hundred million fellow sisters). In *Fanmei Huagong jinyue wenxueji* (Collected literature on opposition to the American treaty excluding Chinese laborers), ed. A Ying. Beijing: Zhonghua shuju chuban, 1960.

Liu Jucai. *Zhongguo jindai funu yundongshi* (A history of modern Chinese women's movement). Beijing: Zhongguo funu chubanshe, 1989.

Liu Xiaoqing. "Xianjing xinwen zhuizong baodao: Sheng Chong shijian" (The pursuit of the Shen Chong incident by Yanjing news). *Minguo chunjiu* (The republican years) 84 (June 2000): 18–19.

Lu Zude. "Zhu Ziqing xiansheng de shengping shiji" (The life story of Mr. Zhu Ziqing). *Wenshi ziliao xuanbian*, no. 6 (1980): 85–104.

Luo Rongqu. "Meiguo yu xifang zichanjieji xinwenhua shuru Zhongguo" (The influx of American and Western bourgeois new cultures to China). In Zhou Yiliang, ed. *Zhongwai wenhua jiaoliushi* (A history of cultural exchanges between China and foreign countries). Henan: Henan renmin chubanshe, 1987.

Mao Zedong. *Jianguo yilai Mao Zedong wengao* (Mao Zedong's manuscripts since the founding of the people's republic). vol. 1, September 1949–December 1950, and vol. 2, January 1951–December 1951. Beijing: Zhongyang wenxian chubanshe, 1987, 1989.

Meng Xianzhang. "Meiguo fuzhi riben mianmianguan" (A comprehensive look at the American policy of building up Japan). *Qinghua yuekan* (May 28, 1948): 3–5.

———. *Zhongguo fan MeifuRi yundong douzhengshi* (The history of Chinese struggle against the U.S. support of Japan). Shanghai: Zhonghua shuju, 1951.

Peng Qian, Yang Mingjie, and Xu Deren. *Zhongguo weishenme shuobu? Lengzhanghow Meiguo duihua zhengce de wuqu* (Why does China say no? Mistakes in post–cold war U.S. China policy). Beijing: Xinshijie chubanshe, 1996.

Qinghua daxue xiaoshi bianxiezu. *Qinghua daxue xiaoshigao* (The history of Qinghua university). Beijing: Zhonghua shuju, 1981.

Qi Youzi. "Ku xuesheng" (Bitter student). In *Fanmei Huagong jinyue wenxueji* (Collected literature on opposition to the American treaty excluding Chinese laborers), ed. A Ying. Beijing: Zhonghua shuju chuban, 1960.

Renmin chubanshe bianjibu, eds. *Zenyangzuo xuanchuanyuan* (How to be a propagandist). Beijing: Renmin chubanshe, 1951.

Shandong daxue bianxiezu, eds. *Zhongguo gemingshi lunwen jiyao* (Essays on the revolutionary history of China). Beijing: Zhonggong dangshi ziliao chubanshe, 1987.

Shanghai daxue. *Xinbian Zhongguo xiandaishi* (A new edition of modern Chinese history). Nanchang: Jiangxi renmin chubanshe, 1987.

Song Bai. *Beijing xiandai gemingshi* (A revolutionary history of modern Beijing). Beijing: Zhongguo renmin daxue chubanshe, 1988.

Song Qiang, Zhang Zangzang, and Qiao Bian et al. *Zhongguo keyi shuobu* (China can say no). Beijing: Zhonghua gongshang lianhe chubanshe, 1996.

Sun Geqin, and Cui Hongjian. *Ezhi Zhongguo: Shenhua yu xianshi* (Containing China: myths and realities). Beijing: Zhongguo yanshi chubanshe, 1996.

Tao Jie. "Heinu yu tian lu—diyibu yicheng zhongwen de Meiguo xiaoshuo" (A black slave's cry to heaven—The first American novel translated into Chinese). *Meiguo yanjiu*, no. 3 (1991): 128–40.

Tao Wenzhao. *ZhongMei guanxishi, 1911–1950* (The history of Chinese-American relations, 1911–1950). Chongqing: Chongqing chubanshe, 1993.

———. "1946 ZhongMei shangyue: Zhanhou Meiguo duiHua zhengcezhong jingji yinsu ge'an yanjiu" (The 1946 Sino-American commercial treaty: A study of economic elements in U.S. China policy in the postwar period). *Jindaishi yanjiu*, no. 2 (March 1993): 236–58.

Tianjingshi wenyijie baowei shijie heping fandui Meidi qinlue weiyuanhui (Committee of the Tianjin cultural circles on safeguarding world peace and opposing American imperialist invasion), eds. *Kangmei yuanchao dumuju xuan* (Selected one-act dramas on resist America, aid Korea). Beijing: Dazhong shudian, 1950.

Wang Guohua. "Sheng Chong shijian shimo" (The whole story of the Sheng Chong incident). *Beijing wenshi ziliao* (Cultural and historical materials of Beijing) 51 (December 1995): 135–42.

Wang Niankun. *Xuesheng yundong shiyao jianghua* (An account of important historical events of student movements). Shanghai: Shanghai chubanshe, 1951.

Wang Ping, and Zhang Liyao, eds. *Zhongguo xiandai fengyunlu* (A turbulent history of modern China). Shanghai: Tongji daxue chubanshe, 1988.

Wang Qing. "Meiguobing gunhuiqu!" (Roll back home, American soldiers). In *Qingnian yundong huiyilu* (Recollections of the youth movement), ed. Zhang Aiping and Xiao Hua. Beijing: Zhongguo qingnian chubanshe, 1978.

Wang Zhichen. "*Dagong bao* yu 'fan MeifuRi' aiguo yundong" (l'impartiale and the patriotic movement opposing the U.S. support of Japan). *Zonghen*, no. 1 (2000): 56–57.

Wei Wei. "Shui shi zui keaide ren?" (Who are the most beloved people?). In *KangMei yuanChao sanwen xuancui* (Selected prose on resist America, aid Korea), ed. Zhang Wenyuan. Beijing: Jiefangjun wenyi chubanshe, 1991.

Wen Liming. "Lun yier yi yundongzhongde daxue jiaoshou yu Lianda jiaoshouhui—Zhongguo sishi niandai de ziyouzhuyi kaocha zhiyi" (A discussion on the university professors and Lianda's faculty meetings during the December 1 movement: One of the examinations on China's liberalism during the forties). *Jindaishi yanjiu* 70 (July 1992): 188–213.

Xi Yongjun, and Ma Zaihuai. *Chaoyue Meiguo: Meiguo shenhua de zhongjie* (Surpass U.S.A.: The end of the American myth). Huhehaote: Neimengu daxue chubanshe, 1996.

Xiao Chaoran et al. *Beijing daxue xiaoshi, 1898–1949* (The history of Beijing University, 1898–1949). Shanghai: Shanghai jiaoyu chubanshe, 1981.

Xinhua shishi congkanshe, eds. *Meijun zhuHua shiqi de xuezhai* (The bloody debts American troops stationed in China incurred). Beijing: Renmin chubanshe, 1950.

Yanda xuesheng zizhihui, eds. "Da bi zhan qian huo" (Around the time of the big verbal fight). In *Yanda sannian* (Three years in Yanda). Beiping: Yanda xuesheng zizhihui, 1948.

Yang Yusheng. "Dayang bian gaigechao de dongfang xiaoying" (The effect of the reform movement at the other side of the Pacific on the East). *Meiguo yanjiu*, no. 2 (1991): 87–117.

———. "Cong yangwu re dao diyue chao" (From the self-strengthening craze to the 1905 boycott). *Meiguo yanjiu*, no. 3 (1991): 77–91.

———. *Zhongguoren de Meiguoguan* (Chinese views of America). Shanghai: Fudan daxue chubanshe, 1996.

Yier yi yundongshi bianxiezu, eds. *Yier yi yundong shiliao xuanbian* (A selected collection of the historical materials on the December 1 movement). Kunming: Yunnan renmin chubanshe, 1980.

Yu Danchu. "Meiguo dulishi zai jindai Zhongguo de jieshao he yingxiang" (The introduction and impact of the history of American independence on modern China). *Shijie Lishi*, no. 2 (1987): 60–81.

Zhang Chunwu. *Guangxu 31 ZhongMei gongyue fengchao* (The 1905 agitation against the Sino-American labor treaty). Taibei: Taiwan shangwu yinshuguan, 1965.

Zhang Aiping, and Xiao Hua et al. *Qingnian yundong huiyilu* (Recollections of the youth movement). Beijing: Zhongguo qingnian chubanshe, 1978.

Zhang Wenyuan, ed. *KangMei yuanChao sanwen xuancui* (Selected prose on resist America, aid Korea). Beijing: Jiefangjun wenyi chubanshe, 1990.

Zhi Qun. "Zhengyue zhi jinggao er" (Second warning on fighting the Chinese exclusion law). In *FanMei Huagong jinyue wenxueji* (Collected literature on opposition to the American treaty excluding Chinese laborers), ed. A Ying. Beijing: Zhonghua shuju chuban, 1960.

Zhonggong Beijing shiwei dangshi yanjiushi, eds. *Kangyi Meijun zhuHua baoxing yundong ziliao huibian* (Collected materials on the movement protesting the brutalities of U.S. troops in China). Beijing: Beijing daxue chubanshe, 1989.

Zhonggong Kunmingshi dangshiban and Yunnansheng danganguan, eds. *1948 nian kunming "fan MeifuRi" yundong* (The 1948 *fan MeifuRi* movement in Kunming). Kunming: Yunnan renmin chubanshe, 1989.

Zhonggong Shanghai shiwei dangshi ziliao zhengji weiyuanhui, eds. *Shanghai renmin gemingshi huace* (A picture album of the revolutionary history of the Shanghai people). Shanghai: Shanghai renmin chubanshe, 1989.

Zhongguo renmin zhengzhi xieshang huiyi Beijingshi weiyuanhui wenshi ziliao yanjiu weiyuanhui, eds. *Beiping dixiadang douzheng shiliao* (Historical materials on the struggles of the Beiping underground party). Beijing: Beijing chubanshe, 1988.

Zhongguo renmin zhiyuanjung kangMei yuanChao zhanzheng zhengzhi gongzuo jingyan zongjie bianweihui. *Zhongguo renmin zhiyuanjun kangMei yuanChao zhanzheng zhengzhi gongzuo* (Political work during the Chinese people volunteers' resist America, aid Korean war). Beijing: Jiefanjun chubanshe, 1985.

Zhongguo shixuehui, eds. *Yangwu yundong* (Self-strengthening movement). Shanghai: Shanghai chubanshe, 1961.

Zhonghua quanguo funu lianhehui funu yundong lishi yanjiushi, eds. *Zhongguo funu yundong lishi ziliao, 1945–1949* (Historical records on women's movement in China, 1945–1949). Beijing: Zhongguo funu chubanshe, 1991.

Zhongyang meishu xueyuan kangMei yuanChao weiyuanhui, eds. *Xuanchuanhua cankao ziliao* (Reference materials for propaganda posters). Beijing: Zhongyang meishu xueyuan, 1951.

Zhou Chengen et al. *Beijing daxue xiaoshi* (A history of Beijing university). Shanghai: Shanghai jiaoyu chubanshe, 1981.

Zhou Wangjian. "Huiyi Shanghai xuesheng fan MeifuRi yundong" (A recollection of the Shanghai student movement opposing the American support of Japan). *Wenshi ziliao xuanji* (A selected collection of cultural and historical materials) 24 (1979): 155–57.

Zi Zhongyun. *Meiguo duiHua zhengce de yuanqi he fazhan, 1945–1950* (The origins and development of U.S. policy toward China, 1945–1950). Chongqing: Chongqing chubanshe, 1987.

ENGLISH LANGUAGE SOURCES

Archival Collections Consulted

Hoover Institution Archives, Stanford, California

Carey, Arch Papers
Chaisson, Hon R. Papers
Calder, Alonzo Bland Papers
Huang, J.L. Papers
Sprouse, Philip D. Papers
Tseng, Chao-lun (Zeng Zhaolun) Papers

U.S. National Archives, Washington, D.C.

Marshall Mission Files. Record Group 59
United States Department of State Decimal Files. Record Group 59
U.S. Department of State Records of the Office of Chinese Affairs, 1945–1955
Press Publications of Records of the Office of Chinese Affairs, 1945–1955

Government Documents Consulted

U.S. Department of State. *The China White Paper: August 1949*. Stanford: Stanford University Press, 1967.

U.S. Department of State, *Foreign Relations of the United States, 1943, China*. Washington, D.C.: Government Printing Office, 1972.

U.S. Department of State. *Foreign Relations of the United States, 1946, The Far East: China*. 2 vols. Washington, D.C.: Government Printing Office, 1972.

U.S. Department of State. *Foreign Relations of the United States, 1947, The Far East: China*. Washington, D.C.: Government Printing Office, 1972.

U.S. Department of State. *Foreign Relations of the United States, 1948, The Far East: China*. Washington, D.C.: Government Printing Office, 1973.

Books and Articles

The American Information Committee. *Japan over China—America's Gain or Loss?* Shanghai, 1939.

Aplington, Henry II. "China Revisited." *Marine Corps Gazette* 57 (July 1973): 25–31.

Arkush, R. David. *Fei Xiaotong and Sociology in Revolutionary China.* Cambridge: Harvard University Press, 1981.

Arkush, R. DavOid, and Leo O. Lee, eds. *Land without Ghosts: Chinese Impressions of America from the Mid-Nineteenth Century to the Present.* Berkeley: University of California Press, 1989.

Barlow, Tani E., ed. *Gender Politics in Modern China.* Durham: Duke University Press, 1993.

Beal, John Robinson. *Marshall in China.* New York: Doubleday, 1970.

Bernstein, Richard, and Ross H. Munro. *The Coming Conflict with China.* New York: Alfred A. Knopf, 1997.

Bianco, Lucien. *Origins of the Chinese Revolution, 1915–1949.* Stanford: Stanford University Press, 1967.

Bland, Larry I., ed. *George C. Marshall's Mediation Mission to China, December 1945–January 1947.* Lexington, Va.: George C. Washington Foundation, 1998.

Bodde, Derk. *Peking Diary: A Year of Revolution.* New York: Octagon Books, 1976.

Borg, Dorothy. "America Loses Chinese Good Will." *Far Eastern Survey* 18 (February 23, 1949): 37–45.

Borg, Dorothy, and Waldo Heinrichs, eds. *Uncertain Years: Chinese-American Relations, 1947–1950.* New York: Columbia University Press, 1980.

Brandt, Conrad, Benjamin Schwartz, and John K. Fairbank. *A Documentary History of Chinese Communism.* Cambridge: Harvard University Press, 1952.

Buckley, Roger. *Occupation Diplomacy: Britain, the United States, and Japan, 1945–1952.* New York: Cambridge University Press, 1982.

Cameron, Craig M. *American Samurai: Myth, Imagination, and the Conduct of Battle in the First Marine Division, 1941–1951.* New York: Cambridge University Press, 1994.

Canning, Charles J. "Peiping Rape Case Has Deep Social, Political Background." *The China Weekly Review* (January 11, 1947): 168–69.

Chang, Maria Hsia. "Chinese Irredentist Nationalism: The Magician's Last Trick." *Comparative Strategy* 17 (1998): 83–100.

Chen, Jerome. *China and the West: Society and Culture 1815–1937.* Bloomington: Indiana University Press, 1979.

Chen Jian. *China's Road to the Korean War: The Making of the Sino-American Confrontation.* New York: Columbia University Press, 1994.

Chen, Joseph T. *The May Fourth Movement in Shanghai.* Leideon: E.J. Brill, 1971.

Chen, Wen-hui. *Wartime "Mass" Campaigns in Communist China: Official Countrywide "Mass Movements" in Professed Support of the Korean War.* Lackland Air Force Base, Tex.: Air Force Personnel and Training Research Center, 1955.

Chiang Kai-shek. *The Collected Wartime Messages of Generalissimo Chiang Kai-shek, 1937–1945.* Ed. and trans. George Kao. New York: The John Day Company, 1946.

———. *Soviet Russia in China: A Summary at Seventy.* New York: Farrar, Straus and Cubahy, 1957.

Chiang, Monlin. *Tides from the West: A Chinese Autobiography.* New Haven: Yale University Press, 1947.

Chow, Tse-tsung. *The May Fourth Movement: Intellectual Revolution in Modern China.* Cambridge: Harvard University Press, 1960.

Chung, Shih. *Higher Education in Communist China.* Hong Kong: The Union Research Institute, 1958.

Clark, George B. *Treading Softly: The U.S. Marines in China from the 1840s to the 1940s.* Pike, N.H.: The Brass Hat, 1996.

————. *Treading Softly: U.S. Marines in China, 1819–1949.* Westport, Conn.: Praeger, 2001.

Cleverley, John F. *The Schooling of China: Tradition and Modernity in Chinese Education.* Boston: George Allen and Unwin, 1985.

Clews, John C. *Communist Propaganda Techniques.* New York: Frederick A. Praeger, 1964.

Clifford, Nicholas R. *Spoilt Children of Empire: Westerners in Shanghai and the Chinese Revolution of the 1920s.* Hanover, N.H.: Middlebury College Press, 1991.

Cohen, Jerome B. "Japan: Reform vs. Recovery." *Far Eastern Survey* 17 (June 23, 1948): 137–42.

Cohen, Paul. *China and Christianity: The Missionary Movement and the Growth of Chinese Antiforeignism, 1860–1870.* Cambridge: Harvard University Press, 1963.

Cohen, Theodore. *Remaking Japan: The American Occupation as New Deal.* New York: New Press, 1987.

Cohen, Warren I. "American Perceptions of China." In *Dragon and Eagle, United States–China Relations: Past and Future,* ed. Michel Oksenberg and Robert B. Oxnam. New York: Basic Books, 1973.

————, ed. *Pacific Passage: The Study of American–East Asian Relations on the Eve of the Twenty-First Century.* New York: Columbia University Press, 1996.

————. *America's Response to China: A History of Sino-American Relations.* 4th ed. New York: Columbia University Press, 2000.

Cook, James A. "Penetration and Neocolonialism: The Shen Chong Rape Case and the Anti-American Student Movement of 1946–47." *Republican China* 22 (November 1996): 65–97.

Cosgrove, Julia F. *United States Foreign Economic Policy toward China, 1943–1946.* New York: Garland Publishing, Inc., 1987.

Deane, Hugh. *Good Deeds and Gunboats: Two Centuries of American-Chinese Encounters.* San Francisco: China Books & Periodicals, 1990.

Deng, Yong, and Fei-ling Wang, eds. *In the Eyes of the Dragon: China Views the World.* Lanham, Md.: Rowman & Littlefield Publishers, 1999.

Dewey, John. "America and the Fast East: The Issues of Pacific Policy." *Survey* 56 (May 1926): 186–90.

Dikötter, Frank. *The Discourse of Race in Modern China.* Stanford: Stanford University Press, 1992.

Donahue, William J. "The Francis Terranova Case." *The Historian* 43 (February 1981): 211–24.

Dower, John D. *War without Mercy: Race and Power in the Pacific War.* New York: Pantheon Books, 1986.

————. *Embracing Defeat: Japan in the Wake of World War II.* New York: W.W. Norton, 1999.

Edwards, Louise. "Policing the Modern Woman in Republican China." *Modern China* 26 (April 2000): 115–47.

Esherick, Joseph W. *The Origins of the Boxer Uprising.* Berkeley and Los Angeles: University of California Press, 1987.

Fairbank, John K. "China's Prospect and U.S. Policy." *Far Eastern Survey* 16 (July 2, 1947): 145–49.

────. *China Perceived: Images and Politics in Chinese-American Relations.* New York: Alfred A. Knopf, 1974.

Fang, C.C. "The Way of the US Aggressor: Korea." *People's China* 2 (December 1950): 5–7.

Fishel, Wesley R. *The End of Extraterritoriality in China.* Berkeley and Los Angeles: University of California Press, 1952.

Forrestal, James. *The Forrestal Diaries.* New York: Viking Press, 1951.

Fung, Edmund S.K. *In Search of Chinese Democracy: Civil Opposition in Nationalist China, 1929–1949.* Cambridge: Cambridge University Press, 2000.

Gao, James. "Myth of the Heroic Soldier and Images of the Enemy." In *America's Wars in Asia: A Cultural Approach to History and Memory,* ed. Philip West, Steven I. Levine, and Jackie Hiltz. Armonk, N.Y.: M.E. Sharpe, 1998.

Goette, John. "China Does Not Hate Us." *The China Monthly.* 7–8 (June 1946): 200–2.

Goldman, Merle. *China's Intellectuals: Advice and Dissent.* Cambridge: Harvard University Press, 1981.

Goldman, Merle and Timothy Cheek, eds. *China's Intellectuals and the State: In Search of a New Relationship.* Cambridge: The Council on East Asian Studies, Harvard University, 1987.

Goncharov, Sergei N., John W. Lewis, and Xue Litai. *Uncertain Partners: Stalin, Mao and the Korean War.* Stanford: Stanford University Press, 1993.

Gray, William. "Friendship Lost? How Stands US Prestige in China?" *Time* 49 (February 10, 1947): 22–23.

Grieder, Jerome B. *Hu Shih and the Chinese Renaissance: Liberalism in the Chinese Revolution, 1917–1937.* Cambridge: Harvard University Press, 1970.

────. "Liang Ch'i-chao 1873–1929 and Hu Shih 1891–1962." In *Abroad in America,* ed. Marc Pachter and Frances Wein. Reading, Mass.: Addison-Wesley, 1976.

────. *Intellectuals and the State in Modern China: A Narrative History.* New York: The Free Press, 1981.

Griggs, Thurston. *Americans in China: Some Chinese Views.* Washington, D.C.: Foundation for Foreign Affairs, 1948.

Hao, C. *Chinese Intellectuals in Crisis: Search for Order and Meaning (1890–1911).* Berkeley: University of California Press, 1987.

Hao, Yufan, and Guocang Huan, eds. *The Chinese View of the World.* New York: Pantheon Books, 1989.

Harding, Harry, and Yuan Ming, eds. *Sino-American Relations, 1945–1955: A Joint Reassessment of a Critical Decade.* Wilmington, Del.: Scholarly Resources, 1989.

Holman, D.S. "Japan's Position in the Economy of the Far East." *Pacific Affairs* 20 (December 1947): 371–80.

Hsiao, Kung-chuan. *A Modern China and a New World: Kang Yu-wei, Reformer and Utopian, 1858–1927.* Seattle: University of Washington Press, 1975.

Huang, Jianli. *The Politics of Depoliticization in Republican China: Guomindang Policy towards Student Political Activism, 1927–1949.* Berne, Germany: Peter Lang, 1996.

Huebner, Jon W. "Chinese Anti-Americanism, 1946–48." *The Australian Journal of Chinese Affairs* 17 (January 1987): 115–25.

Hunt, Michael H. *The Making of a Special Relationship: The United States and China to 1914.* New York: Columbia University Press, 1983.

────. "Themes in Traditional and Modern Chinese Images of America." In *Mutual Images in U.S.-China Relations,* ed. David Shambaugh, 1–17. Occasional Paper, no. 32. Washington, D.C.: Asian Program, The Woodrow Wilson Center, 1988.

———. "Chinese National Identity and the Strong State: The Late Qing–Republican Crisis." In *China's Quest for National Identity*, ed. Lowell Dittmer and Samual S. Kim. Ithaca: Cornell University Press, 1993.

———. *The Genesis of Chinese Communist Foreign Policy*. New York: Columbia University Press, 1996.

Iriye, Akira. *Across the Pacific: An Inner History of American-East Asian Relations*. New York: Harcourt, Brace & World, 1967.

———. *The Cold War in Asia*. Englewood Cliffs, N.J.: Prentice-Hall, 1974.

Isaacs, Harold R. *Scratches on Our Minds: American Images of China and India*. New York: The John Day Company, 1958.

Israel, John. *Student Nationalism in China, 1927–1937*. Stanford: Stanford University Press, 1966.

———. *Lianda: A Chinese University in War and Revolution*. Stanford: Stanford University Press, 1998.

Israel, John, and Donald Klein. *Rebels and Bureaucrats: China's December 9ers*. Berkeley: University of California Press, 1976.

Jeans, Roger B., and Katie Letcher Lyte, eds. *Good-Bye to Old Peking: The Wartime Letters of U.S. Marine Captain John Seymour Letcher*. Athens, Ohio: Ohio University Press, 1998.

Jespersen, T. Christopher. *American Images of China, 1931–1949*. Stanford: Stanford University Press, 1996.

Johnson, Chalmers A. *Peasant Nationalism and Communist Power: The Emergence of Revolutionary China, 1937–1945*. Stanford: Stanford University Press, 1962.

Kidd, David. *Peking Story*. New York: Clarkson N. Potter, 1988.

LaFargue, Thomas E. *China's First Hundred: Educational Mission Students in the United States, 1872–1881*. Pullman: Washington State University Press, 1987.

Lam, Tong. "Identity and Diversity: The Complexities and Contradictions of Chinese Nationalism." In *China Beyond the Headlines*, ed. Timothy B. Weston and Lionel M. Jensen. Lanham, Md.: Rowman & Littlefield Publishers, 2000.

Lapwood, Ralph, and Nancy Lapwood. *Through the Chinese Revolution*. London: Spalding and Levy, 1954.

The League of Nations' Mission of Educational Experts. *The Reorganisation of Education in China*. Paris: League of Nations' Institute of Intellectual Co-operation, 1932.

Levine, Steven I. *Anvil of Victory: The Communist Revolution in Manchuria, 1945–1948*. New York: Columbia University Press, 1987.

Li, Hongshan. "The Unofficial Envoys: Chinese Students in the United States, 1906–1938." In *Image, Perception, and the Making of U.S.-China Relations*, ed. Hongshan Li and Zhaohui Hong. Lanham, Md.: University Press of America, 1998.

Li, Lincoln. *Student Nationalism in China, 1924–1949*. Albany: State University of New York Press, 1994.

Lin, Yu-sheng. *The Crisis of Chinese Consciousness: Radical Anti-Traditionalism in the May Fourth Era*. Madison: University of Wisconsin Press, 1979.

Liu, Kwang-ching. *Americans and Chinese: A Historical Essay and a Bibliography*. Cambridge: Harvard University Press, 1963.

Liu, Lydia H. "The Female Body and Nationalist Discourse: Manchuria in Xiao Hong's *Field of Life and Death*." In *Body, Subject and Power in China*, ed. Angela Zito and Tani E. Barlow. Chicago: The University of Chicago Press, 1994.

Lutz, Jessie Gregory. *China and the Christian Colleges, 1850–1950*. Ithaca: Cornell University Press, 1971.

———. "The Chinese Student Movement of 1945–1949." *Journal of Asian Studies* 31 (November 1971): 89–110.

Lutze, Thomas D. "America's Japan Policy and the Defection of Chinese Liberals, 1947–1948." In *George C. Marshall's Mediation Mission to China, December 1945–January 1947*, ed. Larry I. Bland. Lexington, Va.: George C. Marshall Foundation, 1998.

MacKerras, Colin. *Western Images of China.* Hong Kong: Oxford University Press, 1989.

Madsen, Richard. *China and the American Dream: A Moral Inquiry.* Berkeley and Los Angeles: University of California Press, 1995.

Mann, James. *About Face: A History of America's Curious Relationship with China, from Nixon to Clinton.* New York: Alfred A. Knopf, 1999.

Mao, Tse-tung. *Selected Works of Mao Tse-tung.* Peking: Foreign Languages Press, 1961: 4.

————. *Selected Works of Mao Tse-tung.* Peking: Foreign Languages Press, 1977: 5.

Marolda, Edward J. "The U.S. Navy and the 'Loss of China,' 1945–1950." In *George C. Marshall's Mediation Mission to China, December 1945–January 1947*, ed. Larry I. Bland. Lexington, Va.: George C. Washington Foundation, 1998.

Mazur, Mary G. "Intellectual Activism in China during the 1940s: Wu Han in the United Front and the Democratic League." *The China Quarterly* 133 (March 1993): 27–55.

————. "The United Front Redefined for the Party-State: A Case Study of Transition and Legitimization." In *New Perspectives on State Socialism in China*, ed. Timothy Cheek and Tony Saich. Armonk, N.Y.: M.E. Sharpe, 1997.

McKee, Delber L. *Chinese Exclusion versus the Open Door Policy, 1900–1906: Clashes over China Policy in the Roosevelt Era.* Detroit: Wayne State University Press, 1977.

Melby, John F. *The Mandate of Heaven: Record of a Civil War, China 1945–49.* Toronto: University of Toronto Press, 1968.

Meng, Chih. *Chinese American Understanding: A Sixty-Year Search.* New York: China Institute in America, 1981.

Meng, C.Y.W. "An Interpretation of Student Anti-US Demonstrations." *The China Weekly Review* (3 August 1946): 78–80.

Ng, Vivian. "Ideology and Sexuality: Rape Laws in Qing China," *Journal of Asian Studies* 46 (February 1987): 57–70.

No, Yong-Park. "A Chinese View of the American Character." In *America in Perspective: The United States through Foreign Eyes*, ed. Henry Steele Commager. New York: Random House, 1947.

Oksenberg, Michel, and Robert B. Oxnam, eds. *Dragon and Eagle, United States-China Relations: Past and Future.* New York: Basic Books, 1973.

Patch, Buel W. *Anti-Americanism and Soldiers Overseas.* Washington, D.C.: Editorial Research Reports, 1957.

Pepper, Suzanne. "The Student Movement and the Chinese Civil War, 1945–1949." *The China Quarterly* 48 (December 1971): 698–735.

————. *Civil War in China: The Political Struggle, 1945–1949.* Berkeley: University of California Press, 1978; Lanham, Md.: Rowman & Littlefield, 1999.

————. *Radicalism and Education Reform in 20th-Century China: The Search for an Ideal Development Model.* New York: Cambridge University Press, 1996.

Peterson, Michael, and David Perlmutt. *Charlie Two Shoes and the Marines of Love Company.* Annapolis, Md.: Naval Institute Press, 1998.

Qing, Simei. "Visions of Free Trade and U.S.-China Commercial Treaty Negotiations, 1945–46. " In *China and the United States: A New Cold War History*, ed. Xiaobing Li and Hongshan Li. Lanham, Md.: University Press of America, 1998.

Reardon-Anderson, James. *Yenan and the Great Powers: The Origins of Chinese Communist Foreign Policy, 1944–1946.* New York: Columbia University Press, 1980.

Schaller, Michael. *The U.S. Crusade in China, 1938–1945*. New York: Columbia University Press, 1979.

———. *The American Occupation of Japan: The Origins of the Cold War in Asia*. New York: Oxford University Press, 1985.

———. *The United States and China in the Twentieth Century*. New York: Oxford University Press, 1979, 1990.

Shaffer, Robert. "A Rape in Beijing, December 1946: GIs, Nationalist Protests, and U.S. Foreign Policy." *Pacific Historical Review* 69 (February 2000): 56–60.

Shambaugh, David L. "Anti-Americanism in China." *Anti-Americanism: Origins and Context*, ed. Thomas P. Thornton, special issue of *The Annals of the American Academy of Political and Social Science* 497 (May 1988): 142–56.

———. "Americanization of East Asia: Writings on Cultural Affairs since 1900." In *New Frontiers in American-East Asian Relations: Essays Presented to Dorothy Borg*, ed. Warren I. Cohen. New York: Columbia University Press, 1983.

———. *Beautiful Imperialist: China Perceives America, 1972–1990*. Princeton: Princeton University Press, 1991.

Shaw, Henry I. *United States Marines in North China, 1945–1949*. Washington, D.C.: U.S. Marine Corps, 1968.

Spence, Jonathan D. *The Search for Modern China*. 2d ed. New York: W.W. Norton, 1999.

Spurr, Russell. *Enter the Dragon: China's Undeclared War against the U.S. in Korea, 1950–51*. New York: Newmarket Press, 1988.

Stewart, Fraser, ed. *Chinese Communist Education: Records of the First Decade*. Nashville: Vanderbilt University Press, 1965.

Strand, David. *Rickshaw Beijing: City People and Politics in the 1920s*. Berkeley: University of California Press, 1989.

Stuart, John Leighton. *Fifty Years in China: The Memoirs of John Leighton Stuart, Missionary and Ambassador*. New York: Random House, 1954.

Stueck, William Whitney. *The Road to Confrontation: American Policy toward China and Korea, 1947–1950*. Chapel Hill: University of North Carolina Press, 1981.

———. "The Marshall and Wedemeyer Missions: A Quadrilateral Perspective." In *Sino-American Relations, 1945–1955: A Joint Reassessment of a Critical Decade*, ed. Harry Harding and Yuan Mingo. Wilmington, Del.: Scholarly Resources, 1989.

———. *The Korean War: An International History*. Princeton: Princeton University Press, 1995.

Sun, Yat-sen. *San-min Chu-i: The Three Principles of the People*. Trans. Frank W. Prince. Shanghai: Institute of Pacific Relations, 1927.

Tan, Chester C. *The Boxer Catastrophe*. New York: Octagon Books, 1967.

Thomson, James C., Jr. *While China Faced West: American Reformers in Nationalist China, 1928–1937*. Cambridge: Harvard University Press, 1969.

Ting, Lee-hsia Hsu. *Government Control of the Press in Modern China, 1900–1949*. Cambridge: Harvard University Press, 1974.

Townsend, James. "Chinese Nationalism." *The Australian Journal of Chinese Affairs* 27 (January 1992): 97–130.

Truman, Harry S. *Memoirs of Harry S. Truman: Years of Trial and Hope*. New York: Doubleday Company, 1950.

Tseng Chao-lun (Zeng Zhaolun). "The Disposal of American-Subsidized Schools Is the Foremost Task on the Current Cultural Front Now." In *Chinese Communist Education: Records of the First Decade*, ed. Stewart Fraser. Nashville: Vanderbilt University Press, 1965.

Tsou, Tang. *America's Failure in China, 1941-50*. Chicago: University of Chicago Press, 1963.

Tu, Wei-ming. "Chinese Perceptions of America." In *Dragon and Eagle, United States-China Relations: Past and Future*, ed. Michel Oksenberg and Robert B. Oxnam. New York: Basic Books, 1973.

Tucker, Nancy B. *Patterns in the Dust: Chinese-American Relations and the Recognition Controversy, 1949–1950*. New York: Columbia University Press, 1983.

Unger, Jonathan, ed. *Chinese Nationalism*. Armonk, N.Y.: M.E. Sharpe, 1996.

United Nations. *Security Council Official Records*. No. 68, 526th Meeting, November 28, 1950.

———. *Security Council Official Records*. No. 69, 527th Meeting, November 28, 1950.

Van Slyke, Lyman P., ed. *Marshall's Mission to China, December 1945–January 1947: The Report and Appended Documents*. Arlington, Va.: University Publications of America, 1976.

———. "Culture, Society, and Technology in Sino-American Relations." In *Dragon and Eagle, United States–China Relations: Past and Future*, ed. Michel Oksenberg and Robert B. Oxnam. New York: Basic Books, 1978.

Vandegrift, A.A. *Once a Marine: The Memoirs of General A.A. Vandegrift*. New York: W.W. Norton, 1964.

Varg, Paul. *The Closing of the Door: Sino-American Relations, 1936–1946*. East Lansing: Michigan State University Press, 1973.

Vogel, Ezra F., ed. *Living with China: U.S./China Relations in the Twenty-First Century*. New York: W.W. Norton, 1997.

Wakeman, Frederick, Jr. *The Fall of Imperial China*. New York: The Free Press, 1975, 163–98.

Wang, Ming. "Public Images of the United States," in *In the Eyes of the Dragon: China Views the World*, ed. Yong Deng and Fei-ling Wang. Lanham, Md.: Rowman & Littlefield Publishers, 1999.

Wang, Q. Edward. *Inventing China Through History: The May Fourth Approach to Historiography*. Albany: State University of New York Press, 2001.

Wang, Tsi C. *The Youth Movement in China*. New York: New Republic, 1927.

Wang, Y.C. *Chinese Intellectuals and the West, 1872–1949*. Chapel Hill: University of North Carolina Press, 1966.

Wang Yun-sheng. "Japan—Storm Center of Asia." *Pacific Affairs* 21 (June 1948): 195–99.

Wasserstrom, Jeffrey N. *Student Protests in Twentieth-Century China: The View from Shanghai*. Stanford: Stanford University Press, 1991.

———. "Student Protests in Fin-de-Siècle China." *New Left Review* 237 (September/October 1999): 52–76.

———. "Big Bad China and the Good Chinese: An American Fairy Tale." In *China Beyond the Headlines*, ed. Timothy B. Weston and Lionel M. Jensen. Lanham, Md.: Rowman & Littlefield Publishers, 2000.

Wei, C.X. George. *Sino-American Economic Relations, 1944–1949*. Westport, Conn.: Greenwood Press, 1997.

Wei, C.X. George, and Xiaoyuan Liu, eds. *Chinese Nationalism in Perspective: Historical and Recent Cases*. Wesport, Conn.: Greenwood Press, 2001.

Wei Wei. "Get Them Down." *Chinese Literature* 2 (1953): 115–31

West, Philip. *Yenching University and Sino-Western Relations, 1916–1952*. Cambridge: Harvard University Press, 1976.

———. "The Korean War and the Criteria of Significance in Chinese Popular Culture." *The Journal of American-East Asian Relations* 1 (winter 1992): 383–408.

West, Philip with Li Zhihua, "Interior Stories of the Chinese POWs in the Korean War." In *Remembering the "Forgotten War": The Korean War Through Literature and Art*, ed. Philip West and Suh Ji-moon. Armonk, N.Y.: M.E. Sharpe, 2001.

West, Philip, Steven I. Levine, and Jackie Hiltz, eds. *America's Wars in Asia: A Cultural Approach to History and Memory*. Armonk, N.Y.: M.E. Sharpe, 1998.

Westad, Odd Arne. *Cold War and Revolution: Soviet-American Rivalry and the Origins of the Chinese Civil War, 1944–1946*. New York: Columbia University Press, 1993.

———. "Could the Chinese Civil War Have Been Avoided? An Exercise in Alternatives." In *George C. Marshall's Mediation Mission to China, December 1945–January 1947*, ed. Larry I. Bland. Lexington, Va.: George C. Marshall Foundation, 1998.

———, ed. *Brothers in Arms: The Rise and Fall of the Sino-Soviet Alliance, 1945–1963*. Washington, D.C.: Woodrow Wilson Center Press, 1998

Weston, Timothy B., and Lionel M. Jensen, eds. *China Beyond the Headlines*. Lanham, Md.: Rowman & Littlefield Publishers, 2000.

White, John A. *The United States Marines in North China*. Millbrae, Calif.: by the author, 1974.

Whiting, Allen S. *China Crosses the Yalu: The Decision to Enter the Korean War*. Stanford: Stanford University Press, 1968.

Wilson, David. "The United States and Chinese Nationalism during the 1920s." *Chinese Historians* 5 (fall 1992): 49–58.

Wong, Sin-kiong. "Die for the Boycott and Nation: Martyrdom and the 1905 Anti-American Movement in China," *Modern Asian Studies* 35 (July 2001): 565–88.

Wright, Mary Clabaugh, ed. *China in Revolution: The First Phase, 1900–1913*. New Haven: Yale University Press, 1968.

Wu Ningkun. *A Single Tear: A Family's Persecution, Love, and Endurance in Communist China*. Boston: Little, Brown and Company, 1993.

Yang, Zhiguo. "U.S. Marines in Qingdao: Society, Culture, and China's Civil War, 1945–1949." In *China and the United States: A New Cold War History*, ed. Xiaobing Li and Honngshan Li. Lanham, Md.: University Press of America, 1998.

Ye, Weili. *Seeking Modernity in China's Name: Chinese Students in the United States, 1900–1927*. Stanford: Stanford University Press, 2001.

Yeh, Wen-Hsin. *The Alienated Academy: Culture and Politics in Republican China, 1919–1937*. Cambridge: Harvard University Press, 1990.

Yen, Maria. *The Umbrella Garden: A Picture of Student Life in China*. New York: Macmillan, 1954.

Yick, Joseph K.S. *Making Urban Revolution in China: The CCP-GMD Struggle for Beiping-Tianjin, 1945–1949*. Armonk, N.Y.: M.E. Sharpe, 1995.

———. "The Communist-Nationalist Political Struggle in Beijing during the Marshall Mission Period." In *George C. Marshall's Mediation Mission to China, December 1945–January 1947*, ed. Larry I. Bland. Lexington, Va.: George C. Marshall Foundation, 1998.

Yip, Ka-che. *Religion, Nationalism, and Chinese Students: The Anti-Christian Movement of 1922–1927*. Bellingham: Western Washington University, 1980.

Yu, Frederick T.C. *The Propaganda Machine in Communist China—With Special Reference to Ideology, Policy, and Regulations, as of 1952*. Lackland Air Force Base, Tex.: Air Force Personnel and Training Research Center, 1955.

Yuan Ming. "Chinese Intellectuals and the United States: The Dilemma of Individualism vs. Patriotism." *Asian Survey* 29 (July 1989): 645–54.

———. "The Failure of Perception: America's China Policy, 1949–50." In *Sino-American Relations, 1945–1955: A Joint Reassessment of a Critical Decade*, ed. Harry Harding and Yuan Ming. Wilmington, Del.: Scholarly Resources, 1989.

Yue Daiyun and Caroline Wakeman. *To the Storm: The Odyssey of a Revolutionary Chinese Woman*. Berkeley and Los Angeles: University of California Press, 1985.

Yueh, Tai-yun. *Chinese Intellectuals in Fiction*. Berkeley: Institute of East Asian Studies, 1988.

Zhang, Hong. *"Fan Meifuri*: The Chinese Student Movement Opposing the U.S. Rehabilitation of Japan, 1948." *The Journal of American–East Asian Relations* 5 (summer 1996): 183–208.

————. "Chinese Intellectuals and the 'Resist America, Aid Korea' Political Campaign." *Chinese Historians* 9 (1996): 38–74.

Zhang Leping. *Adventures of Sanmao, the Orphan*. Hong Kong: Joint Publishing Co., 1981.

Zhang, Shu Guang. *Deterrence and Strategic Culture: Chinese-American Confrontation, 1949–1959*. Ithaca: Cornell University Press, 1992.

————. *Mao's Military Romanticism: China and the Korean War, 1950–1953*. Lawrence: University Press of Kansas, 1995.

Zhao, Suisheng. *Power and Competition in East Asia*. New York: St. Martin's Press, 1997.

Zito, Angela, and Tani E. Barlow, eds. *Body, Subject and Power in China*. Chicago: University of Chicago Press, 1994.

Zhu, Pingchao. "The Korean War at the Dinner Table." In *America's Wars in Asia: A Cultural Approach to History and Memory*, ed. Philip West, Steven I. Levine, and Jackie Hiltz. Armonk, N.Y.: M.E. Sharpe, 1998.

Dissertations

Chen, Chang-fang. "Barbarian Paradise: Chinese Views of the United States, 1784–1911." Ph.D. diss., Indiana University, 1985.

Gries, Peter Hays. "Face Nationalism: Power and Passion in Chinese Anti-Foreignism." Ph.D. diss., University of California, Berkeley, 1999.

Guo, Xixiao. "The Climax of Sino-American Relations, 1944–1947." Ph.D. diss., University of Georgia, 1997.

Liu, Yi-rong Young. "Chinese Intellectuals' Sense of Mission and Their Attitude toward Foreign Study." Ph.D. diss., University of California at Los Angeles, 1985.

Lutze, Thomas D. "New Democracy: Chinese Communist Relations with the Urban Middle Forces, 1931–1952." Ph.D. diss., University of Wisconsin at Madison, 1996.

Ting, Yueh-Hung C. "The Intellectuals and the Chinese Revolution: A Study of the China Democratic League and Its Components, 1939–1949." Ph.D. diss., New York University, 1978.

Wang, Guanhua. "The 1905 Anti-American Boycott: A Social and Cultural Reassessment." Ph.D. diss., Michigan State University, 1994.

Yang, Zhiguo. "U.S. Marines in Qingdao: Military-Civilian Interaction, Nationalism, and China's Civil War, 1945–1949." Ph.D. diss., University of Maryland, 1998.

INDEX

About the Author

HONG ZHANG is Assistant Professor of History at the University of Central Florida. Since obtaining degrees at Nankai University and the University of Arizona, she has had articles published in *The Journal of American-East Asian Relations* and *Chinese Historians*.